Cyclopedia of
Young Adult Authors

Cyclopedia of
Young Adult Authors

Volume 3

Han Nolan–Paul Zindel

From
The Editors of Salem Press

Salem Press, Inc.
Pasadena, California   Hackensack, New Jersey

Editor in Chief: Dawn P. Dawson
Project Editors: Kenneth T. Burles
R. Kent Rasmussen
Acquisitions Editor: Mark Rehn
Production Editor: Cynthia Beres
Photograph Editor: Philip Bader
Design: Moritz Design, Pasadena, California
Page Layout and Graphics: James Hutson
Assistant Editor: Andrea E. Miller
Editorial Intern: Heather Pistole

Library of Congress Cataloging-in-Publication Data

Cyclopedia of young adult authors / from the editors of Salem Press.
p. cm.
Includes bibliographical references and index.
ISBN 1-58765-206-4 (set : alk. paper) — ISBN 1-58765-207-2 (vol. 1 : alk. paper) —
ISBN 1-58765-208-0 (vol. 2 : alk. paper) — ISBN 1-58765-209-9 (vol. 3 : alk. paper)
1. Young adult literature, American—Dictionaries. 2. Young adult literature, English—
Dictionaries. 3. Authors, American—Biography—Dictionaries. 4. Authors, English—
Biography—Dictionaries. I. Salem Press.
PS490.C93 2005
810.9'9283'03—dc22
2004027668

First Printing
Printed in Canada

Contents

Volume 3

R

S

T

Cyclopedia of
Young Adult Authors

Han Nolan

Born: August 25, 1956; Birmingham, Alabama

www.harcourtbooks.com/authorinterviews/
bookinterview_Nolan.asp

The characters in **Han Nolan**'s books are most often young women seeking to find and forge their identities despite living in dysfunctional families and having uncertain futures. Religious themes weave throughout the books, not merely at the fringe of the characters' lives but often making up the fabric of their worlds. Nolan's plots are always unusual, sometimes outlandish, yet made believable through deep characterization and an evocative writing style.

Born "Helen" and nicknamed "Han," Nolan was born in the South but reared in the Northeast. As she grew up, she frequently visited relatives in the South and consequently shares sensibilities of both northern and southern cultures. Growing up in an artistic and literate family, she loved books from an early age and credits Louise Fitzhugh's *Harriet the Spy* with inspiring her to begin keeping journals and to ultimately become a writer. In college and graduate school she majored in dance and afterward taught dance for several years. When she and husband Brian Nolan adopted three children, she turned to writing as a career that would enable her to stay home and raise a family. She chose to write for adolescents because she liked her own teenage

Louise Fitzhugh's *Harriet the Spy*

Harriet the Spy **was first published in 1964 and broke new ground for a children's book. Eleven-year-old Harriet spies on everyone around her and takes notes about them. In addition to taking notes on her neighbors' behavior, Harriet also takes notes on her** friends and classmates. When she misplaces her notebook, the other kids find it and read what she has to say about them. Soon Harriet is without friends. Having learned her lesson, Harriet finds a way to win back her old friends and carry on her with her normal life. The book was made into a popular movie in 1996.

years and found the age exciting and passionate.

Though her most frequently read and taught book is her first, *If I Should Die Before I Wake*, Nolan rocketed to fame with her next two books, *Send Me Down a Miracle* and *Dancing on the Edge*. Both were nominated for **National Book Awards** in **p.12?** consecutive years; the first was named a runner-up, and the second was a winner. No other author had ever before been nominated to that award two years in a row. Many of Nolan's other books have been honored by the **American Library Association** as **p.45** **Best Books for Young Adults** or **Popular Paper-** **p.480** **backs for Young Adults**.

In *If I Should Die Before I Wake*, neo-Nazi high **p.501** school student Hilary Burke falls into a coma after a motorcycle accident and slips back in time to trade places with a **Holocaust** victim. The experience **p.50** teaches her empathy. In *Send Me Down a Miracle*, Preacher's daughter Charity Pittman also learns the importance of understanding others as she defends the visionary power of a chair on which her strange new neighbor claims to sit and see Jesus. In *Dancing on the Edge*, Miracle McCloy mixes mysticism and madness to find out the truth about her roots: Her mother committed suicide when she was born, and her father later abandoned her. Another character abandoned by her parents is the gifted singer Janie of *Born Blue*, who renames herself Leshaya and becomes obsessed with jazz culture, including the darker side of drug addiction. p.405

p.233 Han Nolan used a male protagonist for the first time in *A Face in Every Window*. After his grandmother's death, teenage James Patrick realizes that he is functionally the most mature resident of a house filled with lost souls—his father is mentally challenged, his mother is free-spirited, and an odd cast of boarders fills the house's rooms.

– Lisa Rowe Fraustino

Neo-Nazi

The Neo-Nazi movement surfaced in many countries in the late twentieth century. Organized groups have adopted the slogans, salutes, and prejudices of the Nazis from World War II Germany. They are first and foremost anti-Semitic, but they also are prejudiced against foreigners. In addition to protests, they may attack individuals. They also damage property. The Neo-Nazi movement also has a strong presence in Germany and France, where their anger is directed against Jews, Muslims, and Africans. They deface graveyards, set apartments on fire, and beat up individuals on the street. In the U.S., they are called "skinheads," because many of their followers shave their heads.

Charles Nordhoff

Born: February 1, 1887; London, England
Died: April 11, 1947; Santa Barbara, California

www.kirjasto.sci.fi/nordhof.htm

James Norman Hall

Born: April 22, 1887; Colfax, Iowa
Died: July 6, 1951; Papeete, Tahiti, French Polynesia

www.jamesnormanhallhome.pf

TITLES

Mutiny on the Bounty, 1932

Men Against the Sea, 1934

Pitcairn's Island, 1934

Charles Nordhoff and **James Norman Hall** wrote vivid, romantic novels of life at sea that combined careful historical research with their own first-hand knowledge of the South Pacific Ocean. The best of their books feature characters torn between their desire for freedom and their sense of responsibility. Together the two writers created some of the most exciting novels of their time.

Both Hall and Nordhoff were Americans with strong affinities for Great Britain. Hall was born and reared in Iowa. During World War I, he served in the British army's **Lafayette Flying Corps**—a unit whose officers were French and whose pilots were American. He also served in the U.S. Air Service.

p.503

Nordhoff was born in England, but his parents were Americans, and he grew up in Mexico (where he ran a sugar cane plantation as a young man) and California. During World War I he also served with the Lafayette Flying Corps and published a series of letters in the *Atlantic Monthly* magazine describing his experiences. He and Hall both wrote about the war and were afterward commissioned to compile the official history of the Lafayette Flying Corps.

Although the two men did not care for each other at first, they eventually became close friends

Charles Nordhoff

and shared a mutual dislike of modern progress. They traveled together through the Polynesian islands of the South Pacific and collaborated on a series of articles about their journey and experiences. These articles were published in book form as *Faery Lands of the South Seas* (1921). They so liked the South Pacific that they made their homes on the French-ruled island of Tahiti and continued to write. During this time Nordhoff produced two adventure novels for young readers, *The Pearl Lagoon* (1924) and its sequel *The Derelict* (1928), while Hall published several collections of essays.

Several years later Nordhoff and Hall collaborated on a trilogy of novels about one of the most famous incidents in British naval history, the mutiny aboard the HMS *Bounty* in 1789. Under the command of Lieutenant William Bligh, with Fletcher Christian second in command, the *Bounty* had been ordered to carry breadfruit trees from Tahiti to the British **West Indies**, where they were to be replanted and cultivated as a cheap source of food. Nordhoff and Hall wrote the novel from the point of view of young Roger Byam, who is sent on the expedition to complete a Tahitian dictionary. Through his eyes, readers witness Bligh's many acts of cruelty, Christian's efforts to protect the crew, and the act of rebellion in which Christian takes command of the ship and has Bligh and a few loyal crewmen set adrift in the open sea.

Lafayette Flying Corps

The Lafayette Flying Corps was a group of Americans who flew with the French air force beginning in 1914 when war broke out between France and Germany. A group of young Americans living in France wanted to join the air force, but they were not allowed to do so since the U.S. had not entered the war. Instead, they joined the French Foreign Legion and later were allowed to fly for France. They were known as l'Escadrille ("flying squadron") de Lafayette, and later renamed the Lafayette Flying Corps. Once the U.S. entered World War I in 1917, some of the Americans joined the U.S. Air Force, but others remained with the Corps, providing replacements for those who lost their lives. Nordhoff and Hall were both members of the Corps and wrote its official history in 1920.

671

Mutiny on the Bounty, the Movies

The first film version of *Mutiny on the Bounty, In the Wake of the Bounty*, starred Errol Flynn as Fletcher Christian and was released in 1933. It was remade as *Mutiny on the Bounty* in 1935, starring Clark Gable as First Mate Fletcher Christian and Charles Laughton as Captain Bligh. It was a box-office success and won the Academy Award for Best Picture, one of eight nominations it received. The film was again remade in 1962 and starred Trevor Howard as Captain Bligh and Marlon Brando as Fletcher Christian. Moviegoers either loved this version or hated it. The performance of Marlon Brando continues to be discussed by film fans as either brilliant or ridiculous. The 1984 version of the film, *The Bounty*, starring Anthony Hopkins as Bligh and Mel Gibson as Christian, is truest to the original story.

The authors followed *Mutiny on the Bounty* with two sequels. *Men Against the Sea* tells the heroic story of Captain Bligh's voyage with his crewmen in an open boat some 3,600 miles to the East Indies, one of the most extraordinary feats of seamanship ever undertaken. *Pitcairn's Island* describes the violent fate of the *Bounty* mutineers on the incorrectly charted island on which they settled with a number of Tahitian women and men. The entire trilogy proved enormously popular and made its authors world famous.

Nordhoff and Hall later collaborated on several more novels about the South Pacific, including *Botany Bay* (1941), which deals with the early settlement of **Australia** by British convicts. In 1941 Nordhoff returned to California, where he died six years later without publishing any further works. Hall went on to write a collection of comic stories about a Royal Navy surgeon, *Dr. Dogbody's Leg* (1941). His autobiography, *My Island Home* (1952), was left uncompleted at the time of his death in Tahiti in 1951.

Mutiny on the Bounty has been filmed several times.

— Grove Koger

p.46

p.504

Mary Norton

Born: December 10, 1903; London, England
Died: August 29, 1992; Hartland, Devonshire, England

www.sfsite.com/09b/bor41.htm

Long before J. K. Rowling imagined **Harry Potter**, **Mary Norton**'s books were using magic as a useful narrative tool. As with Rowling's later novels, Norton's stories convey the message that magic is not something to play at, as it can have serious negative consequences, especially when things go wrong (as they invariably do).

Norton was born in London but raised in Leighton Buzzard, in the southwest corner of Bedfordshire, about forty miles from London itself. Her father was a physician, and she attended **convent schools** for most of her childhood. During the mid-1920's she was an actress with the Old Vic Theatre Company in London but left the stage to marry Robert Norton, a shipping magnate. The couple had four children. Upon their marriage, the couple moved to Portugal, where they lived until the onset of World War II. On returning to England in 1940, Norton worked for the **British Broadcasting Corporation** (BBC) for a year.

In the early 1940's, Norton began writing the stories that were eventually melded into *Bedknob and Broomstick*. These tell of a set of three children, Charlie, Carrie, and Paul, who are **evacuated** to the country (presumably to escape the bombing raids that were leveling London). There they meet Miss Price, a **spinster** who is learning how to be a witch. In the first story, Miss Price transports herself and the children to a South Seas island, where they encounter cannibals and have other adventures. In the second book, they all travel back to the

p.597

p.506

p.6

p.59

p.507

seventeenth century and save a wizard from being burned at the stake.

Most of Norton's other books are about the Borrowers, a race of tiny people who live within the walls and under the floors of the houses of "human beans" and "borrow" what they need to live from their unsuspecting landlords. The Borrowers are a declining race, however, and when they are first met, the Clock family—father Pod, mother Homily, and daughter Arrietty—are among the few Borrowers living in a country house that formerly contained multitudes. The Borrowers believe their survival depends on remaining hidden from human beans, but they are discovered by a boy who comes to lives in the house, and Arrietty does not see why she cannot be friends with him. Throughout the series of Borrowers adventures, and as they become nomads searching for a place to live in peace, Arrietty is the voice of innovation, challenging the assumptions of Borrower life, sometimes with beneficial results, sometimes with bad. The charm of the books lies in their depiction of the ingenious ways in which the Borrowers adapt human-made objects for their own

Convent Schools

Traditionally, English girls were educated at convent schools, or schools associated with the Catholic Church. As early as the eighth century, convent schools were being established in England. With the Reformation during the sixteenth century, the Church of England split from the Roman

Catholic Church, and the education of women in convent schools came to an end. The nineteenth century saw the reestablishment of girls' convent schools. Today there are more than two hundred Catholic secondary schools in England, both day schools and boarding schools. They are government regulated and provide an authorized education. In addition to the secular subjects, girls in convent schools receive religious instruction as well.

Spinster

The dictionary definition of "spinster" is "a woman whose occupation it is to spin." Of course, this means to spin yarn or cloth, a definition we might already consider somewhat out of date. Today, spinning is largely accomplished by machinery in factories. Likewise, the secondary definition of "spinster," "an unmarried woman of gentle family, an unmarried woman, or a woman past the common age for marrying or one who seems unlikely to marry," is equally archaic. In modern American society, women have the choice to marry or remain single. They enter professions and earn money to support themselves. The definition of "spinster" comes from an age when women had not achieved equality with men and were dependent on the status and material goods provided by their husbands. In some parts of the world, women's dependency on men for survival still continues.

use, such as using postage stamps for paintings and turning a teakettle into a boat when they must escape from their home.

Norton's story *Poor Stainless* is about the Borrowers but takes place before the adventures of the Clocks, harkening back to the time when the Borrowers were more numerous and depicting Borrower society in full swing. *Are All the Giants Dead?* is a story of a boy—who prefers science fiction to **fantasy**—who is nonetheless swept off to a fairyland where he must complete the giant-killing left unfinished by the legendary Jack.

p.87

Mary Norton's novels remain popular among young readers, and some of them have been adapted to the screen. In 1940, Norton received Great Britain's prestigious **Carnegie Medal** for her first Borrowers book.

p.42

— Leslie Ellen Jones

Scott O'Dell

Born: May 23, 1898; Los Angeles, California
Died: October 15, 1989; Mt. Kisco, New York

www.scottodell.com

p.509

p.117

Scott O'Dell was one of the finest writers of historical novels for young adult readers. His young characters are of all races and genders. Most of them live in historical periods, and all of them face the challenges of their times with courage and resourcefulness. He was so honored and beloved for his work that he won several awards in his lifetime, and his books are still read by millions.

O'Dell was born and reared in Southern California, which was the frontier before Los Angeles became a big city. The first sound he remembered hearing was that of a wildcat scratching on the roof of his family's house. He lived part of his boyhood on a place called Rattlesnake Island, near Los Angeles, and watched three-masted ships sail by as he and his friends floated in the surf clinging to logs. He later lived amid the sagebrush foothills of Mount Baldy, east of Los Angeles, among the descendants of the first Spanish settlers of California, and in the Oriflamme Mountains, the ancestral home of the Diegueño Indians. O'Dell's many experiences and love of nature drove him to write about growing up in different historical eras.

O'Dell began writing books during the 1920's but did not take up writing young adult books until he was about sixty years old. His first and most famous young adult novel, *Island of the Blue Dolphins*, is based on a true story of a young Native American woman who was stranded alone on a island off the coast of Southern California during the early nineteenth century. That book won the Newbery Medal.

p.102

O'Dell's other books about Native Americans include *Streams to the River, River to the Sea* and *Thunder Rolling in the Mountains*. He also wrote other exciting historical tales about Inuits, Mayans, African Americans, Spaniards, and Caribbean islanders. His stories about young people in contemporary times include *Alexandra*, in which the title character is a **sponge diver** of Greek descent learning to come to terms with adventure and romance in Tarpon Springs, Florida.

p.510

O'Dell's novels are fast moving and well researched, rich in details of other times, other lands and customs, the frontier, and the sea. *My Name Is Not Angelica* is the story of an African girl sold by Danish slave dealers on the Caribbean island of St. John's in 1733. *The 290* is a stirring sea adventure

Diegueño Indians

The Diegueño Indians, also known as the Kumeyaay, lived in what is now known as the San Diego area of Southern California. When Father Junipero Serra first entered the area in 1769, he encountered a friendly, productive tribe of Native Americans. The Spanish recruited the natives to build the Mission San Diego de Acalá. According to custom, the Spanish named the tribe of 20,000 to 30,000 natives after the mission built in their area. Many of the Native Americans resisted the attempts by the Spaniards to convert them to Christianity. In 1775, a group attacked and burned the mission, killing the padre and another Spaniard, the only Spanish killed by Indians in California. At the time of Mexican independence from Spain in 1821, most of the Diegueño fled into the mountains. Over time, the tribe dwindled to some 2,000, largely because of disease. Their lands were taken from them, but they were eventually granted reservations in the area. Since 1910, the tribal membership has grown. Today, there are about 20,000 descendants of the Diegueños living in the San Diego area, with some 10% living on reservations.

about a British boy who ends up in the Confederate navy during the American Civil War. *The King's Fifth* chronicles the adventures of a young mapmaker to the Spanish explorer Coronado. *The Road to Damietta* is a biographical novel about the early thirteenth century Saint Francis of Assisi. *The Cruise of the Arctic Star* (1973) is a nonfiction saga about O'Dell and his family's voyage up the California coast in the title ship, but it is as thrilling, mysterious, and eventful as his fiction.

Scott O'Dell's many writing awards include three citations for **Newbery Honor Books**, the **Hans Christian Andersen Medal**, and a **Phoenix Honor Award**. In 1984 the Scott O'Dell Award for Historical Fiction was created in his honor, to be awarded annually to authors of the year's best young adult historical novels. In 1987 he received the award himself for *Streams to the River, River to the Sea*.

– Fiona Kelleghan

p.120
p.147
p.51

Sponge Divers

Sponges are simple multi-cellular animals that attach themselves to the ocean floor where they find food. Humans dive to the bottom of the ocean to detach these sponges, bring them to the surface, strip them to the skeleton, and sell them for commercial use. Before diving suits were invented, it was necessary for divers to reach the ocean floor and hold their breath while harvesting sponges. This was a slow and dangerous process. With diving suits and a steady oxygen supply, divers could remain on the bottom longer and harvest more sponges. This, of course, stripped the coastal fields of sponges and pushed the remaining fields further out into the ocean, requiring divers to reacher greater depths. With the introduction of synthetic sponges in the 1950's, the demand for natural sponges has decreased.

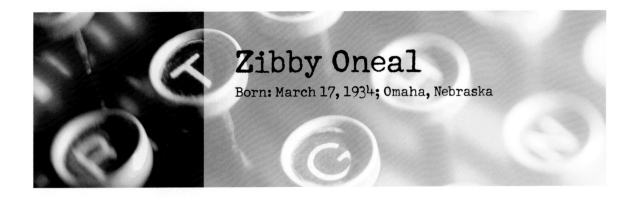

Zibby Oneal

Born: March 17, 1934; Omaha, Nebraska

Zibby Oneal's adolescent novels offer complex portraits of young women dealing with confusing emotions as they approach adulthood. Within the framework of mostly intact families, her protago- p.233 nists face inner conflicts of the maturing self, rather than the problems of dysfunctional families and social conflicts that are more typical of today's adolescent literature. Her third-person narrators guide the action and use language rich in metaphor and allusion.

Born Mary Elizabeth Bisgard, Oneal was the third in a line of Mary Elizabeths and was nicknamed "Zibby" early in her life. Before she could even write, she began making up stories in her head, inspired by her mother, who went around the house quoting lines from classic poetry and prose. Her sister became an artist like their father. After entering Stanford University, Zibby left early to marry Bob Oneal, then a medical intern p.512 training to become a plastic surgeon. She worked as a secretary until she had two children. She then stayed home with the children until they started school, at which time she finished her education at the University of Michigan. She lectured in English there from 1976-1985. Beginning with books for younger children, Oneal wrote stories about protagonists close to the ages of her own children and produced her three young adult novels during the 1980's. After her children were grown, she turned to nonfiction subjects.

Oneal has said that her characters guide the plots of her stories, and this is evident in her narra-

Medical Intern

The education of a future doctor includes a period of training as an intern. Following a four-year course of study in medical school, graduates enter an internship to prepare for independent practice. All new physicians complete their first year of internship in a residency program before receiving a full medical license in the second year of residency. Some interns rotate through the areas of medicine, surgery, pediatrics, and obstetrics, before entering specialized medical training in areas such as radiology, dermatology, and some surgical specialties. The intern is closely supervised during this period. At the end of the internship, the intern must pass a third portion of the standard licensing exam in order to practice medicine and surgery.

tives of change and transformation within family relationships. In *The Language of Goldfish*, for example, Carrie Stokes goes through a mental breakdown and attempts suicide as she struggles with puberty, clinging to memories of the idyllic childhood that she does not wish to leave. In *A Formal Feeling*, Anne Cameron comes home from **boarding school** for p.16 the holidays and must face the grief of her mother's death now that her father has remarried. Kate Brewer of *In Summer Light*, weakened by **mononucleosis**, p.513 must confront her long-simmering anger toward her famous and egotistical artist father before she can finally step out of his shadow to create her own art. All three of these coming-of-age stories show the gradual processes through which adolescents must go to explore their feelings and move beyond their self-absorbed worlds.

Working slowly, and preferring writing in longhand over using a keyboard, Zibby Oneal has produced a small number of books, but they have made a large impact. Although critics have praised *A For-*

mal Feeling as her most nearly technically perfect novel, her earlier novel *The Language of Goldfish* has been her most popular book among young readers and teachers. All three novels received **Notable** and **Best Books for Young Adults** citations from the American Library Association. *A Formal Feeling* won the 1983 **Christopher Award** and the 2002 Phoenix Award, given annually by the Children's Literature Association to a book of the highest literary quality published twenty years prior.

p.480

p.45

p.147

— Lisa Rowe Fraustino

Mononucleosis

Mononucleiosis, also called the "kissing disease," is an acute viral infection that enlarges the lymph nodes. The virus is transmitted through infected saliva or blood. It causes fever, fatigue, and weight loss. Treatment is usually bed rest, limits on physical activity, and medication to relieve fever. The symptoms generally go away after several months of treatment, and there are seldom serious complications. Medical science has not found effective ways to destroy or control viruses, so most information about them comes from studying their effects on the body. "Mono" occurs frequently in young adults and is fairly common in the U.S., Canada, and Europe.

Uri Orlev

Born: February 24, 1931; Warsaw, Poland

www.ithl.org.il/author_info.asp?id=192

The Israeli writer **Uri Orlev** writes mainly on Jewish themes, but his books appeal to young adults of all religious backgrounds. He typically draws on his own childhood because he believes that children experience events much more intensely than adults do. His books are often autobiographical, and they are at once scary, funny, and believable. His young heroes suffer the embarrassments of childhood and puberty as they grow up.

Orlev was born Jerzy Henryk Orlowski in Warsaw, Poland. During World War II, his father was captured by Russians, and his mother was murdered by **German Nazis**. Orlev and his younger brother were reared by their aunt and were eventually smuggled out of Warsaw's **Jewish ghetto** and hidden by Christian Polish families, which is how many Jews survived the war. In 1943 the Germans captured Orlev and his brother and put them in a **concentration camp**, where they suffered terribly until the United States Army liberated the camp. Fourteen-year-old Orlev and his brother then moved to a **kibbutz** in Palestine (now Israel). After working for many years on a cattle farm, Orlev moved to the city of Jerusalem.

The Island on Bird Street recreates Orlev's experiences as a boy in Warsaw's Jewish ghetto. During World War II, Alex hides alone in a bombed-out house. While he waits for his father to return, he takes what he needs from abandoned houses nearby.

p.407

p.515

p.590

p.516

Jewish Ghetto

A ghetto is an area of a city in which a minority or impoverished group is required to live. The term "ghetto" originated with 14th century Italians who used it to designate restricted areas of housing for Jews. Jewish ghettos have existed in Rome, Italy; Venice, Italy; and Frankfurt, Germany. The Jewish residents lived in a small area of the city that often was locked at night to protect the Christian residents of the city from losing their faith. During the Nazi reign in Europe in the twentieth century, ghettos were established in cities such as Warsaw, Poland, and Jews were relocated to live in them. These ghettos became transition areas to the concentration camps. We also refer to neighborhoods where African Americans, Asian Americans, or certain immigrants groups live as ghettos. In this case, they are not forced to live there by law, but economic circumstances and social prejudice leave the members of the group little choice but to live in the ghetto.

His only friend is a white mouse named Snow. Alex has scary adventures when strangers come in to search his hideout. Meanwhile, he learns the tricks of survival under life-threatening conditions.

The Man From the Other Side is set on the outskirts of the Warsaw ghetto in 1942. Fourteen-year-old Marek Jaworski has a bad conscience. With a couple of thuggish school buddies, he robs a frightened Jewish man. When his mother finds the money he has stolen, Marek promises he will find and give the money to a poor Jew. This happens when he sees a stranger in a Roman Catholic church who does not seem to know how to cross himself properly. Marek befriends the man, who is a Jew pretending to be a Christian in order to escape from Nazi persecution. After Marek persuades his grandparents to shelter the man, he learns a secret about his dead father and his racist grandmother learns some truths about humanity in the days before the Warsaw ghetto uprising.

Kibbutz

Kibbutz is the Hebrew word for "communal settlement." Such communities were first founded in what would become Israel some forty years before the founding of the state, in 1948. These rural communities began as cooperative farms. Housing was provided for families, but children all slept in dedicated children's housing. Dining halls, auditoriums, swimming pools, and community medical centers served the entire community. Today there are more than 250 kibbutzim in Israel with populations of forty to one thousand members each. Children now live with their parents in individual housing, but many public buildings still serve the needs of the entire community. In addition to agriculture, most kibbutzim now also engage in industry, producing some commercial products.

Lydia, Queen of Palestine is based on the life of the Israeli poet Arianna Haran. Ten-year-old Lydia describes her childhood escapades in pre-World War II Romania, her struggles to understand her parents' divorce amid the chaos of the war, and her life on a kibbutz in Palestine. She is amusing and likable as she tells about trying to make friends with schoolmates and teachers. A similar novel is *The Lady with the Hat*, in which seventeen-year-old Yulek survives the German concentration camps and joins a group of young Jews preparing to live on a kibbutz in Palestine after the war. He is unaware that his aunt living in London is looking for him. Both Jewish and non-Jewish readers find Orlev's realistic books fascinating. Orlev's writing honors include Denmark's **Hans Christian Andersen Medal** and **Mildred L. Batchelder Awards** for *The Island on Bird Street* and *The Man from the Other Side*.

 p.120   p.46

– Fiona Kelleghan

Judith Ortiz-Cofer

Born: February 24, 1952; Hormigueros, Puerto Rico

www.english.uga.edu/~jcofer/home.html

Judith Ortiz-Cofer has written many books. Only two of them were written as young adult fiction; however, most of her writing deals with coming-of-age situations, particularly those of young women from bilingual or bicultural backgrounds.

Ortiz-Cofer grew up in two worlds: the Puerto Rico of her birth and the predominantly Latino barrio in which her family lived in Paterson, New Jersey, from the time she was four. Her father, J. M. Ortiz, served in the U.S. Navy and was usually stationed at the nearby Brooklyn Navy Yard. The family stayed in New Jersey when the father was home, but the mother and children usually returned to Puerto Rico when he was at sea.

Ortiz-Cofer grew up speaking English even though she lived in what she has called "El Building," an apartment complex in Paterson occupied exclusively by Spanish-speaking Puerto Ricans. When she returned to Puerto Rico, she stayed with grandparents and other relatives who spoke Spanish primarily. Nevertheless, English remained the language in which she felt comfortable.

The twelve stories in *An Island Like You: Stories of the Barrio* are interrelated and focus on young people forced to make decisions that will influence their futures substantially. A

.519
.518

TITLES

An Island Like You: Stories of the Barrio, 1995

The Year of Our Revolution: New and Selected Stories and Poems, 1998

The Meaning of Consuelo, 2003

Call Me Maria, 2004

recurrent theme in these stories is that people must be true to themselves and resist yielding to peer pressure. In nearly all the stories, grandparents and other elders represent the traditions and culture of Puerto Rico, while parents and young relatives prefer assimilation in mainstream American life.

In many stories Puerto Rico represents a place of redemption. In "Bad Influence," Rita's liaison with her boyfriend results in her being sent, quite against her will, to live with her grandparents in Puerto Rico. Through her grandfather, who is a spiritualist, she is redeemed, saved from the bad influence of her boyfriend. In "Arturo's Flight," a studious boy, Arturo, is teased and chased by his classmates because he is reading William Shakespeare. He flees, throwing his copy of Shakespeare's plays into a nearby dumpster. Once this crisis ends, he returns to the dumpster to rescue the book he has discarded. In these stories, young people are faced with problems that seem to them monumental but nevertheless adhere to their principles and survive adolescence.

The Year of Our Revolution is more sophisticated than *An Island Like You*. In its combination of short stories and poems, the first-person narrator, Mary Ellen, also called

Barrio

In the U.S., a barrio is a Latino neighborhood or part of town. In many Southwestern cities, the barrio was the original settlement founded by Spanish explorers and Mexican settlers. As the cities grew, the Latino population became isolated in the barrio much as the Jewish had been in ghettos. While not legally required to live there, the Latinos remained because of community and because prejudice kept them out of other parts of the growing cities. Today, many barrios are enjoying a renewal. The buildings are being renovated and businesses are moving in to help preserve the history and heritage of the original settlers of the Southwest. In other cities, new Latino populations are creating barrios and establishing services to help recent immigrants to the U.S.

Puerto Rico

The Caribbean island of Puerto Rico was first settled by Native Americans from South America. During Columbus's second voyage in 1493, the Spanish discovered the island. Explorer Ponce de León became the leading figure behind the Spanish colonization of Puerto Rico, which had begun by 1508. The lack of Spanish women resulted in the intermarriage of Spanish, Indian, and African slaves, which has resulted in a racially harmonious population. During centuries of Spanish rule, Puerto Ricans developed an economy based on raising cattle, sugar cane, tobacco, and coffee. In 1898, Spain ceded the island to the U.S. as a result of the Spanish-American War. In 1902 Puerto Rico was named a territory of the U.S., and in 1940 Congress granted Puerto Ricans U.S. citizenship. This resulted in the first wave of Puerto Rican immigration to the U.S. In 1952, Puerto Rico became the Commonwealth of Puerto Rico, with its own constitution and government. While the citizens of Puerto Rico retain U.S. citizenship, they still have resisted becoming the fifty-first state of the U.S.A.

Maria Elenita, reveals some of the conflicts of her bicultural background. The stories deal head-on with the conflicts that American-born children of Puerto Rican parents experience in growing up, particularly in the late 1960's, the time frame of this book. The collection includes fables that reinforce many of the themes of its other stories and poems.

Judith Ortiz-Cofer's other books include *Latin Women Pray* (1980), *The Line in the Sun* (1989), *Silent Dancing: A Partial Remembrance of a Puerto Rican Childhood* (1990), and *The Latin Deli* (1993). Although she did not aim them specifically at young adult readers, they are appropriate for younger readers. Her intermixing of prose and poetry is particularly effective in reinforcing the themes that most concern her.

– R. Baird Shuman

George Orwell

Born: June 25, 1903; Motihari, India
Died: January 21, 1950; London, England
http://www.k-l.com/Orwell/

TITLES

Animal Farm, 1945

Nineteen Eighty-Four, 1949

One of the most important writers of the twentieth century, **George Orwell** is best known for his brilliant satires attacking **totalitarianism**. He never wrote specifically for younger readers, but his two most famous books and many of his essays are widely read and appreciated by young adults.

Born in India, where his father was an opium agent in the British colonial service, Orwell grew up as Eric Blair. At an early age he went to England for his schooling, which took him as far the prestigious **Eton College**. Instead of going on to a university, he joined the British colonial service in Burma (later Myanmar), which was then part of British India. Several years of helping to police colonial subjects taught him to hate imperialism. During his first home leave, he resigned his position and decided to become a writer. He did odd jobs in Paris and London and joined the group of unemployed men who were perpetually on the move in southern England. His first book, *Down and Out in Paris and London* (1933) describes those experiences.

Meanwhile, he adopted the pen name "George Orwell." From then until shortly before he died, he made only a meager living as a writer. In 1937 he

p.521

p.32

p.22

p.20

went to Spain with his new wife to report on the 567▸ civil war. Always more than an armchair socialist, he joined an antifascist militia and fought until a bullet in the throat knocked him out of action. He returned to England and wrote a moving memoir of his Spanish experience in *Homage to Catalonia* (1938).

In 1945 Orwell published *Animal Farm*, a brief parable on the Russian Revolution. Fed up with being oppressed by corrupt humans, the animals on a farm rise up, drive the humans out, and create a socialist state under the leadership of the pigs—who represent the Russian Revolution's ruthless **Bolshe-** 576▸ **viks.** At first, conditions on the farm improve, but gradually the pigs take on the worst characteristics of the humans and transform the farm into an oppressive totalitarian state.

Although Orwell had no high hopes for this book, it was an immediate **best-** 384▸ **seller** whose success suddenly lifted him to prosperity. However, by then his health 522▸ was broken by **tuberculosis.** He spent his last few years working on the book that would be recognized as his masterpiece and that would make the term "Orwellian" a synonym for totalitarian nightmare.

A savage satire on totalitarianism, *Nineteen Eighty-Four* targets not only

Totalitarianism

Totalitarianism is a form of government that controls not only political life but also every aspect of an individual's private life. The goal of a totalitarian state is to achieve a perfect, harmonious society. Such regimes often come into power to control the chaos left by war or collapse of a corrupt government. They usually are led by a dictator, a single government authority. They do not allow for debate or views contrary to the leader's policies. They frequently employ secret police to spy on individuals and their activities and attitudes. Totalitarian governments in recent history include Adolf Hitler's Germany, Joseph Stalin's Soviet Union, and Chairman Mao Tse-tung's China.

p.227 **communism** and fascism but also aspects of the Britain in which Orwell lived. Its **protagonist**, p.23 Winston Smith, works for a government controlled by a remote figure known only as "Big Brother." A perpetual war among three superstates gives the government a justification for every form of control imaginable over its citizens. Cameras watch everyone everywhere in a sort of universal, paranoia-inspiring reality show. Television screens that can never be shut off constantly indoctrinate people, and the state maintains its control by constantly rewriting history. It also works to dumb-down the language—a form of English called Newspeak—to make it impossible for people even to think subversive thoughts. In the midst of this nightmare, Winston falls in love with a woman named Julia. Together, they try to find privacy to express their love and their mutual hatred of the state but are ultimately reduced to Big Brother-loving drones.

Nineteen Eighty-Four is easy to read but painful to experience. While Orwell did not intend it as a prediction of the future, he did want it to be a warning of the dangers of government power. Since his novel was published, writers of every political stripe have interpreted it as an attack on the political philosophies that they oppose. That fact in itself is a confirmation of George Orwell's concern for the manipulation of language.

— Fiona Kelleghan

Tuberculosis

Tuberculosis is a highly infectious lung disease that destroys tissue. It is caused by bacteria that spread easily in overcrowded, unsanitary conditions. The bacteria are found in the droplets released when a person with active tuberculosis sneezes, coughs, or even talks. This mist of droplets can remain aloft for hours. When a person inhales these droplets, the bacilli can be carried to the lungs, causing infection. Most people will not become infected with the disease, and of those who become infected, most recover. Those who do not recover experience destruction of the tissue in the lungs. Control of tuberculosis in the U.S. has come from early diagnosis. The tuberculin skin test is a common diagnostic test for tuberculosis. Current treatment includes antituberculosis drugs and antibiotics so that those infected are no longer contagious. In developing countries, there is a greater incidence of tuberculosis, and living conditions make it difficult to bring it under control through preventative measures.

Linda Sue Park

Born: March 25, 1960; Urbana, Illinois

www.lspark.com

The courageous young teenagers of **Linda Sue Park**'s books all live in Korea. While they battle typical problems such as sibling rivalry, girls versus boys, and family issues, they also live in extraordinary times. The historical eras of Park's novels range from the Middle Ages to World War II. Against a carefully historically and richly described social background, her young protagonists face important challenges. The world of Park's characters is fascinating, dangerous, and always exciting.

Born in Illinois, Park is the daughter of parents who immigrated to America from Korea. Her father was a computer analyst and her mother a teacher. Park grew up loving to read and write and sold her first haiku poem to *Trailblazer Magazine* at the age of nine. She gave the one-dollar check she received to her father, who framed it on Christmas day, 1969. After studying English at Stanford University, Park wrote publicity releases for an oil company. After marrying an Irishman, she moved to Europe, where she studied literature and taught English. She returned to America in 1990. While raising her two children and teaching, she began to write young adult fiction. Her love for Ko-

Haiku Poetry

Haiku refers to a Japanese poetic form. It is dictated by three units, the first of five syllables, the second of seven syllables, and the third of five syllables. In classical Japanese poetry, this form was part of a longer poem. However, in the 1890's, Masaoka Shiki defined a new independent poetic form. Haiku is not only strictly defined by form, it is also defined by content. Each poem should be a response or observation of the poet to daily life. Also, each Haiku must contain an expression that defines a season, such as snow for winter, or cherry blossom for spring.

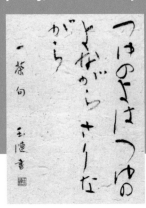

rea and her talents at storytelling have made for wonderful books well beyond the ordinary.

Park's first novel, *Seesaw Girl*, takes place in aristocratic Korea of the seventeenth century. Beautiful illustrations help transport readers into the world of twelve-year-old Jade Blossom. Korean custom of the time period required girls and women of the upper class to stay in their homes until they were married. Jade Blossom rebels and is smuggled out in a market basket. Back home, she continues to rely on her imagination and creativity to make life more exciting.

The Kite Fighters focuses on sibling rivalry between two teenage brothers in the year 1473. Kee-sup is excellent at making fighting kites. His younger brother, Young-sup, is a master at flying them. When Korea's boy king asks Young-sup to design and fly the royal kite at the New Year's Day competition, the brothers build a kite whose flying lines have razor-sharp pottery pieces slicing the competitors.

A Single Shard tells how a twelve-year-old orphan boy, Tree-ear, becomes a potter's **apprentice** during the Middle Ages. With courage and determination, he travels to present Korea's king with two glazed pots. Even encountering bandits does not deter him.

p.24

When My Name Was Keoko takes place in Korea during World War II, when the whole country suffered at the hands of the occupying Japanese forces. Like other Koreans, Sun-hee, a spirited girl who is ten in 1940, and her older brother Tae-yul must take new Japanese names. Brother and sister tell the story in alternating chapters, as they survive perilous situations. p.525

Linda Sue Park has quickly established her reputation as an award-winning storyteller whose characters are as imaginative as their historical settings are fascinating. Her teenagers live in a world different from contemporary America, and encounter many adventures. Among the awards she has received is a Newbery Medal for *A Single Shard*, which was chosen as one of the American Library Association's Best Books for Young Adults. p.234 p.102 p.480 p.45

– R. C. Lutz

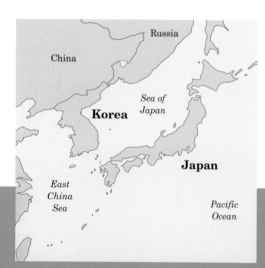

Japanese Occupation of Korea

Japan occupied Korea in 1910 and held control of the country until the end of World War II in 1945. During that time, the Japanese ruled the Koreans. Some 750,000 Japanese resided in Korea and had control of the government and the economy. Japan did modernize Korea by building roads, harbors, dams, railroads, and factories. However, all of this moderniziation was to support Japan's military goals. Meanwhile, the Koreans remained uneducated. It was not until 1998 that Japanese Prime Minister Obuchi apologized to the Korean government and people for the colonial occupation of Korea earlier in the century.

Katherine Paterson

Born: October 31, 1932; Qing Jin, China

www.terabithia.com

Katherine Paterson's young adult novels usually feature realistic, young teenagers who are struggling with feelings of isolation and abandonment in their most important relationships: those with parents, siblings, and close friends. Although their feelings of isolation are common, the reasons for having such feelings are many, including separation by death, parental abandonment, sibling rivalry, and being different from peer groups.

Born in China to **missionary** parents, Paterson led a life that eventually brought her around the world to the United States, back overseas to Japan, then ultimately back to the United States. For a long time, she did not realize that she wanted to be a writer. Instead, she planned to be a missionary. Her plan was not realized; she spent her early adult years teaching elementary students and raising a family. When she later returned to college, a class project led her to write her first published book, *The Sign of the Chrysanthemum*. This novel, like many of her earlier works, is set in Japan, a country she grew to love during her time there. In it, a boy searches for his **samurai** warrior father, from whom he has been separated.

This theme of separation continues in *Bridge to Terabithia*. In this novel, young Jesse Aarons must deal with grief and loss in the aftermath of the death of his best friend, Leslie. The book, one of the first fiction books expressly written for young adults dealing with

p.527

p.528

p.34

Christian Missionaries in China

The Protestant missionary movement in China did much to foster understanding of China in Western countries from the 1850's through 1949, when the Communist regime took control of China. First the British, then the Americans flocked to China to find converts to Christianity. In 1900, the Boxer Rebellion saw the Chinese fight to expel this western influence from their country, but the missionaries continued their work. Perhaps their greatest contribution was in opening up Chinese society. They established schools, universities, and research institutions to bring education to more Chinese. They also brought an understanding of China to the West. Two children of missionaries to China, Henry Luce, founder of *Time* magazine, and Pearl S. Buck, the Nobel-Prize winning author of popular novels set in China, did much to popularize China through their publications. Other children of missionaries have served such important roles in furthering East-West relations as ambassadors from the United States to China.

the death of someone from within their own age group, also tackles other ways in which people can be separated, such as by differences in gender and socioeconomic background.

The Great Gilley Hopkins deals with an eleven-year-old girl in foster care who has trouble relating to anyone who tries to be close to her because of her confusion over the loss of her natural parents. Paterson shows Gilley's sometimes terrible behavior as part of her struggle to cope. This theme of dealing with the loss of a parent is common in Paterson's work. It recurs in books such as *Flip-Flop Girl*, in which siblings struggle to cope with their grief over the loss of their father. It also returns in *Jip*. In this novel, a young boy who has been abandoned lives on a struggling farm and ultimately seeks and finds his true identity.

p.123

KATHERINE PATERSON

Chrysanthemum

The chrysanthemum is the symbol of the Japanese monarchy and is visible on the royal coat of arms. This monarchy is the oldest in the world, dating from 660 B.C. The sixteen-petal flower is a common ornament on Japanese lacquerware. It even adorned the rifles used in World War II, indicating that each one belonged to the Emperor.

With her use of varied times, places, and male and female narrators, Paterson provides for young adult readers a view of children and teens who are all similar in their need to build meaningful relationships with others and their struggles to overcome the losses that sometimes accompany that closeness.

Katherine Paterson is one the most honored of contemporary writers of young adult fiction. She has received several awards for her realistic portrayals including **Newbery Medals** for *Bridge to Terabithia* and *Jacob Have I Loved* and the Scott O'Dell Award for Historical Fiction for *Jip*.

p.10

p.51

— Emma Harris

Jill Paton Walsh

Born: April 29, 1937; London, England

www.greenbay.co.uk/jpw.html

Most of **Jill Paton Walsh**'s novels for young adults are historical fiction. Their determined realism often extends into brutal violence and stark tragedy, and her novels set in the present are dominated by fascination with the past.

Born Gillian Bliss, Paton Walsh was educated at St. Michael's Convent in Finchley and St. Anne's College, Oxford. Afterward, she worked as a teacher until she married Anthony Paton Walsh in 1961.

Her first book, *Hengest's Tale* is a vividly dramatic account of the Dark Ages. *The Dolphin Crossing* and *Fireweed* are both accounts of young people who are emotionally devastated when they become involved in key events of World War II—the evacuation of Dunkirk in the former, the London Blitz in the latter. Paton Walsh's first contemporary novel, *Goldengrove*, also features a key character devastated by the war, a portion of whose suffering is communicated to his adolescent descendants; its sequel, *Unleaving*, is a powerful tale of recovery, beautifully illuminated by its Cornish setting. The shorter contemporary novel *Gaffer Sampson's Luck*, set in Norfolk, is distinctly lackluster by comparison, although it won the **Smarties Prize**.

Paton Walsh set *The Emperor's Winding Sheet* in Constantinople during the period in which the last remnant of the old Roman Empire was falling to the Turks. It is a vivid historical reconstruction and a fine novel, although its record of decay and destruction is profoundly disturbing. *A Parcel of Patterns*, which describes how the people of the Derby-

p.117

p.506

p.41

.530

Fall of the Roman Empire

The decline and eventual fall of Rome began with the reign of Emperor Marcus Aurelius, a brutal persecutor of the Christians, who reigned from 161-180 C.E. There followed a succession of rulers and a long period of internal strife. The vast empire began to fall, with the collapse of Roman settlements on the Rhine and Danube rivers and the invasion of the eastern provinces by the Persians. When Constantine the Great assumed control of the Roman world, he reunited the Western and Eastern Roman Empires. He converted to Christianity and made it the official religion of the Empire. He established the seat of government in Byzantium, later named Constantinople in his honor (modern-day Istanbul). Following his death in 337, there was a period of civil wars. By 395, the empire was divided into the Roman Western and the Greek Byzantine Eastern empires. The Eastern Empire lived on until 1435, when it was conquered by the Turks. The Western Roman Empire was overrun by Germanic tribes. The conquest of Africa by the Vandals and the seizure of Gaul and Italy by the Huns soon followed. The city of Rome was plundered in 410 by the Visigoths and by the Vandals in 455. In 475, Orestes, a former lieutenant of Attila the Hun, crowned his young son Romulus emperor of the Roman Empire. Orestes, at odds with his Germanic army, was slain in 476, and the mercenary leader Odoacer overthrew the child emperor on September 4, 476, finalizing the fall of ancient Rome.

shire village of Eyam heroically quarantined themselves when invaded by the plague, is similarly harrowing.

In the brilliant time-slip *fantasy* p.87 *A Chance Child*, an unwanted child makes his way along a canal from a present-day rubbish dump to the early days of the Industrial Revolution. p.531 There he shares the experience of child laborers, initially as a kind of ghost but eventually as a wholehearted participant. The fact that he can find more to engage him emotionally in the difficult past than the unbearable present is a particularly poignant tragedy. These issues are explored in Paton Walsh's fine allegorical adult fantasy *Knowledge of Angels* (1994).

Torch is a more effective trip into science fiction than Paton Walsh's rather awkward novel for younger readers *The Green Book* (1981), although it is similarly stylized. Its pro-tagonists, p.23 living in a post-technological society after a ecological catastrophe, embark upon a quest to learn about the wonders of "Ago" and rediscover Olympian ideals by means of the "torch of Olim." *Grace* scrupulously reconstructs the story of Grace Darling, the lighthouse-keeper's daughter who became an early heroine—and victim—of press hype when she helped her father rescue survivors of a wreck. As with almost all of Paton Walsh's young adult fiction, it shows that even when virtue does not go unrewarded, its rewards usually come with severe penalties—a hard lesson, but one that needs to be learned.

Jill Paton Walsh's writing honors include a **Whitbread Children's Book of the Year award** for *The Emperor's Winding*, a Boston Globe-Horn Book Award for *Unleaving*, and a Phoenix Award for *A Chance Child*.

p.747
p.147

– Brian Stableford

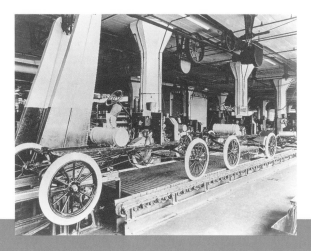

Industrial Revolution

The period of invention from the beginning of the eighteenth century to the beginning of the nineteenth century is known as the Industrial Revolution. It began first in Great Britain but quickly spread to the rest of the modern world. It was ushered in by the invention of machines that could do work that previously was done by people. This shifted workers from fields to factories, and the population began the move from farms to the cities. By 1813, British industry employed more workers than did agriculture. The invention of the steam engine by James Watt was a major contribution to the Industrial Revolution. Soon steam provided power for machines, then locomotives, and finally boats. Not only was the way in which products were created changing, but also how they were distributed throughout the world. With increased productivity came a higher output of products, which in turn reduced prices. However, the Industrial Revolution also brought problems. Industry resulted in pollution of air, water, and soil. Working conditions were brutal and hours were long. The heritage of the Industrial Revolution has continued to the present day. As we find ways to improve productivity, we continue to cope with how to improve the working environment.

Gary Paulsen

Born: May 17, 1939; Minneapolis, Minnesota

www.randomhouse.com/features/garypaulsen

For **Gary Paulsen**, the wilderness that remains beyond the massive urban developments where most of the people of the United States live is a valuable and misunderstood resource. In his books, young men displaced from dysfunctional but conventional lives in the cities—both contemporary and historical—find that they are truly at home in undeveloped country and are able to realize and appreciate strengths of character that have previously been dormant. Frequently, their contacts and connections with animals or older people who have sought solitude reveal aspects of themselves that superficial relationships with other humans have not touched.

When Paulsen was born in Minnesota in 1939, his father was away serving in the army. Their initial meeting took place in 1946 when the family was reunited in the Philippines. Paulsen grew up undisciplined and unruly. He was an indifferent student who had read only one book until a librarian offered him p.35 a membership card when he entered a library to warm up while delivering newspapers. After serving in the army for several years, he became a satellite repair technician but left that job abruptly to work as a magazine proofreader so he could write at p.533 night. He completed his first novel during a winter in Minnesota while living in a cabin in the woods.

Finding the rural setting congenial, Paulsen combined writing with a fascination for dogs, eventually completing Alaska's fabled Iditarod dog-sled p.42 race twice. When a heart condition forced him to limit his participation in rigorous sporting activities, he focused his energy on writing, employing the same rigor that he had used in the eighteen-to-twenty day dog-sled races. His dedication resulted in a continuous production of books through three decades.

Among Paulsen's earliest works, *Dogsong* is particularly powerful and compelling. Its **Eskimo protagonist** on the threshold of adulthood must establish a deep understanding of animal nature to survive. On a journey of discovery through an arctic wilderness and into his psyche, he recovers a lost heritage, becomes attuned to a harsh landscape and accepts the responsibilities that his strengths demand. Vivid description, deep psychological insight and a command of the subject make the novel very compelling. *Foxman* and *Night of the White Deer* are similar in portraying alienated teenagers who learn about life from an older person separated from society.

.534
p.233

In addition to Paulsen's many other books based on human interactions with animals as an aspect of developing the resources necessary to live in a harsh environment, Paulsen has also written candidly about controversial issues. His experiences in the army led to *Soldier's Heart*, a novel illustrating his belief that nothing about the American Civil War was nice. *The Rifle* is a message novel that traces the path of a weapon that damages the life of every person who handles it; the novel directly

Proofreader

When any document is published, it must first be typeset. In today's world, we use the computer to transfer words into electronic documents that can be formatted and printed directly or sent to a commercial printing company to be professionally printed. Prior to the computer, printing companies gave written or typed manuscript to a typesetter, who set type by placing the individual letters into trays and creating an impression on paper. The first printed copy was called a proof. Readers were employed to read the proof, comparing it to the manuscript to make sure the typesetter had not made errors. A series of proofreaders' marks gave the typesetter instructions to make certain changes: correct spelling, add a comma or other punctuation, transpose two words, etc. Today, we still need proofreaders to read for errors in documents that are created on the computer.

Eskimos

The term Eskimo is used to describe a large number of Native American groups living in the Arctic region. Many Canadian Arctic natives prefer the name "Inuit." The first contact between Eskimos and Europeans probably occurred in Greenland around 985. From the sixteenth century on, there were many expeditions seeking the Northwest Passage through Canada that brought increased contact with native peoples. The arrival of Russian fur traders in 1741 proved devastating to the native population. A combination of disease, warfare, and forced labor wiped out 80 to 90% of the Aleuts, the natives living in the Aleutian Islands. American and Scottish whalers also had an impact on the Eskimos, with disease taking its toll. The whaling industry eventually collapsed, and many Eskimos turned to fur trapping. Eventually, they lost most of their traditional lifestyle. Up until the 1960's, the Eskimo struggled with the advances of a new society, which resulted in poverty, high infant death rate, and high rates of tuberculosis. The government intervened, moving the Inuit from isolated hunting camps into organized communities, which were intended to provide employment, education, and health care.

confronts the issue of the American obsession with firearms. Paulsen's strong sense of social justice is prominently displayed in *Nightjohn* and *Sarny*, accounts of racism and slavery in the nineteenth century.

Although Paulsen's work is generally intense and dramatic, he has also created a lighter, comic milieu in *The Boy Who Owned the School* and in *Harris and Me*. Paulsen likes to develop a sequential narrative, following a central character through a historical period, as in the Francis Tucket novels, or returning to a basic situation as in the books detailing a young man's struggles to survive in the wilderness, *Hatchet*, *The River* and the two Brian Robeson books.

Among Gary Paulsen's numerous writing awards, *Hatchet*, *Dogsong* and *The Winter Room* have been listed as **Newbery Honor Books**, and *Soldier's Heart* was chosen as a *Publishers Weekly* **Best Book of the Year** and one of the **American Library Association's Best Books for Young Adults**.

p.10
p.14
p.45
p.48

– Leon Lewis

Philippa Pearce

Born: January 23, 1920; Great Shelford,
Cambridgeshire, England

www.oup.co.uk/oxed/children/authors/pearce

Philippa Pearce
grew up in rural England, where her father
was a miller. After completing her education at
p.5 **Girton College, Cambridge**, she worked for
the British civil service
p.6 and the **British Broadcasting Corporation** (BBC) and later became an
.536 editor for **Oxford University Press**. However, she
did not begin to write until she was forced to rest fol-
p.522 lowing a bout with **tuberculosis**. Moved by a powerful nostalgia, she reconstructed her childhood environment in the beautifully executed adventure
story *Minnow on the Say*. She then progressed to a
fictional meditation on the recovery of lost time and
the inevitability of change in one of the great children's books of the modern era, the brilliant **Carnegie Medal**-winning timeslip romance *Tom's Mid-*
p.42 *night Garden*. Although the plot of the novel has
something in common with Robert Nathan's classic
romance *Portrait of Jennie* (1940), in that Hatty, the
mysterious girl Tom encounters in the magically
transformed garden, grows older at each meeting,
Pearce employs the motif in a very different way,
progressing toward a profitable meeting of minds.

The distinction of producing a masterpiece is a
rare one, and it is not surprising that Pearce never
recovered the intensity of her first two books. She
did, however, continue to write stylish fiction, much

Oxford University Press

Oxford University first began printing books in 1478, two years after William Caxton introduced the first printing press to England. By 1586, the University had official permission to print books, Delegates were appointed to oversee the operation of the Press, and by 1668 Oxford University Press was organized as it exists today. The press obtained the right to print the King James Authorized Version of the Bible in the seventeenth century, which resulted in two centuries of profitable publishing. Selling bibles is big business. The American office was opened in 1896 and printed religious books as well as scholarly works. OUP is the largest publisher in the United Kingdom and the world's largest university press. As a department of the university, OUP contributes approximately 30% of its profits to the university. As a not-for-profit organization, all of OUP's earnings are reinvested in the press or the university.

of it for younger readers. *A Dog So Small* is an unusual and neatly moralistic story about the art of making do, whose young protagonist tries to make p.23 the best of his disappointment at receiving a present of a picture of a dog rather than a living creature. *The Children of the House* (also known as *The Children of Charlecote*) is an adaptation of a nostalgic story initially written by her coauthor about the exploits of his young forebears in the years preceding World War I. *The Way to Sattin Shore* belatedly attempted to revisit the same imaginative territory as *Tom's Midnight Garden* but it could not muster the same emotional intensity. The same is also true of such short stories as "Miss Mountain" and "Her Father's Attic" in *The Shadow-Cage*, and "The Fir Cone" in *The Rope*.

Pearce's short fiction is, however, always polished and well plotted, and often very witty; the stories in *The Elm Street Lot*, and such later items as "The Nest-Egg" (in *The Rope*) are celebrations of inventive approaches to personal problems, in much the same vein as *A Dog So Small*. The best items in *The Shadow-Cage* and *Who's Afraid?* are ghost stories firmly, if sometimes rather lightly, in the tradition of M. R. James.

Given that the achievements of so many modern writers for young adults are spread across large numbers of books, frequently running into several dozens, the products of Philippa Pearce's endeavors over nearly half a century may seem thin. However, its compensating virtue is a remarkable concentration of effort and attention. *Minnow on the Say* and *A Dog So Small* are both fine works, while *Tom's Midnight Garden* stands out as a landmark of its kind, its genre, and its era.

– Brian Stableford

M. R. James

M. R. James (1862-1836) was Provost of King's College, Cambridge, and later the prestigous English boarding school Eton, but he is best known as the father of the modern ghost story. His ghost stores are the perfect example of quality over quantity. Although he wrote stories over a forty year period, his complete tally is only thirty-six stories. Almost all of James's stories have a common approach and content. They are told by an antiquarian, meaning that the incidents are linked to the study of old documents or buildings. They develop the theme of "a little knowledge is a dangerous thing," as the antiquarians in his stories always suffer from delving a little too far into things best left alone.

Richard Peck

Born: April 5, 1934; Decatur, Illinois

http://richardpeck.smartwriters.com/index.2ts

Richard Peck's books are about youths who stand apart from their peers. Their independence becomes an isolating factor as they mature and alienates them from their peers, their parents, and authority figures with whom they interact daily. Peck considers independence of thought and action the mark of worthwhile people—the kind of people who make compelling fictional protagonists.

Peck published his first young adult novel at the age of thirty-seven. A high-school English teacher, textbook editor in Chicago, and teacher at Hunter College and Hunter College High School in New York City, he has had realistic perspectives on the concerns of youths. He collaborated on various collections, but not until 1972 did his first young adult novel, *Don't Look and It Won't Hurt You*, appear. More books followed over the next three decades.

Peck's stature as a writer of young adult fiction is indicated by the fact that his earlier novels remain in print and are still read by adolescents. Also, when the Young Adult Services Division of the American Library Association issued its list of the **Best of the Best Books, 1970-1982**, Peck was one of only two writers from a field of seventy-five honorees who had more than two books on the list; he had three.

Born in Illinois, Peck came from a closely knit extended family that included his grandmother and her four sisters. After his father incurred a war injury that prevented him from farming, he moved his family into town where he ran a gas station. Peck's mother was a **dietitian**. While hanging around his

p.23

p.45

p.539

father's gas station, Peck was exposed to locals who were inveterate story tellers. One of his high school English teachers challenged him to become a writer. At about the same time, he spent a summer in New York City visiting relatives. These factors represented turning points in his life.

Peck's fiction deals with teenage pregnancy, the deaths of loved ones, suicide, and rape. He approaches these wrenching topics in ways that offer hope and encourage young readers to work on developing self-confidence in the face of daunting problems. His first novel, *Don't Look and It Won't Hurt You*, deals unabashedly with the unwanted pregnancy of a young woman, whose fifteen-year-old sister tells the story and, in an interesting role reversal, becomes a surrogate parent herself.

Are You in the House Alone?, deals directly with the sensitive subject of rape. *Close Enough to Touch* is a book about dating told from the viewpoint of a young boy. With the sudden death of the girl he loves, Matt reveals emotions seldom shown in fictional adolescent males. Among Peck's later fiction, *A Long Way from Chicago* is representative. Joey and his sister spend a week every summer with their eccentric grandmother and revel in her iconoclastic handling of hypocrites and **Holy Rollers**.

.540

Dietitian

A dietitian or nutritionist is a person who plans food and nutrition programs, supervises the preparation and serving of food , and promotes healthy eating habits. Today dietitians earn a bachelors degree in dietetics, food and nutrition, or food service management before becoming employed, most frequently in hospitals or schools. On the job, dietitians provide education about healthy eating habits and work with individuals to promote dietary changes that contribute to good health.

Holy Rollers

Holy Rollers is a term applied to charismatic Christians who believe that they can be filled with the spirit of the Holy Ghost, one of the three members of the Christian Holy Trinity. Frequently associated with the Pentacostal Church, Holy Rollers speak in tongues, or unknown languages, when moved by the spirit. They also may dance or roll in the aisles of the meeting house as a manifestation of the spirit, hence the name Holy Rollers.

Peck unflinchingly handles topics many people ignore, even though they present genuine coming-of-age problems. His novels are tempered by a compassionate understanding of the adolescent mentality and by a gentle wit.

Richard Peck's many writing honors include an **Edgar Allan Poe Award** for *Are You in the House Alone?*, a **Newbery Medal** for *A Year Down Yonder*, and five American Library Association awards for **Best Books for Young Adults**. In 1990 the Young Adult Library Services Association of the American Library Association gave him the **Margaret A. Edwards Award** for lifetime achievement.

– R. Baird Shuman

p.72
p.10
p.48
p.33

Robert Newton Peck

Born: February 17, 1928; rural Vermont

myathenet.net/~blahnik/rnpeck/about.htm

In most of **Robert Newton Peck**'s novels, teen-age protagonists confront conflict, danger, responsibilities, and needs. Often, though they are severely tested, they typically rise to their challenges. In the process, they move toward greater maturity and early adulthood. Most of his stories also feature adult figures who significantly aid the adolescents as they struggle toward understanding and resolution.

Peck was born on a small farm in Vermont and raised there during the **Depression** years. He attended a one-room country school, where his teacher inspired him to read and encouraged his lively imagination. At an early age, Mark Twain's *The Adventures of Tom Sawyer* (1876) became a shaping force in his view of story, style, and audience. When Peck was older, he worked as hog butcher and lumberjack, served in the army as a machine-gunner, graduated from college, studied law, and worked in **advertising**. However, he would discover through the success of his first novel that he could make a living at writing stories that both children and young adults loved to read. After making that discovery, Peck never stopped writing.

Peck's first book, *A Day No Pigs Would Die*, came out of his personal experience as a farm-boy who at the age of thirteen had to assume the family responsibilities when his father died. Many other stories succeeded this poignant tale before Peck turned back to his sudden coming-of-age experience in *A Part of the Sky*, a sequel that focuses on the eco-

p.233

p.437

.542

.657

TITLES

nomic hardships of the Depression and the steadying force of personal values. Peck also has a love for research and history. His next two books, *Fawn* and *Hang for Treason*, center on the Battle of Ticonderoga during the Revolutionary War. Both books' protagonists experience war's savagery and their conflicting loyalties toward the opposing sides. Another book that highlights the crucible of a loyalty conflict is *Justice Lion*, in which Muncie Bolt's father must prosecute lifelong friends for making bootleg liquor.

p.543

A recurrent theme in many of Peck's stories is the need for family. In *Dukes* and *Horse Thief*, the family is a thrown-together, motley collection of people that need one another. In *Hallapoosa*, an old bachelor becomes a family man when his seven orphaned nephews and nieces move in with him; in *Extra Innings* a great

Mark Twain's
The Adventures of Tom Sawyer

Mark Twain's style is characterized by the use of exaggeration, irreverence, seriousness, cynicism, and commentary on the human condition. All of this is masked in an uncomplicated, straightforward narrative introducing everyday expression into American fiction. Twain's nostalgic recollections of his own youth became the basis of *The Adventures of Tom Sawyer*, in which he balances romantic and realistic, humor and pathos, and innocence and evil. In the end, it is, as Mark Twain put it, "the history of a boy." Tom is the all-American boy, defining in himself the concept of American boyhood as he passes from one obsession to another, always showing a child's ability to concentrate all of his energies on one thing at a time. *The Adventures of Tom Sawyer* is a true American classic.

Battle of Ticonderoga

Fort Ticonderoga was an American stronghold during the Revolutionary War. It is located about ninety-five miles north of Albany, New York, between Lake George and Lake Champlain. In Iroquois, it means "place between two waters." As the French Fort Carillon, it was the site of a 1758 battle in the French Indian Wars, during which the French turned back the British attackers. The British finally captured the fort in 1759 and renamed it Fort Ticonderoga. In 1775, Ethan Allen, an American revolutionary soldier, and the Green Mountain Boys overtook the fort. In 1777, the British forced the Americans from the fort; they later abandoned and burned it. In 1909, the fort was restored and turned into a museum.

grandfather and an adopted black great-aunt heal a boy after an airplane crash destroys his family. Courageous protagonists in *The Horse Hunters, Cowboy Ghost,* and *Nine Man Tree* rise to heroic stature as would-be healers, saviors, and survivors of families in distress. All these stories stress the values of endurance, sacrifice, and basic human goodness.

At his best, Peck is highly entertaining through his vivid style, well-developed and interesting characters, and fast-paced action. Through his books and making personal appearances in classrooms, he has carried forward the work of his beloved first childhood schoolteacher by helping to make the young excited about reading.

Robert Newton Peck is one of the most frequently honored authors of young adult books. Among his many awards are five citations for **American Library Association** **Best Books for Young Adults,** a **Newbery Medal** and a **Newbery Honor Book** award, and the **Margaret A. Edwards Award** for Outstanding Literature for Young Adults.

p.45

p.102

p.339

p.480

– Henry J. Baron

K. M. Peyton

Born: August 2, 1929; Birmingham, England

K. M. Peyton's books reveal her obsession with horses, which shows up even in her stories about boys. Her interest in horses remained evident throughout her writing career, which has spanned more than half a century; it is the main dramatic focus of her earliest novels. Peyton's many readers value the forthrightness of her outlook as much as the clean-cut candor of her literary style.

Born Kathleen Wendy Herald, Peyton was moved to begin writing at an early age by the frustration of her desire to own a pony—an impractical ambition for a girl raised in a city. It is the main dramatic focus of her earliest novels, which include her early Ruth Hollis novels *Fly-by-Night* and *The Team*, the historically inclined novels *Right Hand Man* (which was filmed in 1987) and *Dear Fred* (after whose publication Peyton damaged her spine in a riding accident), *Free Rein*, *The Sound of Distant Cheering*, *Darkling*, *Poor Badger*, *The Wild Boy* and *Queen Moon* and the trilogy begun with *The Swallow Tale*. *The Last Ditch* and *Blind Beauty* both feature the foremost **British steeplechase race**, the Grand National, the latter constituting a stirring modernization of the plot of Enid Bagnold's classic *National Velvet* (1930). Peyton's other sports stories, including the comedies *Who Sir, Me Sir?* and its sequel *Downhill All the Way*, are conspicuously lighthearted by comparison.

p.545

p.546

Peyton's greatest commercial and artistic success was the Flambards series, whose second volume, *The Edge of the Cloud*, won the **Carnegie Medal**. She extended the initial trilogy after its popularity was boosted by a successful television adaptation. This story is about an orphan girl who is abruptly transplanted to a country house in the early years of the century. There she enters into complex relationships with the two sons of the family and a groom. It is unusual in following its heroine from the age of twelve into her adulthood, when she becomes a mother. It thus presents a much fuller account of growing up than books narrowly aimed at particular age groups.

p.42

Peyton's earnest and highly effective ghost stories are equally distinguished; *A Pattern of Roses* and *Marion's Angels* redeploy the fascination with nineteenth century featured in such early works as *Windfall* and *The Maplin Bird*. *Unquiet Spirits* is closer in theme and tone to the sentimental *Snowfall*. *Firehead* is a more **melodramatic** excursion into the violent era of King Cnut.

p.198

Peyton's early collaborations with her husband Michael—whose initial she later included in her

British Steeplechase Race

The British Steeplechase Race is a horse race on a closed course of obstacles, including hedges and walls which the rider and horse must navigate. Originally it was a race for fox hunters over open country. Church steeples were used as course landmarks, giving the steeplechase its name. In 1839, the Grand National began, a closed course in which the riders complete two rounds for a total of 4.48 miles and 31 jumps. The Grand National Hunt Committee is the controlling body of the sport. Steeplechase is also popular in Ireland, France, and the U.S.

own byline—consisted of serials written for *The Scout Magazine*. She retained an interest in boys' adventure fiction, exemplified in such works as the historical spy story *Thunder in the Sky*, the melodramas *Prove Yourself a Hero* and its sequel *A Midsummer Night's Death*, and the Hitchcockian thriller *The Boy Who Wasn't There*. Peyton's male characters—including Will in the Flambards series and the hero of the overlapping trilogy begun with *Pennington's Seventeenth Summer*—are usually unruly, often driven to delinquency by their passionate nature. In effect, the boys are human equivalents of the unmanageable but gifted horses who can only be tamed by her spirited heroines. Humans are, alas, always the poorer investment; Will is killed in pursuit of his fascination with flying and Ruth Hollis, who is recruited to the Pennington saga in *The Beethoven Medal*, fails to keep Pat out of jail. They also tend, when they are old enough, to get the heroines pregnant. This mildly cynical frankness is, however, precisely what endears Peyton's work to many readers,

p.19

p.11

p.21

– Brian Stableford

Enid Bagnold's *National Velvet*

National Velvet, published in 1935 for young adult readers, is the story of Velvet Brown, a young English girl who lives with her family in a village by the sea. Velvet loves horses and dreams of becoming the best rider in England. When she wins the Piebald, an unruly horse known for jumping out of his pasture, in a village raffle, Velvet and Mi, the family's live-in helper, begin to train for the Grand National. Velvet's mother puts up the entry fee, and Velvet, diguised as a boy, is the rider. The Pie outjumps and outruns his competitors in the race only to be disqualified when Velvet is exposed as a girl: Women are not allowed to ride in the race. Suddenly, Velvet is at the center of the public's attention and gains the nickname "National Velvet."

Rodman Philbrick

Born: 1951; Boston, Massachusetts

www.rodmanphilbrick.com

.695

Once a longshoreman and **boat builder**, **Rodman (W. R.) Philbrick** began writing short stories in sixth grade. He even wrote a novel in high school, although it was never published. He continued to write several more novels, but these went unpublished until 1982 when *Shooting Star* debuted.

Before he began writing for young adults, he had published more than a dozen novels for adults, particularly mysteries and detective novels. In 1993, he won the Private Eye Writers of America's **Best Novel** award for *Brothers and Sinners*, coincidentally the same year as his first young adult novel appeared, *Freak the Mighty*. This book earned Philbrick multiple awards as well. The story of two unlikely friends, it was inspired by a boy who lived a few blocks from Philbrick. The book was adapted to the screen in 1998 as *The Mighty*, with theme music by Sting.

The sequel, *Max the Mighty*, focuses on a more confident Max, because of his friendship with Kevin or "Freak." Kevin is gone now, and Max finds himself befriending a young girl who is so voracious a reader her classmates call her "Worm." Once again, Max becomes a champion.

The idea for *The Fire Pony* came when Philbrick and his wife Lynn Harnett were driving in the Southwest. Philbrick's love of the land-

TITLES

Freak the Mighty, 1993

The Fire Pony, 1996

Max the Mighty, 1998

REM World, 2000

The Last Book in the Universe, 2000

The Journal of Douglas Allen Deeds: The Donner Party Expedition, 1846, 2001

The Young Man and the Sea, 2004

The Donner Party

What became known as the Donner Party was a group of people who left Springfield, Illinois, in the spring of 1846 on a 2,500 mile trek to the Mexican territory of Upper California. In July, the Donner Party split from the other travelers to try a shortcut through the barren Great Basin. The difficult crossing left them short of supplies and behind schedule. When they reached the Sierra Nevada mountains of eastern California, it was later October. An early blizzard trapped them in the mountains, where they spent five months struggling to survive. During the winter of 1846-1847, almost half of the 87 people in the party died, one third of the women and children and two thirds of the men. Those who survived were forced to resort to cannibalism to stay alive until they were rescued by an expedition from Sacramento.

scape and California's then rash of fires seemed to meld into this story of a pony, a boy, and his arsonist older brother. Philbrick also admits that Faulkner's short story, "The Barn Burner" may have nurtured its conception. It won the Washington, D.C., **Capitol Choice Award**.

Philbrick explored another genre in *REM World*, a **fantasy** tale, and then created *The Last Book in the Universe*, named a **Best Science Fiction Selection** by Voice of Youth Advocates, as well as a **Best Young Adult Book of the Year** by the **American Library Association**. Originally published as a short story, this novel grew out of Philbrick's unsatisfied imagination.

Next to be published was *The Journal of Douglas Allen Deeds*, a pseudo-journal of the Dear America/ My Name Is America series. Subtitled *The Donner Party Expedition, 1846*, this **historical fiction** novel reveals what might have occurred during the ill-fated journey west.

Philbrick, with Harnett, has also written three trilogies, two in the horror genre: The House on Cherry Street series—*The Haunting, The Horror,*

p.549

p.8

p.45

p.548

p.11

and *The Final Nightmare* (1995), and the Werewolf p.377 Chronicles—*Night Creature, Children of the Wolf,* and *The Wereing* (1996), and the third in the science-fiction genre, the Visitors series–*Strange Invaders, Things,* and *Brain Stealers* (1997). The pair discuss story ideas, Philbrick writes an outline, Harnett writes the first draft, and after more discussion, they create a final version. Additionally, they co-created *Abduction* (1998).

While Rodman Philbrick's series books are typically fast-paced and action-oriented, making them ideal for reluctant young adult readers, the characters of his principal young adult books all have a very human side to which young adults readily respond. Humor, wisdom, and compassion describe his body of work. While his mission is to tell a great story, life lessons emerge gracefully and compellingly.

— Alexa L. Sandmann

WASHINGTON, DC

Washington, D.C.'s Capitol Choice Award

Capitol Choice is a committee of librarians, teachers, booksellers, specialists, and editors who work in and around the Washington, D.C. area. These are people with a passion for children's books. Each year they discuss the merit of books for children and young readers up to age sixteen published the previous calendar year. The selected books must appeal to the young reader, plus show "clarity, accuracy, credibility, and …distinguished writing and illustration." The group was inspired by the work of Margaret Coughlan at the Library of Congress and has published the list of choices each year since 1996.

Meredith Ann Pierce

Born: July 5, 1958; Seattle, Washington

http://moonandunicorn.com

Fantasy writer **Meredith Ann Pierce** uses swords and sorcery to clothe the real and human issues of growing up, changing, and loving. While the settings of her novels are supernatural, the envies, fears, and sorrows that her characters experience mirror the real everyday problems that young adults face. p.55

Pierce has written two fantasy trilogies. The first book of her Darkangel trilogy is *The Darkangel* about a slave girl named Ariel whose mistress, Eoduin, is carried away by the vampire Darkangel, who wishes to drink her blood, steal her soul, and add her to his harem. While trying to rescue Eoduin, Ariel instead becomes a slave to Darkangel and his wives. Ariel sets off on a quest for the talisman she needs to free the vampire from his evil ways. In the second book, *A Gathering of Gargoyles*, Ariel marries the redeemed Darkangel, now named Irrylath; however, the marriage is not happy. Ariel sets off on another quest, hoping to find the magic that will earn her Irrylath's favor. In *The Pearl of the Soul of the World*, Ariel continues her quest, but this time the stakes are even higher. The world is dying of drought, and only Ariel can persuade the White Witch, the mother of seven darkangel sons, to end it. p.8 p.3

Pierce's Firebringer trilogy takes place in a world populated by unicorns displaced from their home- p.55

Sorcery

A sorcerer is a person who practices an ancient form of magic. Using charms, spells, rituals, or potions, a sorcerer uses energy to accomplish his or her goal, which can be for good or for evil. To those who believe in sorcery, it is all about controlling energy. A sorcerer also is called a wizard. Recently, the character of Harry Potter in the J. K. Rowling novels has introduced many readers to the concept of a sorcerer or wizard. Sorcerers also communicate with spirits of the dead, gaining information from the past or from the hereafter.

land, the Hallow Hills. In *Birth of the Firebringer*, readers meet Aljan (Jan), a unicorn prince eager to prove his worth. Soon to become a warrior, Aljan sets off on a pilgrimage that discloses his destiny as the legendary Firebringer and the prophesied liberator of his nation. In *Dark Moon*, Jan is attacked and lost at sea then rescued by humans who enslave horses. He escapes, seeking to conquer his enemies and free his people. The trilogy concludes with *The Son of Summer Stars*, in which Jan succeeds at last in returning the unicorns to the Hallow Hills.

Although Pierce is best known for her trilogies, she has also written several stand-alone works that have earned both awards and critical acclaim. *Treasure at the Heart of the Tanglewood* is one example. It is the story of Hannah, who lives by a magical forest with some animal companions. Flowers grow from Hannah's head, and she must pull them out and make them into tea for a wizard who lives in the woods. Hannah falls in love with a knight, whom the wizard turns into a fox. Hannah sets out on a journey to restore the fox to human form. In the process, she discovers her own identify and destiny.

Meredith Ann Pierce's writing is rich in description and poetry. The fantastical worlds she creates are visually appealing, and her imaginative characters seem real. Although good and evil battle on

MEREDITH ANN PIERCE

Unicorns

The Unicorn in Western legend is a horselike, white animal with one horn in the middle of its head. No one has proved the existence of the Unicorn, but in legend it is known for its purity and the magical power of its horn. The most famous depiction of the Unicorn is in a series of sixteenth century Belgian tapestries about a hunt. The tapesteries depict the unsuccessful hunt; the capture and taming of the Unicorn by a virgin, as is told in the medieval legend; and the captured unicorn chained to a tree in a fenced enclosure. The tapestries are on display at the Cloisters, a museum in New York City that is part of the Metropolitan Museum of Art.

mythical landscapes, Pierce never oversimplifies. Her characters must discern right and wrong in the face of ambiguity, and Pierce never denies them opportunities for deliverance. Her skill in the fantasy genre has earned her numerous awards. *The Darkangel* appeared among *Booklist*'s **Best Books of the Decade**. In 2002, *Treasure at the Heart of the Tanglewood* earned the **Best Book** honors from both the American Library Association and the Young Adult Library Services Association.

p.14

p.4

– Faith Hickman Brynie

Sylvia Plath

Born: October 27, 1932; Boston, Massachusetts
Died: February 11, 1963; London, England
www.sylviaplathforum.com

Although **Sylvia Plath** is best known as a poet, her novel *The Bell Jar* was one of the first works to examine the origins and growth of the artistic consciousness of a young woman. In several significant ways, it parallels J. D. Salinger's *The Catcher in the Rye* (1951), particularly in its protagonist, who is working as a guest editor of a woman's magazine in New York in 1953. Like Salinger's Holden Caulfield, Plath's Esther Greenwood is witty, ironic, self-aware, and set apart from the conformist tendencies of her contemporaries. Her accounts of her experiences are marked by an exasperated dismissal of conventional modes of thinking and acting, a means of shielding an inner sensitivity that cannot prevent her from eventually suffering a serious mental breakdown while attempting to write a novel. After being subjected to a brutally ineffective type of treatment, she is transferred to a private hospital, where she gradually recovers with the assistance of a compassionate woman psychiatrist.

The parallels between Esther Greenwood and Plath herself are clear. Plath based her novel on journal entries she had kept since she was seventeen. The college Greenwood attends is similar to Plath's **Smith College**; Esther's boyfriend

TITLE

The Bell Jar, 1963

is drawn from Plath's own college boyfriend; and her internship in New York is similar to Plath's at *Mademoiselle* magazine. Finally, Esther's suicide attempt, commitment to a state mental hospital, and psychotherapy resemble Plath's but are compressed for dramatic effect. The novel reaches beyond its autobiographical foundation, however, in terms of Plath's desire to examine the rigid social conventions that made it difficult for a woman to follow a path other than one designed to provide social and monetary security, preferably in a domestic arrangement in which any creative impulses were expected to be channeled toward the support of a husband and family.

In spite of her psychic fragility, Plath had the courage and spirit to move beyond this mode. She was awarded a **Fulbright Scholarship** for postgraduate study that she took at **Cambridge** in England, where she met and married the poet **Ted Hughes** in 1956. She taught in the United States and the United Kingdom during the late 1950's, wrote continuously during that time, and published her first book of poetry, *The Colossus*, in 1960, the

p.80

p.554

p.5

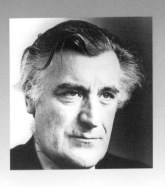

Ted Hughes

Ted Hughes was an English student at Cambridge University in 1956 when he met Sylvia Plath, a young American college student. They were married four months later. Hughes and Plath were both poets and they influenced each other's writing. They had two children, Frieda, born in 1960, and Nicholas, born in 1962. That same year, their marriage began to disintegrate. Plath sank into a depression and committed suicide in February, 1963. Hughes developed a reputation as a poet and was named poet laureate of England in 1984. However, his reputation was often overshadowed by the ghost of Plath. As her literary executor, he often refused permission to quote from her works and would not talk about their marriage. He surprised the literary world in 1998 with the publication of *Birthday Poems*, a collection of prose poems about his life with Plath. The book won major awards, and Hughes was made a member of the Order of Merit. He died the same year.

Sylvia, the Movie

The 2003 British movie starring Gwyneth Paltrow as Sylvia Plath tells the story of the relationship between Plath and her husband, Ted Hughes. By focusing on the marriage, the movie suggests that Plath's depression was caused by her husband's affairs with other women and her resulting jealousy, downplaying the depth of her depression before meeting Hughes. Frieda Hughes, their daughter, refused to cooperate with the filmmakers, limiting the quotations from Plath's work that could be used in the film. Readers of Plath's journals, poetry, and novel, *The Bell Jar*, will gain a better understanding of Plath's life and art as a writer.

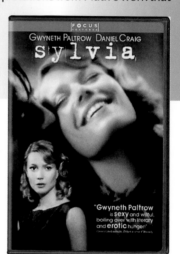

year her first child was born. She wrote *The Bell Jar* the following year but delayed publication so that she could accept a grant and revise the manuscript. Her second child was born in 1962, the year she and Hughes separated. While living alone in London in 1963, she committed suicide one month after the novel was published under the pseudonym Victoria Lucas.

Although *The Bell Jar* was not intended specifically for young adults, its depiction of an energetic, perceptive young woman entering the world of work after the excitement of a brilliant academic performance remains relevant and appealing, especially so for women whose artistic inclinations and literary sensibility resemble Plath's. The poetic power that Plath brought to her work is apparent in *The Bell Jar*, and its concerns with romance, social responsibility and mental illness are presented in a manner that has not made them seem dated or limited to a particular era. The film version of the novel made in 1979 is uneven, lacking the kind of charismatic performance that might have given Plath's protagonist something of the edge and verve the novel projects.

— Leon Lewis

Carol Plum-Ucci

Born: August 16, 1957; Atlantic City, New Jersey

Carol Plum-Ucci's novels are genuine page-turners, with compelling plots that are filled with unexpected twists and turns. They also address problems and issues faced by contemporary young adults. Issues addressed in her books include bullying, runaways, suicide, labeling and predetermined perceptions of reality, post-traumatic stress syndrome, **eating disorders**, surviving cancer, homophobia, alcoholism, parental infidelity, and the common desire to be popular. Plum-Ucci clearly has her finger on the pulse of modern teenage culture. Her teenage characters speak the language of today and communicate by cell phones and e-mail.

p.557

p.10

p.263

Plum-Ucci was reared on an island near Atlantic City, New Jersey, where she was born. The fact that she is a descendant of ten generations of sea captains may account for the strong sense of place in her novels. Her books are set on the South Jersey Shore, and close-knit small town life is an element in her writing.

Plum-Ucci trained in journalism and business writing, for which she has won a number of awards. Her message to young writers is to be persistent. It was persistence that led to the publication of her first novel, *The Body of Christopher Creed*, ten years after she began writing fiction. This book is a realistic and complex mystery. One day, Chris Creed, an unpopular boy who is the target of bullies, simply disappears. He leaves only an e-mail message behind, saying that he wishes he were someone else, that he wishes only to be gone. Is he a runaway? A suicide? Has he been murdered?

One of Chris's classmates, Torey Adams, is not satisfied with the theories about Chris's disappearance and decides to do something about it, even though he seems to have everything: friends, athletic ability, and a beautiful girlfriend. Torey's doubts lead him to befriend a troubled girl and a boy with a juvenile record, and he learns that all is not as idyllic as it seems in his affluent hometown. The final scenes are chilling, as Torey reaches a turning point in his life.

Plum-Ucci's second published novel, *What Happened to Lani Garver*, is an intense novel about a disturbing character, a newcomer to tight-knit Hackett Island. Lani is oddly **androgynous**; at first it is unclear to others whether he is a boy or a girl. He is a sensitive individual who helps high school sophomore Claire face her fears about a recurrence of her childhood **leukemia** and her eating disorder. The story takes a violent twist when outsider Lani is persecuted as a **homosexual**, and Claire's loyalty to her popular crowd is tested. This story explores the arts as outlets for expression, a subtle

558
p.237
p.57

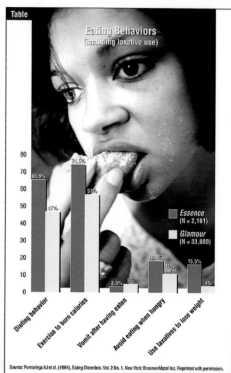

Table

Eating Behaviors
(including laxative use)

Essence (N = 2,161)
Glamour (N = 33,000)

Dieting behavior — 65.5% / 47%
Exercise to burn calories — 74.5% / 57%
Vomit after having eaten — 3.5% / 5%
Avoid eating when hungry — 18.5% / 11% (use?)
Use laxatives to lose weight — 16.5% / 4%

Source: Pumariega AJ et al. (1994). Eating Disorders. Vol. 2 No. 1. New York: Brunner/Mazel Inc. Reprinted with permission.

Eating Disorders

Eating disorders are psychological disorders that are characterized by an abnormal relationship between body image and eating. While obesity caused by overeating is an eating disorder, we most often think of anorexia nervosa and bulimia nervosa when we discuss this emotional and physical problem. Anorexia nervosa is characterized by a desire to be thin and a fear of gaining weight. It afflicts more women than men and often begins in adolescence. Loss of weight does not reduce the fear of becoming fat, leading to unhealthy weight loss. Bulimia nervosa refers to binge eating followed by self-induced vomiting. It is almost as damaging to health as anorexia.

mysticism, and compassion, suspense, and mystery. What causes Lani's appearance at the very moment when Claire needs help? What has happened to Lani Garver?

Carol Plum-Ucci's novels are tightly plotted and paced. Elements of mystery and suspense predominate as each main character befriends an outsider or underdog, gains insights into human nature, and grows through the events of the novel. Her books explore issues of concern to contemporary young adults, and once opened, they are difficult to put down. *The Body of Christopher Creed* has won several awards, including **Michael L. Printz Honor Book** and **American Library Association Best Books for Young Adults**, and was a finalist for the **Edgar Allen Poe Award** for Best Young Adult Mystery.

p.488

p.480

p.4

p.7

— Susan Butterworth

Androgyny

Androgyny defines something that has the characteristics of both male and female or, on the other hand, not seeming specifically masculine or feminine. In contemporary society, we most commonly associate androgyny with individuals who try to blur their gender identity. In popular culture, we can think of musician Marilyn Manson who, while a male, dresses in non-traditional clothes and make-up. We also can look at actress Diane Keaton's dress in Woody Allen's movie *Annie Hall*, in which, while a woman, she often wears mens clothing.

Edgar Allan Poe

Born: January 19, 1809; Boston, Massachusetts
Died: October 7, 1849; Baltimore, Maryland

www.poemuseum.org/index.html

Edgar Allan Poe was one of the earliest writers in the gothic genre in the United States. He created tales of horror and melancholy menace that still have the power to run chills up readers' spines more than a century and a half after he died. He is also credited with giving birth to the mystery genre with his stories of the detective C. Auguste Dupin and with sowing the seeds of science fiction in tales such as "The Conversation of Eiros and Charmion" and "The Unparalleled Adventure of One Hans Pfaall."

Poe was the son of actors David and Elizabeth Poe. His father ruined his career through alcoholism and abandoned his wife and child when Poe was only one year old. He died of tuberculosis in 1810, and Poe's mother died of the same disease when Poe was only two. Afterward, he was adopted by John and Frances Allan, a wealthy couple who treated him well and gave him a good education. Frances Allan had been the driving force behind Poe's adoption, and after her death, Poe fell out with his adoptive father and set out to support himself through a literary career.

In 1835, at the age of twenty-six, Poe secretly married his thirteen-year-old cousin Virginia Clemm. He had inherited his father's predisposi-

Gothic Genre

The gothic genre in literature describes writing that focuses on horror and the supernatural. It developed in the eighteenth century, and common examples include Matthew Gregory Lewis's *The Monk* (1796), Ann Radcliffe's *The Italian* (1797), and Mary Wollstonecraft Shelley's *Frankenstein* (1818). The stories of Edgar Allan Poe also are examples of the gothic genre. Jane Austen satirized the gothic genre in her novel *Northanger Abbey* (1818).

tion for drink, although he was employed sporadically at several magazines and made a name for himself as a literary critic. His short stories and poems brought in barely enough money to live on until his poem "The Raven" (1845) brought him some celebrity. Thereafter his income increased slightly, but he was still plagued by poverty and alcoholism. His wife died of tuberculosis in 1847. Poe rallied after suffering for a year from ill health and depression himself, but he disappeared in Baltimore in September, 1849, and was finally found five days later in a state of inebriation from which he never recovered. He died a few days later of causes that are still disputed—alcohol poisoning, brain fever, nervous prostration, cerebral epilepsy, apoplexy, or syphilis. p.56 Some go so far as to see some sinister conspiracy in his five-day disappearance before his death. In 1949, the centenary of Poe's death, a mysterious figure dressed in black began leaving a partially consumed bottle of cognac and three roses on Poe's grave on his birthday each year.

Poe's most famous short stories are notable for their hallucinatory imagery and their gruesome nature. Death, when it comes (as it always does) is either swift, savage, and bloody, as in "The Murders in the Rue Morgue," in which two women are torn to pieces by an escaped gorilla, or bloodless, prolonged, and horrifying, as in "The Cask of Amontillado," when a man is walled up alive by his enemy for some undefined insult. Madness lurks in every corner and under every facade; it comes to the surface through visions, dreams, brooding, hypnotism, or journeys to desolate regions of the world. Yet, in the midst of this chaos of hallucination, Poe also pioneered the notion of detection as a ruthlessly logical attention to detail, a conceit developed to its fullest by Arthur Conan Doyle's Sherlock Holmes.

– Leslie Ellen Jones

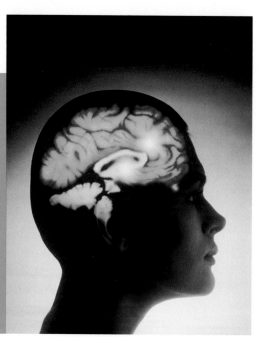

Apoplexy

Apoplexy is a medical term that describes bleeding in the brain caused by a ruptured artery or an obstruction of an artery in the brain caused by a blood clot. It is commonly referred to as a stroke and can cause loss of the ability to control movement or certain functions of the body, loss of conciousness, or death.

Sheena Porter

Born: September 19, 1935; Melton Mowbray,
Leicestershire, England

www3./shropshire-cc.gov.uk/people/porter.htm

TITLE

Nordy Bank, 1964

Sheena Porter is best known for her many children's books and has also written the highly acclaimed young adult novel *Nordy Bank*. Animals of some kind are important characters in all her books, including *Nordy Bank*. One reason her stories are so convincing is that every animal in them is modeled after a real animal she has known. The settings of her books, too, are places important in her life.

Porter was born and raised in the small town of Melton Mowbray in England. She always loved books. During World War II, when books were scarce in England, she felt that deprivation almost as much as the country's serious shortage of food. After the war, she became a voracious reader. When her mother's illness prevented her from leaving home to attend a university, she became a library assistant in nearby Leicester City. After her mother died, Porter attended a library college then took charge of a mobile library in Worcestershire. A brief stint as a nanny revealed to her that, next to books, she loved children. Soon afterward, she became regional children's p.35 librarian for all of Nottinghamshire.

A chance encounter with an editor from the Ox- p.536 ford University Press resulted in Porter's writing her first children's book, *The Bronze Chrysanthemum* (1961). It featured her own dog Angus and was set in a place that she remembered from her travels in Worcestershire. After spending a year as an editorial assistant at Oxford University Press, during which she produced a second children's book, Porter accepted a position in Shropshire as regional children's librarian. However, after her third book appeared, she gave up her job and began writing full time.

Porter's inspiration for *Nordy Bank* came from an experience she had when she and her older sister were exploring the Ludlow area, near the Welsh border. As she was making her way up a hill, she suddenly felt that she was being watched. Later she found out that very spot had been the gateway of an **Iron Age** fort. She immediately knew that her next book would be an adventure story set in an Iron Age camp. The result was *Nordy Bank*, in which a quiet Welsh girl named Bron goes on a holiday visit to a similar Iron Age site and is attacked by the spirit of an ancient woman bent on possessing her. The animal character in *Nordy Bank* is a German shepherd named Griff—a dog much like those Porter had seen being trained at an army camp near Melton Mowbray during the war. Bron captures Griff, who has escaped from the army, and from him gains the strength to defy the malevolent spirit.

Porter later returned to the hill country, settling in Shrewsbury. In 1966 she married the artist Patrick Lane, with whom she had two daughters. She continued

Iron Age

Archaeologists refer to the Iron Age as the period in the development of technology when people worked with iron to make tools, implements, and weapons. It follows the Stone Age and the Bronze Age. This stage of development was reached by different cultures at different times in history. Therefore, there is no one exact date for the Iron Age. In classical Greece, the Iron Age was in full bloom around 500 B.C.E.

SHEENA PORTER

Radio Serial

Before World War II, Americans listened to the radio much the same way we watch television today. In addition to news and music, there were radio serials. In fact, *Star Trek*, the popular television series, began life as a radio serial in the 1920's and 1930's. Each episode ran about fifteen minutes, and listeners tuned in on schedule to hear the next episode. Popular serials also included mysteries, such as *The Shadow*; courtroom stories, such as *Perry Mason*; comedies, such as *My Favorite Husband* (starring actress Lucille Ball); adventures, such as *Captain Midnight*; and westerns, such as *The Lone Ranger*.

Many of these radio serials (such as *My Favorite Husband*, later re-named *I Love Lucy*) made the transition to television in the 1950's as T.V. series.

to write until Oxford University Press, the publisher of all nine of her books, disbanded its children's books department. Porter's last published work, *The Hospital*, appeared in 1973.

Sheena Porter's sense of place and of history, along with her affection for animals, account for her popularity with older children and young adults. In 1964 she was awarded the **Carnegie Medal** for *Nordy Bank*. The book was translated into a number of languages and was also made into a **radio serial**.

– Rosemary M. Canfield Reisman

p.42

p.56

Chaim Potok

Born: February 17, 1929; New York, New York
Died: July 23, 2002; Merion, Pennsylvania
www.lasierra.edu/~ballen/potok

Most of **Chaim Potok**'s central characters are Orthodox Jews searching for ways to integrate their religious and secular lives. With one notable exception, his protagonists are male characters who are confused about their identities.

The child of Orthodox Chassidic Jewish parents, Potok was born and reared in New York's Bronx borough and attended an Orthodox Jewish day school. He earned a bachelor's degree in English literature from Yeshiva University, an Orthodox university in New York, but like some of his characters, he broke from Orthodox Judaism and later received his rabbinate from the Conservative Jewish Theological Seminary in 1954.

Potok's first published work, *The Chosen*, received the **Edward Lewis Wallant Award for Jewish Fiction**. It treats the developing friendship between Reuven Malter and Danny Saunders despite the fact that Danny is a member of an ultra-Orthodox Chassidic community descended from Polish Jewish mystics of the eighteenth century, and Reuven comes from a family with an extremely different view of Judaism and the world. The novel ends with Danny's deciding to go to Columbia Uni-

p.233

.566

p.278

TITLES

The Chosen, 1967

The Promise, 1969

My Name Is Asher Lev, 1972

Davita's Harp, 1985

The Gift of Asher Lev, 1990

versity in Manhattan to study psychology and Reuven's becoming a rabbi. In 1982, *The Chosen* was made into a motion picture. Meanwhile, Potok examined the later lives of Danny and Reuven in *The Promise*. This novel focuses on Danny's ability to succeed as a psychologist without sacrificing his Chassidic beliefs.

My Name Is Asher Lev is about another Chassidic Jew who wants to be an artist. Asher's parents are distrustful of pictures in general because they associate them with idol worship and discourage him from becoming an artist. Only after the leader of their Jewish community says that Asher should study art do his parents relent. However, at the book's end, Asher decides that he must be true to his art. He paints a picture of his mother that distresses her and leads to his separation from his parents and community.

In *The Gift of Asher Lev*, Asher, now a famous artist, returns from Europe with his wife and children to Brooklyn. His wife and children love living in the Chassidic community in Brooklyn, and Asher's father desperately wants his grandson to stay. Asher is determined to pursue his art career in Europe, so he must decide whether to let his

Orthodox Chassidic Judaism

Chassidic or Hasidic Judaism is a movement that began in Eastern Europe in the eighteenth century. It is characterized by devotion to a spiritual leader called a Rebbe, studying the Torah, and wearing distinctive clothing. Men wear beards, hats, and dark clothes. Women dress modestly and wear scarves or other head coverings. Hasidic Jews observe the same laws about the sabbath, prayer, and food as other Orthodox Jews. There are many groups of Hasidic Jews, and the largest populations are found in the U.S., Israel, and Canada. One of the best known groups is the Lubovitchers, headquartered in Brooklyn, New York. This group is very political and is often featured in the press because of its public voice.

Spanish Civil War

In 1936, in Spain, the Republican government had, in five years in power, been unable to gain the support of the people. A group of military leaders, with support of those who wanted to restore the monarchy, wanted to overthrow the government and control the country. When they announced their takeover, the Republicans armed the workers and the trade union members, and civil war broke out. A group of fascists, the Nationalists, also wanted control of the country. They enjoyed support from Adolf Hitler in Germany and Benito Mussolini in Italy, while the Republicans had the support of the Soviet Union. The Western powers avoided involvement in the civil war. Francisco Franco, leader of the Nationalists, united the right-wing groups and by 1939 had toppled the Republicans. Franco held dictatorial power over Spain until his death in 1975, when Prince Juan Carlos became king of Spain.

wife and children remain behind in Brooklyn or take them with him.

Potok's female protagonist in *Davita's Harp*, Ilana Davita Chandal, is the daughter of a Protestant man and a Jewish woman. However, both forsake their religions and join the **Communist Party**, and the father dies in the **Spanish Civil War**. p.567 When Davita's mother learns of the pact between the Soviet Union and Adolf Hitler's Nazi regime in 1939, she revolts against communism and begins a journey back to the Judaism of her youth. Davita attends a Jewish school. When she discovers that her accomplishments as a scholar are overlooked because she is female, she decides to attend a public high school.

p.227

Although most of Chaim Potok's novels deal with forms of Jewish Orthodoxy, they appeal to a much wider readership. Because they treat problems of growing up and adjusting to the world, many readers consider his novels universal in meaning.

– Richard Tuerk

Terry Pratchett

Born: April 28, 1948; Forty Green (now Beaconsfield),
Buckinghamshire, England

www.terrypratchettbooks.com

TITLES

Discworld series:

The Colour of Magic, 1983

The Light Fantastic, 1986

Equal Rites, 1987

Mort, 1987

Sourcery, 1988

Eric, 1989

Pyramids, 1989

Moving Pictures, 1990

Guards! Guards! (with Gray Jolliffe),
1991

Reaper Man, 1991

Small Gods, 1992

Men at Arms, 1993

Soul Music, 1995

Feet of Clay, 1996

Jingo, 1997

Carpe Jugulum, 1998

Hogfather, 1998

The Last Continent, 1999

The Fifth Elephant, 2000

Terry Pratchett may be the only writer to be legitimately compared to both **J. R. R. Tolkien**, the father of twentieth century fantasy, and P. G. Wodehouse, the father of twentieth century farce. Pratchett grew up in Buckinghamshire, England, and began writing stories when still in school. After he published a story in his school paper and had it denounced by the headmaster as immoral, he promptly sold it to *Science Fantasy* magazine, using the proceeds to buy himself a typewriter and begin a career as a newspaper journalist. He spent several years of learning to meet deadlines no matter what, developing a work ethic to which he attributes his voluminous literary production. In 1978 he became the press officer for an electricity board, which involved releasing updates on the doings of four nuclear power plants. The job allowed him enough free time to continue with his own writing, and by 1983, with the publication of his first Discworld novel, Pratchett was making enough money from fiction to give up his day job.

The Discworld novels are Pratchett's best-known works. The Discworld is based on the ancient concept of the Earth as a round, flat plate balanced

p.10
p.87

on the back of a primordial animal; in this case, the Discworld is held up by four elephants (Berilia, Tubul, Great T'Phon, and Jerakeen) who themselves stand on the back of a cosmic turtle named Great A'Tuin. Discworld exists on the very fringe of Reality, and thus is highly susceptible to absurdity. One of Pratchett's major influences was the role-playing game **Dungeons & Dragons**, and so the society of Discworld bears a strong resemblance to the pseudo-heroic, magical universe of that game. However, Pratchett uses his world not so much as an environment for adventures with wizards, dragons, witches, elves, and dwarves (although all exist in Discworld), but as an opportunity to play with absurdity: Death is threatened with death himself when he is deemed to be too sympathetic to those he must carry off, the witch Granny Weatherwax does not believe in magic, and the Night Watch of the Discworld capital, Ankh-Morpork, includes a six-foot-tall dwarf (he was adopted).

Pratchett has also written a number of non-Discworld novels, although all are permeated with his typical irreverent humor. *Good Omens*, co-

Dungeons & Dragons

Dungeons & Dragons, a fantasy roleplaying game, was first marketed to the public in 1974. Since then, it has been revised several times. In this exercise of the imagination, the Dungeon Master creates a world in which players experience adventures. Each player defines his or her character. The rule books define the game, the qualities that characters and monsters can possess, and the nature of the weapons. This is a world before science. Weapons are spears and crossbows. A game can consist of many sessions and can even go on for years. A movie released in 2000, based on the board game and the 1980's television series, attempted to recreate the experience of playing the game, but most devoted players felt it was unsuccessful.

p.570

written with Neil Gaiman, is a tale of the **Apocalypse**; unfortunately, the Antichrist has accidentally been raised in a small English town as a normal English boy and therefore has missed out on all his training in evil, which does not bode well for a really satisfying End of the World. In the Bromeliad trilogy, Pratchett (along with Gaiman yet again in *Wings*) creates another alternate world, this one populated by four-inch-high, winged Nomes, who live in a department store and worship the Arnold Bros. department store (established 1905) as their god. When the department store is slated for demolition, the Nomes must escape, find a new home, and—in subsequent novels—attempt to find their way back to the planet from which they came.

Terry Pratchett's humor is of the kind that readers find either hilarious or childish. Those who like his books, however, are lucky that there is always another one to read. His *The Amazing Maurice and His Educated Rodents* was named one of the **American Library Association**'s **Best Books for Young Adults** in 2002.

p.45
p.48

— Leslie Ellen Jones

The Apocalypse

The Apocalypse is the story of the triumph of Good over Evil as told in the last book of the Bible, the Book of Revelations. It tells of violent crises on earth, wars, famines, disease. The Antichrist is a ruler who gains control of Earth with the help of the false prophet, a religious leader. Together, they write the rules that govern the world. They are opposed by the people of God and two prophets called the two witnesses. The overthrow of the evil rulers ends with the return of Jesus Christ and the establishment of the Kingdom of God.

Philip Pullman

Born: October 19, 1946; Norwich, England

www.philip-pullman.com/index.asp

Philip Pullman is the son of an English airman, and after his father died, his mother married another airman. As a result, Pullman spent the first ten years of his life traveling as his family was posted to Southern Rhodesia, **Australia**, London, and **Wales**. He spent his teenage years in North Wales, in the ancient city of Harlech, and then attended Exeter College at the University of Oxford. A life-long storyteller, Pullman majored in English in order to learn how to write but concluded that academic study of literature was little use for creative endeavor. After graduating, he worked for several years in a men's clothing store and then in a library to support himself while he attempted to write a novel. He married and took a teaching job, all the while continuing to write.

Pullman's Sally Lockhart series was his first major success. These books are set in **Victorian England**, beginning in 1872, and follow the adventures of a young woman from the ages of sixteen into her twenties. Although realistic in tone, Pullman's plots were inspired by nineteenth century **melodramas**. In the first novel, Sally tries to discover the mystery behind a ruby left to her by her dead father and becomes involved in intrigues, murder, and the London underworld. In the second novel, set in 1878, Sally has graduated from **Cambridge University** and become a financial consultant, once again becoming embroiled in financial skullduggery, spiritualism, and a superweapon. In

p.461

p.18

.572

p.198

p.5

TITLES

Sally Lockhart series:

The Ruby in the Smoke, 1985

Shadow in the North, 1987 (publ. in England as The Shadow in the Plate)

The Tiger in the Well, 1990

His Dark Materials trilogy:

The Golden Compass, 1995 (publ. in England as Northern Lights)

The Subtle Knife, 1997

The Amber Spyglass, 2000

Lyra's Oxford, 2003

Victorian England

Victorian England refers to the period of time between 1837 and 1901 when Victoria was queen of England. She came to the throne in 1837, married her German cousin Albert, had nine children, and continued to rule until her death. The Victorian Era followed the Industrial Revolution, so society had to deal with the problems of the new workers and city dwellers. A fascination with invention and finding solutions to technical problems continued to characterize the era. It also was a period of overseas power and expansion. Between 1850 and 1900, the British Empire expanded from a population of some 20 million to one of 410 million people in Britain, India, Australia, New Zealand, South Africa, Rhodesia, Hong Kong, Gibralter, islands in the West Indies, and colonies on the coast of Africa.

the third, Sally is harassed by an unknown person who conspires to strip her of her daughter, her job, her home, and her sanity. She must seek the answer to her plight by becoming involved in the London Jewish community.

Pullman has received most attention, however, for the *His Dark Materials Trilogy*. *The Amber Spyglass* won the **Whitbread Award** in 2002, the first "children's" novel ever to win this prestigious English award. Unlike the many fantasy series p.8? that derive from pre-Christian mythologies of the world, *His Dark Materials* trilogy is based on the much more challenging Christian mythology of the seventeenth century writer John Milton. Pull- p.573 man's alternate universe is an evocative blend of Victorian technology, Renaissance occultism, and futuristic invention. Everyone in this world has a "daemon," an animal-shaped spirit who is emotionally bound to them. The main character is Lyra, an orphan under the guardianship of her uncle, Lord Asriel. Lyra's daemon is Pantalaimon. Lyra discovers that children are being stolen and subjected to experimentation in order to separate them from their daemons. In the second novel, Lyra meets a boy named Will Parry; the two of them are the subjects of an ancient prophecy that makes them the new Adam and Eve after Lord Asriel restages the revolt of the angels against God—a senile and sadistic deity, unlike the story recounted by Milton in *Paradise Lost*. In the third novel, Will and Lyra descend to Limbo to free the souls of the dead. When Lyra and Will finally kiss and achieve a sexual awakening, as did Adam and Eve, the old world ends and a new one begins.

Philip Pullman's fantasy world is one of hard moral decisions and grave challenges; he has stated that fiction writers must wrestle with questions of moral conduct in a world overrun by religious and political fanaticism or risk becoming trivial and irrelevant.

– Leslie Ellen Jones

John Milton

John Milton was the seventeenth century English Renaissance poet—ranked as one of England's greatest—who created the epic poem, *Paradise Lost*. His masterpiece narrates all important events in the earthly and spiritual history of humankind. It tells not only the story of man's fall from God's grace, but also man's restoration and his ability to gain immortality. The twelve books of the epic do not follow the story in chronological order, but they tell of the battle between Satan and God, of the creation of the earth, of Adam and Eve in the Garden of Eden and their fall from grace, Christ's birth, and the establishment of the Christian church and its history until Judgment Day.

Arthur Ransome

Born: January 18, 1884; Leeds, Yorkshire, England
Died: June 3, 1967; Manchester, England
www.arthur-ransome.org/ar

Arthur Ransome was born in Yorkshire the son of a college history professor, and he spent his summer vacations near Lake Windermere in the **Lake District of Cumbria** in northern England. p.575 Windermere is the largest lake in Britain—more than ten miles long, one mile wide, and 220 feet deep—and has been noted as a beauty spot since the time of the Romantic poets. Picturesque views, scenic walks, and water sports have continued to draw tourists for over two hundred years. Ransome was impressed by the beauty of Windermere's wildness as a child, and for the whole of his life, he returned there as often as he could. His love of the place inspired his popular children's books, the Swallows and Amazons series, which focus on sailing adventures on Windermere.

Ransome attended **Rugby**, the prestigious English public school, and Yorkshire College, the predecessor of Leeds University. His first job out of p.599 school was working in a publishing house as an office boy, assistant, reader, and ghost and **freelance writer** between 1901 and 1905. He then became the p.368 assistant **editor** of *Temple Bar* magazine. In 1913 p.2 he moved to Russia and commenced a career as a foreign correspondent for several English newspapers, covering the **Bolshevik Revolution** and subse- p.576 quent events under communist rule. Ransome was known to be left-wing in his politics, friendly with many of the insiders of the **Communist Party**, even p.22 marrying Communist revolutionary Leon Trotsky's secretary as his second wife. However, in 2002, previously classified documents were made public revealing that Ransome had been a spy for British military intelligence operation throughout his journalism career.

In 1922 Ransome set out on his yacht *Racundra* for a sailing trip around the Baltic Sea with his Secret Intelligence Service superior but fell ill while at sea and had to give up journalism and take up a quiet life in England. He retired to his beloved Lake District and began writing adventure stories for and about children.

Ransome's books were ground-breaking in that they are narrated from the child's point of view. The "Swallows" of his series are the Walker children, John, Susan, Titty, and Roger, who come to the Lake District on vacation and discover a boat called the *Swallow*, which they adopt. Their sometime friends, sometime foes, the "Amazons" are local girls Nancy and Peggy Blackett. In *Swallows and Amazons* the six children camp on a small island on the lake and become embroiled in adventures partly deriving from their imaginative games and partly from real interactions with the people living on and around the lake. Subsequent books recount further adventures of the Swallows and Amazons on the lake, off the Norfolk Broads, and

Lake District of Cumbria

Located in northwest England, the Lake District is a beautiful place for sightseers and hikers. It is home to the Lake District National Park, which preserves 880 square miles of nature. The park also is home to England's tallest mountains, four at only 3,000 feet each. Visitors to the Lake District can enjoy the scenery from the water on one of the sixteen lakes, from the highway, or from hiking trails. There are many historic homes and gardens in the Lake District that tourists can visit. Part of Hadrian's Wall, a Roman fortification from the 120's A.D., can also be seen in Cumbria.

Bolshevik Revolution

In 1917, following many serious defeats for Russia in World War I, a Marxist group known as the Bolsheviks overthrew the provisional parliamentary government, which had taken control of Russia from the last Romanov czar earlier that same year. In the following months, the Bolsheviks fought resistance outside of the capital of Petrograd. With Vladimir Illich Lenin at the head, the new government held elections for the Constituent Assembly, then dissolved it after one meeting. Lenin also severed all ties between the church and the state. The lands that had been promised to the peasants instead became property of the state. In 1918, Lenin concluded a formal peace with Germany, made Moscow the new capital, and adopted the name "Communist Party" for his movement.

elsewhere, tales involving a great deal of sailing and seamanship lovingly and accurately described—and indeed illustrated by Ransome himself, who could not find an **illustrator** who could draw sailboats to his exacting specifications. p.3

Arthur Ransome's books present an idealized picture of golden childhoods in a simpler time, but the adventure and the realism of his stories have made them beloved for decades. His awards included a **Carnegie Medal** for *Pigeon Post* and a **Caldecott Medal** for illustration. p.4

– Leslie Ellen Jones

Wilson Rawls

Born: September 24, 1913; Scraper, Oklahoma
Died: December 16, 1984; Cornell, Wisconsin

www.ifpl.org/rawls

Wilson Rawls's two novels are set in the Ozark Mountains of northeastern Oklahoma. They are realistic fiction, stories about following dreams with determination and hard work. *Where the Red Fern Grows* is a classic story about the love between a boy and his dogs. *Summer of the Monkeys* is an adventure story in which a boy meets a challenge with joy, humor, and self-reliance. A strong plot, love for the hills and river bottoms of the Ozarks, authentic details of country life in the early twentieth century, the strength of the family, and nostalgia for a simpler time when self-reliance and determination were more important than money or possessions are integral qualities of Rawls's novels.

Rawls wrote about what he knew. He grew up on the isolated farm he describes in his novels. His mother taught her children at home, and Rawls fell in love with Jack London's *Call of the Wild* (1903) as a boy and decided that he wanted to be a writer. When he was fifteen years old the family moved into town, and Rawls was able to go to school and read books from a library. However, the Great Depression hit the country soon afterward and Rawls left school and traveled around the country working as a carpenter. He wrote several manuscripts

TITLES

Where the Red Fern Grows, 1961

Summer of the Monkeys, 1976

during these years but showed them to no one because he was ashamed of his spelling, grammar and punctuation, and lack of education.

In 1958 Rawls married and confided his dream of being a writer to his wife, Sophie. She encouraged him and helped him with editing and **proofreading**. p.53 After *Where the Red Fern Grows* was published, Rawls began to speak in schools and libraries, encouraging young people to follow their dreams and continue their education.

Where the Red Fern Grows has won numerous awards and become a beloved American classic. Its young **protagonist**, Billy Colman, desperately p.233 wants a pair of hunting hounds. He saves every penny for two years and finally is able to buy two coonhound puppies. Billy and his dogs, Old Dan and Little Ann, become the best hunting team in the region. They overcome many obstacles, and win a gold cup in the annual raccoon-hunting contest, but a battle against a mountain lion turns to tragedy.

Summer of the Monkeys is another tale set in the Ozarks. When a troupe of monkeys escapes from a traveling circus, fourteen-year-old Jay Berry Lee is determined to capture them and claim the reward money with the help of his hound and his grandfather. Trapping those clever monkeys turns out to be a greater challenge than Jay Berry and his grandpa anticipate, and along the way Jay Berry learns what he really wants.

Ozark Mountains

The Ozark Mountains, also called the Ozark Plateau or the Ozarks, are found in Southern Missouri, Northern Arkansas, and Northeastern Oklahoma between the Arkansas and Missouri Rivers. They are characterized by wide plateaus broken up by eroded peaks, with the highest reaching only 2,000 feet. The forests attract tourists who come to view the colorful foilage in spring and fall. The many streams and hot springs also make the Ozarks a popular tourist site.

Carpenter

A carpenter is a person who works with wood to build things. Training can be either on the job or through a formal apprenticeship program combining instruction and on-the-job experience. In the building trades, a carpenter cuts, fits, and assembles wood and other materials. Some carpenters specialize and may build forms for concrete, erect scaffolding, frame walls, install doors and windows, lay wood floors, or build and install cabinets.

In both of Wilson Rawls's novels, young boys meet challenges with a sense of joy and adventure. Rawls embodies the qualities of loyalty, faith, courage, and love for his home and family. As each boy hero keeps trying to reach his goal, the reader is drawn in, wanting to find out what happens next, and daydreaming about the freedom to roam the countryside with nothing but a dog, a plan, and one's own cleverness and ingenuity.

– Susan Butterworth

Erich Maria Remarque

Born: June 22, 1898; Osnabrück, Germany
Died: September 25, 1970; Locarno, Switzerland

www.kirjasto.sci.fi/remarque.htm

Although all of **Erich Maria Remarque**'s works have been praised for their interesting characters and balance, none have received the critical acclaim and success of *All Quiet on the Western Front*. Set in the trenches of World War I, this antiwar novel depicts the horrors of war from the point of view of the ordinary soldier. Narrated in the first person, the novel is semiautobiographical and has earned praise for its stark simplicity and unemotional style. However, its content sparked a storm of controversy. Because of Remarque's failure to glorify German militarism, his books were banned in Germany during the 1930's, and *All Quiet on the Western Front* was ordered burned by the Nazis.

Remarque was born in northwestern Germany to parents of modest means. He entered the University of Münster as Germany was fighting in World War I and was forced into the army at the age of eighteen. While fighting on the Western Front he was wounded several times. He had aspired to become a pianist, but his hopes of a musical career were shattered when he was hit in the wrist by shrapnel. After his discharge from the army he worked as a teacher, stonecutter, drama critic, salesman for a tombstone company, advertising copywriter, and organist in an insane asylum.

p.40

p.65

YOUNG ADULT AUTHORS

Remarque began his writing career as a sports journalist, but his first novel, *All Quiet on the Western Front*, brought him fame. He was also known as a frequenter of cafés and **cabarets**—a habit that may have contributed to his marital difficulties. He divorced and remarried several times. In 1938, while the Nazis were in power, Remarque lost his German citizenship. He obtained **United States citizenship** in 1947 but the next year settled in Switzerland, where he remained the rest of his life.

p.581

p.359

All Quiet on the Western Front begins in 1917 after a battle in which half of the narrator Paul Baumer's company has been killed. The book reveals earlier events of Baumer's life through flashbacks, juxtaposing the horrible reality of the wartime front with his teacher patriotically encouraging his students to go off to war. The naïve Baumer constantly finds himself questioning what is happening around

Cabaret

A cabaret is a type of nightclub or place of entertainment. Berlin, Germany, was known for its cabaret culture during the Weimar Republic, the period of time between the end of World War I and Adolf Hitler's rise to power in the 1930's. The clubs served alcoholic beverages and provided live entertainment. A well known 1972 movie, *Cabaret*, provides a dramatized version of such a club. Today, we refer to many small clubs where live vocal music is performed as cabarets.

him. Ironically, in the summer of 1918, a week or so before the armistice that will end the war, Baumer is killed. The novel's sequel, *The Road Back*, deals with the collapse of the German army after the war and the fate of the survivors.

All Quiet on the Western Front has been translated into more than two dozen languages and even at the time of Remarque's death had sold more than 40 million copies worldwide. In addition, three separate film versions have been made. Erich Maria Remarque was awarded the **German Grand Cross of Merit** and has been called the most published German author of all time.

– Kathleen M. Bartlett

German Grand Cross of Merit

In 1951, the Federal Republic of Germany established the Order of Merit, an award given in eight classes to honor noteworthy persons on behalf of the state for their contributions to the country. The awards are given for achievement in politics, economics, social causes, and creative work. Remarque was awarded the *Grossesverdientskreuz* (Grand Cross of Merit) in 1967 for his literary contribution.

Louise Rennison

Born: October 11, 1951; Leeds, England

www.georgianicolson.com/index.html

Louise Rennison has said that her motto is "I came, I saw, I conga-d." That is precisely what her teenage hero Georgia Nicolson does in a series of sidesplitting diaries. These books do not merely tickle the reader's funny bone, they gyrate it. At the same time, they capture the real-life ironies of growing up with deft skill. Annoyed by her parents, ridiculed by her best friend, embarrassed by her attack cat, Angus, and embroiled in a love-hate relationship with her soggy-diapered baby sister, Georgia faces all the usual teen girl crises, including boys, boys, and boys. Since Georgia is English and a virtuoso of a rich British slang, American readers need the glossary at the back of each book to translate such Briticisms as nunga-nungas (breasts) and snogging (kissing and related activities, the degrees of which are captured on Georgia's ten-point scale, which runs from hand-holding to "the full monty").

Born in northern England, Rennison has worked as a newspaper writer, radio broadcaster, comedian, and comedy writer. After the success of her one-woman autobiographical show, *Stevie Wonder Felt My Face*, she accepted an English publisher's challenge of producing a teenage girl's diary. The results have often been compared to British writer Helen

Helen Fielding

Helen Fielding was a British journalist with one published novel to her name when she began writing a comical newspaper column about a fictional female character and her

daily problems and concerns. She was working on a serious novel when her publisher suggested she make a novel out of her columns about this fictional women, Bridget Jones. The rest is history. Fielding's novel, *Bridget Jones's Diary*, became a best-seller in both Britain and the U.S. and was also adapted as a popular movie.

Fielding's popular adult novel, *Bridget Jones's Diary* (1999). Like Fielding, Rennison draws from real life what is funniest about her own life and the people she knows. She gives her characters a knack for outrageous dialogue and lets the plot expand amoeba-like. The result is rollicking humor and good fun for teen girls who are willing to laugh at themselves.

p.58

Georgia begins her journal at the age of fourteen in *Angus, Thongs, and Full-Frontal Snogging*. Having made the fatal mistake of going to a party dressed as a stuffed olive, her only hope for a social future rests in her all-consuming passion for a seventeen-year-old sex god named Robbie. Robbie, tragically, has his eye on a bombshell named Lindsay, who is brazen enough to wear a thong. Georgia's day-by-day (sometimes minute-by-minute) accounts furnish enough giggles and guffaws to last from one of her crises to the next.

Georgia's crises keep coming. In the second book, *On the Bright Side, I'm Now the Girlfriend of a Sex God*, Georgia must cope with the threat of a family move to Kiwi-a-gogo land (**New Zealand**), a rejection from the SG (sex god), suspension from Stalag 14 (school), and a red bottomosity (pimple on her derriere). In the third book, *Knocked Out by My*

p.45

Nunga-Nungas, Angus the cat faces sexual surgery, while Georgia must endure a family trip to Scotland. A serious snogging session with a rejected boyfriend, Dave the Laugh, gives Georgia second thoughts about Robbie. Throughout it all, Georgia remains self-absorbed, rebellious, impudent, and fabulously flighty. It is the stuff of brash humor and the stuff of teen reality.

The adventures of the irrepressible Georgia have earned Louise Rennison many awards. *Angus, Thongs, and Full-Frontal Snogging* was a **Michael L. Printz Honor Book** and an **American Library Association Best Book for Young Adults**. It also made *Booklist*'s **Top 10 Youth First Novels** in 2000 and was a 2001 **Quick Pick for Reluctant Young Readers** of the American Library Association.

488
143
p.45
p.480

– Faith Hickman Brynie

Chick Lit

Following the success of *Bridget Jones's Diary*, a number of books about young career women in their 20's and 30's trying to balance the demands of work and love were published to success. A new contemporary genre was born: chick lit. Short for chick literature, the genre became a publishing sensation. Most of the books were written by women who were like their main characters. They worked in okay jobs, worried about their weight, and were always looking for the right man. Readers saw in these books women like themselves, characters more true to life.

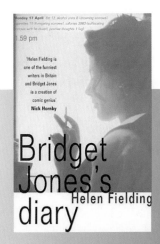

Anne Rice

Born: October 4, 1941; New Orleans, Louisiana

www.annerice.com/index.htm

Vampires have been staples of horror fiction ever since the publication of Bram Stoker's *Dracula* in 1897. However, fashions in vampire stories have come and gone. The original Dracula was a figure of pure dread, completely alien to mortal comprehension, so innately evil that any hint of empathy for him was a sign that he had gotten his fangs into the empathizer, who was well on the way to vampirization. p.3

The first sexy vampires appeared in films produced by Great Britain's **Hammer Studios** in the 1960's and were often played by British actor Christopher Lee. The real popularizer of sexy and empathetic vampires in fiction, however, was **Anne Rice**. p.58

Born Howard Allen O'Brien, Rice was raised as a Roman Catholic in New Orleans, but her family moved to Texas when she was fourteen after her mother died, and she left the church at the age of eighteen. She and her husband, poet Stan Rice, started their married life in San Francisco in 1961, but moved back to New Orleans in 1988, and Rice herself returned to Catholicism in 1998.

Many critics have suggested that the late twentieth century fascination with vampires arises from anxieties over blood-born diseases such as acquired immunodeficiency syndrome (AIDS). Rice's inspiration, however, was a different blood disease, **leukemia**, which killed her first child, Michele, at the age of six in 1970. Rice wrote *Interview with the Vampire* as a way of working through her heartbreak at losing her child, p.2

Hammer Films

Hammer Films was founded in 1934 and produced only a few films before World War II broke out and production stopped. Following the war in 1947, it was reborn and by the 1950's new production deals had been forged with U.S. studios and producers. This led to Hammer's specialty, the horror movie of the 1950's and 1960's. Hammer produced both Frankenstein and Dracula movies that were popular at the box office. By the 1970's, horror films had grown stale, but Hammer discovered new life in television comedy series. In the 1980's they brought the horror series to British television, but their luck again ran out in the 1990's. Recently, Hammer has signed a production deal to make low-budget horror movies aimed at the teen market. Hammer Films may soon be a familiar name to a new generation of filmgoers.

along the way creating the character of the vampire Claudia, an eternally youthful child with Michele's ringleted hair, also afflicted with a disease of the blood. The focal figure of Rice's developing Vampire Chronicles, however, is Lestat, originally an aristocrat in pre-Revolutionary France. In many ways, Lestat, indeed all vampires, epitomize the amoral, perverse, decadent, parasitic society that the French Revolution intended to destroy.

Bram Stoker's *Dracula* was narrated by the humans who battled the ancient evil; Rice's novels are narrated by the vampires themselves, who become complex and fascinating characters grappling with the existential quandaries posed by eternal life purchased at the price of violating the most basic human taboo, that of murder. The immortal Lestat is always an aristocrat of whatever society he inhabits, whether it is eighteenth century France as the son of a marquis or twentieth century America as a rock music star. Nonetheless, he is an aristocrat in a world that began rejecting aristocracy even in his mortal lifetime, and thus he is always an outsider, a reject, an object of horror. Rice's vampires transgress multiple boundaries of life and death, sexuality, morality, belief, even physicality, when Lestat trades bodies with a mortal in *The Tale of the Body Thief*. Above all, however, they transgress the boundaries of good and evil, for nearly all of Rice's vampires sooner or later come to question their own evil.

Anne Rice's novels are sometimes criticized for being too talky, for spending too much time on background or tangential issues. The development of the Vampire Chronicles, however, has been a process of fleshing out secondary characters in earlier novels, starting with Lestat himself, who was originally seen through the eyes of his protege Louis; later novels move on to Armand, a vampire who also first appeared in *Interview with the Vampire*, and Marius, Lestat's own mentor.

— Leslie Ellen Jones

Interview with the Vampire, the Movie

In 1994, Neil Jordan directed the movie version of Anne Rice's novel. He cast Tom Cruise as the vampire Lestat and Brad Pitt as his protégé Louis de Pointe du Lac and worked on the screenplay with Anne Rice. While there are minor differences between the book and the film, with Rice on board, it is difficult to complain about them. The film with lavish sets and costumes, was generally well received by both reviewers and the public. Those who are squeamish might object to the amount of blood or sexual content.

Hans Peter Richter

Born: April 28, 1925; Cologne, Germany
Died: November 19, 1993; Munich, Germany

p.407

Hans Peter Richter wrote three young adult novels on Nazi Germany from the German point of view. These books do not mitigate the horrors of life in Germany during Adolf Hitler's era, especially the Nazi treatment of Jews, the destruction of Germany, and life in battle. Richter's matter-of-fact prose makes the events absorbing and affecting, and the episodic structure of the stories gives the impression of a true-to-life recollection. All three of his novels offer honest, unapologetic, and convincing pictures of why Richter lost his faith in Hitler's cause. Richter's message is all the more convincing because it comes from one who witnessed the events, suffered many of the horrors himself, and participated as an idealistic German soldier and then as a disillusioned veteran of battle.

Richter was born in Germany and grew up while Hitler and the Nazi Party were rising to power. During World War II he served as an officer in the German army. These experiences gave him a firsthand knowledge of wartime Germany, which forms the basis of his three novels. *Friedrich* focuses on two boys who are best friends, one a Jew, the other a non-Jew. The story begins in 1925 and continues to 1942, contrasting the fortunes of the Jew, Friedrich Schneider, and the novel's unnamed narrator. At the beginning, Friedrich's family is well-to-do until the Nazis take everything from them; the mother is killed, and the father is sent to a concentration camp. In the p.590 end, Friedrich himself is killed during an air raid after being denied entrance to an air-raid shelter because he is a Jew.

TITLES

Friedrich, 1961

I Was There, 1962

The Time of the Young Soldiers, 1967

p.59

I Was There looks at Nazi Germany from the perspective of three friends who join the Hitler Youth and eventually serve in the German army. Their enthusiasm for Hitler's ideals turns to disillusionment as they experience the savagery of battle. Their story ends in a hail of bombs and bullets raining down on the narrator. *The Time of the Young Soldiers*, the third novel in the series, begins with a quotation from Benjamin Franklin to the effect that no war is good and no peace is bad. This point is underscored by the narrator's experiences of war from basic training into battle. He is wounded so severely that his arm is amputated, but he remains on active service, is decorated for bravery, and is commissioned an officer. His endurance suggests the strength of his early idealism and loyalty to Germany, and the amputation of his arm symbolizes his loss of faith in the Nazi ideals.

After the war, Richter continued his formal education at several universities, earning a doctorate in

Concentration Camp

Adolf Hitler's policy in Third Reich Germany was to move people from society who were considered undesireable to camps. These groups included Jews, political opponents, members of certain religious groups, homosexuals, and others deemed socially or racially inferior. In some camps, prisoners were forced to work for the war effort for no pay, exist with little food, and live in poor conditions. The death camps were constructed for the mass murder of these undesirable people. While historians most frequently document camps with familiar names such as Dachau, Buchenwald, Mauthausen, Theresienstadt, and Auschwitz-Birkenau, in reality there were some one thousand additional camps in countries occupied by the German forces. Many camps were destroyed by the Germans before the end of the war; others were liberated by the Allied troops. In all, more than six million individuals died in the camps, the majority of them Jews. This event is known, tragically, as the Holocaust.

Hitler Youth

The Hitler Youth organization was created in the 1920's for German boys and girls. By 1933 there were 100,000 members; by 1936 membership became mandatory for all German children. There were separate organizations for boys and girls ages 10 through 18. Boys were trained for military service by learning to march, drill, and dig trenches. Girls were trained for motherhood. The highest achievement for a girl was to give birth to a racially pure German baby boy. As Germany neared defeat, many boys from the Hitler Youth, some as young as age 15, were sent to fight in the war. As the number of troops dwindled and Germany's efforts became more desperate, even some girls manned machine guns alongside young boys.

social psychology in Hanover. He married Elfriede Feldmann in 1952 and fathered four children. In 1954, he began writing professional works and more than twenty books for children, most of which remain untranslated into English. He also wrote many **scripts for radio** and television and served as a broadcaster.

Friedrich received awards from Germany, France, and Japan. In the United States, the novel won both the **Woodward School Book Award** and the **Mildred L. Batchelder Award** from the **American Library Association** as the year's most outstanding book translated from a foreign language into English.

– Bernard E. Morris

p.564

p.468

p.45

Ann Rinaldi

Born: August 27, 1934; New York, New York

www.annrinaldi.com/index.htm

Ann Rinaldi melds fact and fiction to portray young female protagonists during various periods of American history. Some of her protagonists are modeled after historical figures, such as **Phillis Wheatley** and Sarah Revere, others are entirely fictional creations depicted against backdrops of notable historical events, such as President Abraham Lincoln's assassination, the Salem witch trials, or one of America's wars. Despite the distances of time, Rinaldi's readers are able to identify with her protagonists, whose jealousies and fears are not much different from the readers' own.

p.23

p.593

For such a prolific writer, Rinaldi had an unusually nonliterary upbringing. Her mother died soon after she was born, and her father and stepmother not only discouraged her from writing but also prevented her from going to college. It was not until after she married in 1960 and began having children that Rinaldi tried to become a novelist. After meeting no success, she turned to journalism and wrote a column for a local newspaper. In 1979, however, she finished a short story, entitled "Term Paper," which she lengthened into her first novel of the same title. The story is about Nicki, a girl trying to come to terms with death. The novel was accepted by the first publisher who read it and led immediately to its sequel, *Promises Are for Keeping*.

.594

p.117

After Rinaldi's son became involved in **Revolutionary War reenactments**, Rinaldi turned to writing **historical fiction**. At first publishers were leery about offering history-based books to young adults. However, *Time Enough for Drums*, Rinaldi's first historical novel about Jemima Emerson's role during the Revolutionary War, proved their apprehensions were ill-founded, as did Rinaldi's ensuing historical work.

Ann Rinaldi's books depict historical events from a much-needed female point of view, and they inspire girls to become interested in American his-

Phillis Wheatley

Phillis Wheatley is often considered the first African American poet. In 1773 she became the first black American to publish a book of poetry: *Poems on Various Subjects, Religious and Moral*. Wheatley was born on the west coast of Africa, but she was kidnapped as a child by slave traders and brought to the American colonies. She was purchased by John Wheatley, a prosperous tailor in Boston, and became Mrs. Wheatley's personal maid. The Wheatleys saw that Phillis learned to speak, read, and write English. She also studied Latin, the Bible, Greek and Roman works of litera-ture, and British poetry. Her masters encouraged her to write poetry while still in her teens. When Mrs. Wheatley died, Mr. Wheatley set Phil-lis free. She continued to write poetry, married a freed slave, and died at age thirty-one.

tory. In 1987 Rinaldi won the **New Jersey Author's Award** for *Time Enough for Drums*. That same book, *The Last Silk Dress*, *Break with Charity* and *Wolf by the Ears* were named American Library Association **Best Books for Young Adults**. *Wolf by the Ears* also won the American Library Association **Best of the Best Award** and the **Pacific Northwest Library Association Young Readers' Choice Award**.

p.45

p.48

– Cassandra Kircher

Revolutionary War Reenactment

A Revolutionary War reenactment usually takes place at the site of a Revolutionary War battle. Groups of people devoted to the activity dress in reproduction uniforms or clothing and act out the actual battle with period weapons and tactics. The historical reenactment often extends to other activities of daily life, such as women in historically accurate dress preparing food as in the Colonial period.

J. K. Rowling

Born: July 31, 1965; Sodbury, Gloucestershire, England

http://www.jkrowling.com

The immense success of **Joanne Kathleen Rowling**'s Harry Potter series was one of the wonders of the 1990's publishing world. Not only have all her books been spectacular **best-sellers**, but the interest in reading that they have generated among young people has been credited with almost single-handedly reviving the genre of young adult **fantasy** and planting a love of reading in children all over the world. Read by children, young adults, and adults with equal pleasure, Rowling's novels rank among the most popular books of any genre of modern times.

Born in England, Rowling has revealed little to the public about her early life. During her twenties, she worked as a secretary for **Amnesty International** and as an English teacher in Portugal. She married, had a daughter, and divorced, and finally settled in Edinburgh, Scotland, as a single mother with an ambitious story idea in her mind.

Rowling planned the Harry Potter series books as a series from the beginning, outlining seven novels that would take the eleven-year-old Harry from his first year at Hogwarts School of Witchcraft and Wizardry through his graduation. Like all good fairy-tale heroes, Harry is marked as special—in this case literally. He has a lightning-bolt scar on his forehead that he acquired in an encounter in his infancy with the evil wizard Voldemort—a fact of which is he unaware until he is eleven. The encounter with Voldemort killed both his magic-practicing parents, leaving him an orphan to be raised by his

p.384

p.87

.596

TITLES

Harry Potter and the Sorcerer's Stone, 1997

Harry Potter and the Chamber of Secrets, 1998

Harry Potter and the Prisoner of Azkaban, 1999

Harry Potter and the Goblet of Fire, 2000

Harry Potter and the Order of Phoenix, 2003

Harry Potter and the Half Blood Prince, 2005

Amnesty International

Amnesty International (AI) was founded in 1961 as an independent organization not affiliated with any government, political group, or religion. AI works to assure that all people enjoy the human rights outlined in the Universal Declaration of Human Rights. People should be free of physical and mental abuse, enjoy freedom of expression and thought, and be free from discrimination.

AI now has some 1.8 million members in more than 150 countries and territories around the world.

loathsome "Muggle" (nonmagic) relatives, the Dursleys.

The Dursleys try to shield Harry from any knowledge of magic, but on his eleventh birthday he receives a notification that he has been admitted to Hogwarts and he enters a brand new world, one in which he is far from an unwanted nobody. In fact, as the only person ever to have thwarted Voldemort and survived, he is renowned in the magic world. Soon after entering his new school, Harry acquires steadfast friends—Ron Weasley, from a chaotic but loving magical family, and Hermione Grainger, a witch with a pure Muggle background. He also acquires protectors—Hagrid, the giant Hogwarts groundskeeper who has a terrible fondness for monstrous pets, and Professor Dumbledore, a powerful wizard and the wise headmaster of the school. There are enemies, as well; these include Draco Malfoy, a snobbish Pureblood wizard-in-training, mean Professor Snape, and, of course, Lord Voldemort, who lurks in the wings, waiting for the chance to regain his full powers.

Much of the charm and excitement of the Harry Potter stories arises from Rowling's imaginative and detailed descriptions of a life of magic and **sorcery**, in which "all-flavor" jelly beans really can taste like anything under the sun, including earwax;

p.55

witches do ride broomsticks, mostly in order to play the extremely tricky sport of Quidditch; and a cloak of invisibility may be used to play pranks, or to gain important information about an enemy's sinister plans.

In one way, the Harry Potter books are in a direct line of descent from Thomas Hughes's *Tom Brown's School Days* (1857) and other p.572 Victorian and Edwardian novels of British public school life. They also bear a strong resemblance to the early works of P. G. Wodehouse, who began by writing stories about schoolboys at perpetual war with overbearing headmasters, sneaky fellow students, and suspicious teachers who attempt to thwart their every move, though the heroes always triumph, and even do so in the name of fair play. As the Harry Potter series has progressed, however, Rowling's plots have taken a steadily more serious turn as the stakes have grown higher; it is no longer a question of outsmarting a supercilious Professor Snape but one of the eternal battle between Good and Evil.

In addition to setting unprecedented sales records and being adapted into blockbuster ,597 films, J. K. Rowling's Harry Potter novels have earned many prestigious awards, including the Carnegie p.42 Medal and numerous American Library p.45 Association Best Books for Young .480 Adults awards.

— Leslie Ellen Jones

Harry Potter, the Movies

Harry Potter is as popular with filmgoers as he is with readers. The first three films have taken in more than $900 million at the U.S. box office alone. In the first weekend of release, *Harry Potter and the Sorcerer's Stone* took in $90.3 million, *Harry Potter and the Chamber of Secrets* took in $88.4 million, and *Harry Potter and the Prisoner of Azkaban* took in $93 million. With no sign of losing movie audiences, the fourth film, *Harry Potter and the Goblet of Fire* has begun filming and is scheduled for a November, 2005 release. Producers are already talking to directors for the fifth film, *Harry Potter and the Order of the Phoenix*, with an anticipated release date in Summer, 2007.

Salman Rushdie

Born: June 19, 1947; Bombay, India

www.kirjasto.sci.fi/rushdie.htm

Salman Rushdie is best known not for young adult fiction but for the controversy aroused by his 1988 novel *The Satanic Verses*, which Iran's late Ayatollah Ruhollah Khomeini pronounced blasphemous to Islam. Khomeini issued a religious edict sentencing Rushdie to death and calling upon Muslims everywhere to carry out his sentence. As a result of this edict, Rushdie had to live in hiding for a decade. By the beginning of the twenty-first century, however, Rushdie had slipped to a fairly minor position on the list of causes of Islamic outrage, and Iran's new rulers had rescinded Khomeini's death sentence. Meanwhile, the publicity surrounding Rushdie transformed him into a world celebrity.

Rushdie was born in Bombay barely two months before India gained its independence from Great Britain. His father was a Cambridge-educated businessman. After early schooling in India, Rushdie was sent to England to attend **Rugby**, the famous public school, and then Cambridge, where he received a degree with honors in history. During Rushdie's school years in England, his Muslim parents moved from mainly Hindu **India** to predominantly Muslim Pakistan. These multiple uprootings left Rushdie with a sense of permanent exile; he seemed neither sufficiently Indian, Pakistani, nor English to fit in anywhere. After graduating from **Cambridge** in 1968, he attempted to work as a writer in Pakistan but left when one of his teleplays was censored for

p.599

p.32

p.5

Rugby School

Rugby is one of the leading co-educational boarding schools in England. It was founded in 1567 for the boys living in the towns of Rugby and Brownsover. Such famous authors as Matthew Arnold, Lewis Carroll, and Salman Rushdie attended Rugby, as did former Prime Minister Neville Chamberlain. Rugby was also the founding place of the game of rugby football around 1823. The rules of the game were written in 1845. American football grew out of the game of rugby. Today, Rugby school is thoroughly modernized and incoming pupils arrive with laptops. Girls were first admitted in 1975, but it was not until 1995 that they were allowed to enroll in every class. There are approximately eight hundred students at the school.

including the word "pork," a food that is forbidden to Muslims. He then returned to England and worked as an **advertising** copywriter and actor in experimental theater. However, by 1975 he had completed his first novel and his career as a fiction writer was established.

Rushdie's work has always had an element of **Magical Realism** about it, often using folktale and folk religious elements as themes. *Midnight's Children* is based on the premise that all the children born in India and Pakistan within the first hour of those countries' independence from Britain (between midnight and 1 A.M. on August 15, 1947) were imbued with extraordinary powers. However, their gifts of transmutation, flight, prophecy, and wizardry cannot prevent the frustrations, set-backs, and often early deaths the children experience, mirroring the experiences of the newly created nations.

The Satanic Verses, the novel that caused such trouble for Rushdie, is not particularly out of keeping with the trend that he had established in his earlier novels: It is a magical, outrageous, metaphorical, mythological story under and behind which can be seen the outlines of the historical experiences of Indians in Britain and also of the history of the foundation of Islam. The section of the novel that aroused outrage depicted the scribe who is taking down the words of the prophet "Mahound" interpolating his own ideas and opinions into Rushdie's imaginary Koran-like text. Ultraconservative Muslims regarded this as a deliberate attempt to cast doubt upon the legitimacy of the real **Koran**. However, this feature is only one small part of a complex web of stories within the novel, all of which revolve around the demands that religion places on its believers.

p.60

Rushdie's next book, written while he was in hiding, was *Haroun and the Sea of Stories*. It tells of Rashid, a storyteller whose tap into the sea of story—located on a moon called Kahina—is accidentally disconnected, leaving him high and dry. His son Haroun sets out on a series of adventures to restore his father's storytelling powers. The book's underlying message seems clearly related to the censorship that Rushdie himself was experiencing at the time he wrote the book. Most of Rushdie's work since the early 1990's has been increasingly realist, although still satirical in intent.

– Leslie Ellen Jones

The Koran

Also spelled Qur'an, this is the Islamic holy book. Muslims consider the Qur'an the word of God exactly as revealed to the Prophet Muhammad over a twenty-two year period. It consists of 114 chapters and 6,236 verses. While it contains many of the same people found in the Jewish Torah and the Christian Bible, the details of the stories differ. The Qur'an was originally spoken, and the faithful memorized the stories. Before Muhammad's death in 632 B.C., his followers wrote down the words he recited. Even today, many of the faithful memorize the Qur'an and believe it remains unchanged from the words God delivered to the Prophet.

Cynthia Rylant

Born: June 6, 1954; Hopewell, Virginia

www.cynthiarylant.com

Cynthia Rylant's young adult fiction writings feature adolescents questioning the values held by their friends and families and exploring how they fit into the world around them. In the process of learning about themselves, the characters grapple with issues ranging from religion and love to the politics of war.

A versatile writer, Rylant has written novels, short stories, and poetry for young adults as well as stories for children. When she was growing up in a small town in **West Virginia**, few real books were available for her to read. However, she enjoyed reading comic books. Her interest in writing developed after she reached adulthood. She became seriously interested in literature when she was in college. She earned a master's degree and later taught English classes at several universities. When she finally began writing books, her first books were for children, and she remains a popular writer of children's books.

Rylant's young adult novel *A Fine White Dust* won the **Newbery Medal** in 1987 and was listed by the **American Library Association** as one of the year's **Best Books for Young Adults**. Its thirteen-year-old **protagonist**, Peter, seeks religious meaning and understanding. When the Preacher Man comes to town to host

602

p.102

p.45

p.480

p.233

a revival, Peter thinks he has found what he has been missing. He plans to go with the evangelist when he leaves town. However, the Preacher Man instead runs off with a local woman. In the time that follows, Peter contemplates what the events have meant and decides how they will influence his attitudes toward religion and other members of his non-religious family.

p.603

In *A Kindness*, fifteen-year-old Chip has always lived alone with his mother. When she again becomes pregnant, she will not name the baby's father. Chip must face his anger and possessiveness and accept that his mother is going to have the baby despite his hopes that she will get an abortion. As in *A Fine White Dust*, Rylant's protagonist faces painful disappointment but learns about himself and his place in the world because of it.

I Had Seen Castles portrays an elderly man reflecting on his experiences in World War II. Its vivid descriptions of the war support its antiwar message. Even the book's love story helps build this theme, as its protagonist's girlfriend is a pacifist who gives concrete voice to the book's underlying antiwar message.

p.5

Rural West Virginia

West Virginia's location and geography have limited its commercial development. The state is mountainous and rugged. Travel and transportation have often been difficult and even hazardous, creating a sense of isolation in the state. This has resulted in a high number of rural communities with small populations. These rural communites have existed largely from farming, not for outside markets but for their own consumption. This leaves West Virginia among the states with the highest poverty rate and the lowest per capita income. The growing trend to close small rural schools and bus children to larger regional schools has cost money that was used to educate children, resulting in a lower level of education for these rural children.

Revival Meeting

Revival means to bring to life again, and an old-fashioned Christian revival meeting is intended to do that in a religious sense. It is a special event, often featuring a preacher from another region, where Christians revive their faith and newcomers awaken their interest in religion. There is often singing and, in some cases, manifestations of the spirit, such as healing by the laying on of hands and speaking in tongues. Some traveling preachers hold revival meetings in large tents which they erect in towns as they travel throughout the country.

In *The Islander*, Daniel's meeting with a mermaid helps him to find a connection with his grandfather. Rylant skillfully incorporates both mystical and allegorical elements such that the plot and themes are inseparable. As in *I Had Seen Castles*, the device of a character looking back on events that happened some years earlier is used. This device allows the characters to have a thoughtful understanding of the significance of the events.

Cynthia Rylant is a careful stylist who does not waste words. Her writing effectively portrays the thoughts and emotions of her young adult characters and endows them with significance. Her writing honors include a **Newbery Medal**, Boston Globe-Horn Book Awards, and a **Newbery Honor** Book award.

– Joan Hope

Louis Sachar

Born: March 20, 1954; East Meadow, New York

http://louissacher.com

Louis Sachar is the author of many books for children but only one young adult novel. However, that novel, *Holes*, has enjoyed extraordinary popularity and acclaim.

Sachar's books reflect his memories of his childhood in East Meadow, New York, and Orange County, California. He began reading widely when he was in high school and developed an interest in Russian literature in college. When he took an elective college course as a teacher's aide, he discovered that he loved working with children.

Sachar's first book for children is a collection of stories about children with the same names as the students he met at the school in which was a teacher's aide. That first book was accepted for publication during his first week of law school. For many years, Sachar struggled between being a writer and a lawyer. He worked as a lawyer part time and wrote also. Eventually he decided to become a full-time writer.

After finishing school, Sachar moved to Texas. He used that state as the setting for *Holes*. The novel not only highlights the Texas heat and the barrenness of the landscape but also borrows the exaggerations of the **tall tale**, a story form common in southwestern folktales. The novel

p.605

tells the story of Stanley Yelnats, a boy sent to Camp Green Lake, a juvenile detention facility, after being mistakenly accused of stealing a baseball player's shoes. The camp is located in a desert, the site of what was once the largest lake in Texas. Everyday, every boy in the camp must dig a hole five feet deep and five feet across. Although the boys are told that their hole digging builds character, they are actually helping the camp warden look for a treasure he believes is buried in the area.

Stanley blames his bad luck in being sent to Camp Green Lake on a curse that a one-legged psychic named Madame Zeroni once placed on his great-great-grandfather after he broke his promise to carry her up a mountain, where he was to sing her a certain lullaby and let her drink water from the stream. Stanley breaks the curse by finding the buried treasure and escaping with his friend Zero. His friend's real name is Hector Zeroni; he is a descendant of Madame Zeroni. As the boys escape, Stanley carries Zero to the water and sings the same lullaby his ancestor was to have sung. The reversal of his fortunes that follows seems appropriate for a boy whose first name is the same as his last name spelled backward.

The reader's involvement with *Holes* may not end with the book's last page. Near the end of *Holes*, the narrator invites the reader to con-

Tall Tale

Tall tales are a form of American folklore. In the days before radio and television, people entertained themselves by telling stories. Tall tales are part of this storytelling tradition. What characterizes a tall tale is a hero who is larger than life, such as Paul Bunyan. As this hero encounters problems, he solves them in a way that is humorous and stretches reality. A tall tale is full of exaggeration. Since tall tales were told before they were written down, they use everyday spoken language. There are many versions to the popular American tall tales.

tinue the novel's powerful storytelling. Readers are told that it is up to them to fill in the holes in the narrative.

Louis Sachar's *Holes* received many of the most prestigious awards given to literary works, including the **Newbery Medal** and the **National Book Award**. In 2003 the story was made into a successful film. *Holes* blends humor with vivid realistic details, thoughtful observations about boyhood, and elements from folktale and myth to create an intriguing and powerful story.

p.102

p.606

p.12

– Joan Hope

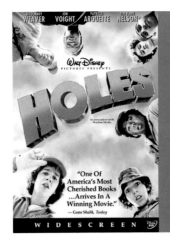

Holes, the Movie

Disney adapted the popular book *Holes* as a movie in 2003 and succeeded not only in pleasing kids, but also adults. This excellent adaptation, with a screenplay by author Sachar, was well received at the box office by audiences and reviewers.

J. D. Salinger

Born: January 1, 1919; New York, New York

www.salinger.org

Although **J. D. Salinger** published a number of short stories, his literary reputation rests almost entirely on his single novel, *The Catcher in the Rye*. This book has been popular with young adults since its publication in 1951. Its protagonist, Holden Caulfield, has become emblematic of alienated youth.

Jerome David Salinger was born in New York City, the son of a Jewish father and Christian mother. This mixed religious background caused Salinger to question his own social identity and to be keenly aware of social divisions and prejudices. Like Holden Caulfield, he grew up in New York City, where he attended public school and then went to **boarding school**—in his own case, a military academy. He also attended New York University, Ursinus College, and Columbia University but never graduated from any of them because he wanted to devote his time to writing. After serving in the U.S. Army during World War II, he began publishing short stories, the most successful of them in *The New Yorker* magazine.

The Catcher in the Rye opens with Holden Caulfield being expelled from Pencey Prep because he is failing all but one class. Seeing no point

TITLE

The Catcher in the Rye, 1951

The New Yorker

This popular weekly magazine began publication in 1925. While providing a guide to the current art and cultural happenings in New York City, the feature articles, poetry, and fiction have long attracted a national audience. Some of the greatest writers of recent history have contributed short stories and poems to *The New Yorker*. The magazine also contains cartoons by famous cartoonists, respected book and movie reviews, and is famous for its whimsical cover art.

in finishing the last few days of the school term but not wanting to go home to face his parents, who have not yet received the letter informing them of the expulsion, he spends several days on his own in New York City. Holden acts less from rebellion than from profound unhappiness and alienation from the upper-class society to which he belongs. When his sister Phoebe asks him to name something that he really likes, he cannot think of an answer. Much of Holden's unhappiness stems from his younger brother Allie's death several years earlier. Holden's thoughts turn repeatedly to his brother and to death in general.

Holden seeks comfort through connections with his other siblings, his brother D. B. and his sister Phoebe. However, his parents are almost absent from the novel. His mother is still saddened by Allie's death, and his father is too involved in his work as a corporate lawyer to provide emotional support to Holden. The novel is told as a flashback after Holden has been sent to a mental institution in California. His brother, who lives nearby, visits often, but his parents remain in New York.

Despite the book's somber elements, its enduring popularity derives largely from the humor and seeming honesty of Holden's first-person narration. His observations are at once naïve and profoundly truthful. The novel's frank language and social critique, which shocked readers in the early 1950's, are tame by current standards. Salinger admired the writing of American novelist Ernest Hemingway, also known for frank observations and for heroes at odds with social conventions.

J. D. Salinger published all his known works before 1960. Since then he has lived as a recluse in New Hampshire and has refused to grant interviews. It has been rumored that he may have continued to write after 1960.

— Joan Hope

Dream Catcher

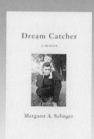

Salinger's daughter Margaret, published the memoir *Dream Catcher* in 2000, revealing some details of their highly secretive family life. She was criticized by some for invading the privacy of her reclusive, private father. Two years earlier, Joyce Maynard, a journalist and novelist, published *At Home in the World*, a memoir, in which she revealed details about her affair with J. D. Salinger in the 1970's. In 1999, she auctioned the letters he wrote to her at that time. They were bought by philanthropist and software entrepeneur Peter Norton and returned to Salinger to protect his privacy.

Graham Salisbury

Born: April 11, 1944; Philadelphia, Pennsylvania
http://www.grahamsalisbury.com

Graham Salisbury's stories reflect his background in Hawaii, where his family had lived since the early nineteenth century. He is a frequently honored writer of books for young adults, and his accomplishments honor his youth, which he spent working on boats, fishing, surfing, and learning that every person has the power to choose what is right.

Born in Pennsylvania, Salisbury grew up in Hawaii, and went to college in California. He later earned a master of fine arts degree from Vermont's **Norwich University**, where he became a founding member of the faculty of a master's program in writing for children. He eventually settled with his family in Portland, Oregon.

p.611

A career in writing for children is a surprising development for a person who has admitted, with some embarrassment, that he did not become a serious reader himself until he was in his thirties. Before then, he read only what he had to read. However, after his son was born, he read Alex Haley's **historical novel**, *Roots: The Saga of an American Family* (1976), and the experience changed his life. First, he became a voracious reader, then he felt a need to write stories himself. He began writing memory pieces, but soon those pieces began to be shaped with actions and feelings of his own creation. He soon realized that he enjoyed writing fiction best, de-

p.117

Norwich University

Norwich University, located in Northfield, Vermont, is the oldest private military college in the U.S. Founded in 1819 by Captain Alden Partridge, Norwich's mission was to train for both war and peace with a liberal education that prepared students for the responsibilities of American citizenship. In 1972, Norwich merged with Vermont College, thereby becoming co-educational and expanding its base of curricula offerings to give students a chance to pursue a non-military education.

spite coming from a family with a century-long tradition of newspaper writing.

Salisbury's *Blue Skin of the Deep* is a series of eleven stories about Sonny Mendoza and his cousin Keo, who grow up in a Hawaiian fishing village. Praised for its ability to depict island life, this book began a theme that Salisbury's later work continued: adolescent boys who endeavor to answer life's questions for themselves. His debut work was named a **Best Book** by *School Library Journal* and the American Library Association and also received a **Parents' Choice Award**.

p.195

p.45

p.153

Under the Blood-Red Sun, Salisbury's next novel, won several awards, including the Scott O'Dell Award for Historical Fiction. This story explores the impact of Japan's attack on **Pearl Harbor** in 1941 on Tomikazu Nakaji, an American-born thirteen-year-old resident of Hawaii and his Japanese-born parents. Another story set in Hawaii, *Shark Bait* features twelve-year-old Mokes, who is supposed to stay home when navy ships are in port. However, when the sailors are in town, Mokes's village is anything but quiet, and he breaks his family's rule in order to stand by his friends.

p.51

p.612

Jungle Dogs is a story of courage and determination as sixth grader Regis learns to win his own battles—and not necessarily by having to fight. *Lord*

Pearl Harbor

In 1941, the U.S. had not entered World War II. While anxiously watching German dictator Adolf Hitler's progress in Europe, U.S. leaders also were concerned about the growing Japanese empire. In 1940, Japan had signed a pact with Germany and Italy and officially became an Axis power. The U.S. had imposed an embargo on aviation gasoline to Japan in 1940 and on scrap iron and steel later the same year. In 1941, Japanese assets in the U.S. were frozen and an oil embargo was imposed. Negotiations regarding the embargo stalled late in 1941. On Sunday morning, December 7, 1941, Japanese squadrons attacked Pearl Harbor in Honolulu. They strafed and bombed rows of aircraft at Wheeler Field and the Naval Air Station, while torpedo planes and dive-bombers attacked Battleship Row in the harbor. After a second round of attacks, the Japanese planes left, less than two hours after the attack had begun. The attack left 2,403 dead and 1,178 wounded. Three battleships were sunk, one lay capsized, and four others were damaged. Japan had succeeded beyond its hopes. President Franklin D. Roosevelt, reluctant to enter the war up until then, declared war on Japan, and on December 11, Germany and Italy, the other Axis allies, declared war on the U. S.

of the Deep, winner of the 2002 Boston Globe-Horn Book Award for Fiction and Poetry, features thirteen-year-old Mikey who is working with his stepfather on a char- p.747 ter boat. This is a true coming-of-age story, in which both Mikey and the reader are wiser at its conclusion. *Island Boyz* is a rich collection of short stories of the islands.

– Alexa L. Sandmann

Jack Schaefer

Born: November 19, 1907; Cleveland, Ohio
Died: January 24, 1991; Santa Fe, New Mexico

www.aristos.org/schaefer/js-page.htm

Nearly all of **Jack Schaefer**'s writing reflects his affinity with the American West. He idealized the West as the right place to build human communities based on justice, peace, hard but honest labor, courage, endurance, and character. However, real human beings sometimes violate such virtues. They become ambitious and selfish and use their power as a destructive force. Accordingly, Schaefer's fiction includes cattle rustlers, greedy capitalists, and cattle barons on the one hand, and sturdy **homesteaders** longing for stable farms and security on the other hand. Between the two is the gunslinger, who is most often employed by the strong against the weak. When that equation is reversed, the gunslinger rises to the level of a physical and moral hero.

Schaefer was born and raised in Cleveland, Ohio, in a home that encouraged reading and a love for the West. An avid reader from an early age, Schaefer began practicing his creative writing skills in high school when he joined the staff of its literary magazine. He continued his interest in writing at **Oberlin College** and eventually became a reporter for United Press. Meanwhile, the history of the West and the novels of **Zane Grey** had always fascinated him, so he started writing fiction himself. His first novel, *Shane*, reflected that interest and won wide-

TITLES

Shane, 1949

The Canyon, 1953

spread acclaim. Its hero is forced to use violence against the land-grasping ranchers to insure the survival of the beleaguered community of homesteaders.

Although Schaefer had still never personally visited the West, he continued to write novels and short stories featuring Western heroes in search of, or trying to escape from, community. However, the need for community is always affirmed, as when Little Bear in *The Canyon* learns that no man is an island and that a quest for wholeness is doomed in isolation.

Eventually Schaefer moved to **New Mexico** to find the kind of homecoming that he idealized in his fiction. That move also allowed him to see that the American notion of civilization was slowly but surely destroying the land and ruining the beauty of the environment. Disenchanted, he stopped writing fiction after completing *Mavericks* (1967), which he wrote as a lament for the passing of the Old West.

Schaefer was skillful in creating vivid and authentic heroes who must know themselves before

p.2

Zane Grey

Zane Grey (1872-1939) was the best-selling Western writer of all time. He published some ninety books in his lifetime, sixty of them Westerns. He was born into a family that had settled as pioneers in the Ohio Valley. Their stories first piqued his interest in the Westward movement. His first success came in 1910 with *Heritage of the Desert*. He moved West with his family settling in Altadena, California, and later purchased a hunting lodge in Arizona. Each year he would spend some months fishing, hunting, and exploring the western states; the rest of the year he wrote, incorporating his experiences into his writing. Zane Grey was responsible for establishing the Code of the West as it is portrayed through movies and Western adventure stories.

Oberlin College

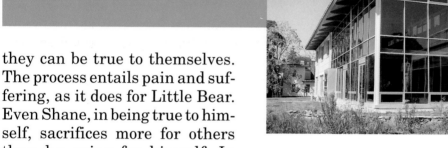

In 1833, two young missionaries reached the Western frontier, in what is now Ohio, to found a colony and a college named for the Alsatian pastor John Frederick Oberlin. They attracted settlers and a first class of twenty-nine men and fifteen women. The college had a commitment to educating both men and women, and also encouraged students of every race to attend. By 1900, one-third of all African American college graduates in the U. S. had graduated from Oberlin College. In 1867 the music division was founded, and today Oberlin continues to educate professional musicians and music teachers in the School of Music.

they can be true to themselves. The process entails pain and suffering, as it does for Little Bear. Even Shane, in being true to himself, sacrifices more for others than he gains for himself. In writing his body of literature, Schaefer was also true to his own sympathies as he depicted the plight of the fringe members of society and the innocence and demise of the American frontier.

Among Jack Schaefer's books, only *Shane* continues to be widely read as a classic literary Western. A number of his novels have been adapted as films, including *Shane*, whose 1953 adaptation earned five Academy Award nominations. A television adaptation of *Shane* appeared in 1966. Jack Schaefer was honored with an **honorary doctorate** in literature from his alma mater, Oberlin College, in 1989.

.204

– Henry J. Baron

Sandra Scoppettone

Born: June 1, 1936; Morristown, New Jersey

www.imt.net/~gedison/scoppett.html

p.57

p.101

Sandra Scoppettone is one of the first young adult authors to write convincingly and honestly about homosexuality, homophobia, and alcohol abuse. The books she wrote during the 1970's may seem old-fashioned because of the social changes that have occurred since her principal young adult novels were first published. Nevertheless, those books rank among the first to feature young gay and lesbian characters and discuss the social pressures brought to bear upon them. Her second novel, *The Late Great Me*, concerns the effects of alcohol abuse upon a seventeen-year-old who begins drinking as a way to overcome her shyness; it was made into an Emmy Award-winning program for television.

Born in New Jersey in 1936, Scoppettone knew from an early age that she would become a writer. Over her parents' objections, she skipped college in order to begin her writing career. Before she undertook her first young adult novel, she wrote children's books and for television, theater, and film. She finally wrote her first young adult novel, *Trying Hard to Hear You*, after directing a youth production of the popular Broadway musical *Anything Goes*. Incidents related to the youngsters in that play and to her own homosexuality spurred her to write the novel, which is set in **Long Island**. It is peopled by a young cast of characters mounting a production of *Anything Goes*.

The narrator of *Trying Hard to Hear You*, Camilla Crawford, is attracted to an actor named Phil in the production. She seeks opportunities to be alone with him, but he is more interested in her neighbor, Jeff. Camilla gradually realizes that Phil and Jeff are gay and are involved with each other. Other members of the production also realize this, and they treat Phil and Jeff with violence and contempt. Phil dies in a car accident after a night of heavy drinking and an attempt to prove his "manliness" by having sex with a willing girl; his death teaches Camilla a lesson about the human cost of intolerance.

Happy Endings Are All Alike also deals with homosexuality, this time it focuses on a lesbian couple, Jaret and Peggy, and the hostility with which their relationship is met. After one of them is raped by a deranged neighbor who condemns her lesbianism, both women face the indifference of law enforcement officers, who assume any lesbian rape victim is "asking for it." The rape, the trial, and its aftermath all strain the girls' relationship, their families, and their community. Once again, the travails of a marginalized and victimized community member serve as a means of educating others about their complicity in wrongdoing, as well

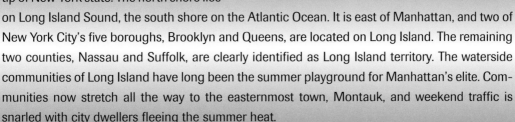

Long Island

Long Island is located at the southeastern tip of New York state. The north shore lies on Long Island Sound, the south shore on the Atlantic Ocean. It is east of Manhattan, and two of New York City's five boroughs, Brooklyn and Queens, are located on Long Island. The remaining two counties, Nassau and Suffolk, are clearly identified as Long Island territory. The waterside communities of Long Island have long been the summer playground for Manhattan's elite. Communities now stretch all the way to the easternmost town, Montauk, and weekend traffic is snarled with city dwellers fleeing the summer heat.

SANDRA SCOPPETTONE

as the limits of their own tolerance of differences in others.

Sandra Scoppettone's young adult novels deal principally with the devastation that results from people trying to coerce others, or themselves, into limited and limiting behaviors. Geri, in *The Late Great Me*, and Jeff, in *Trying Hard to Hear You*, both learn to accept who they are, and to be comfortable with themselves.

– Angela M. Salas

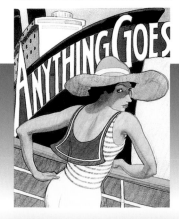

Anything Goes

Anything Goes was one of the hit Broadway musical comedies of 1934. With songs and lyrics by Cole Porter, the story takes place on a luxury liner crossing the Atlantic from New York to England. A movie version was released in 1936. It enjoyed a successful stage revival on Broadway in 1987 and includes the memorable Porter songs "I Get a Kick Out of You," "All Through the Night," "You're the Top," and "Blow, Gabriel, Blow."

Ouida Sebestyen

Born: February 13, 1924; Vernon, Texas

Ouida Sebestyen's novels focus on young human beings caught in the painful process of growing up in a confusing, often cruel world that threatens their longing for wholeness. Her characters struggle with prejudice and hate, loss of parents, difficult relationships and conflicting loyalties, and the need for independence. However, although their plights are often grim, her characters invariably move toward growth in understanding and wisdom and therefore have hope, supported by such timeless values as companionship and compassion.

Sebestyen grew up as an only child whose books were her best friends. She first aspired to become a writer at the age of six. She submitted her first novel manuscript to a publisher when she was twenty, and even though she got back almost nothing but rejection slips, she kept writing. Only a few of her stories were accepted for publication. Eventually she moved to Colorado with her young son. There she continued to hone her writing. However, it was not until Sebestyen reached the age of fifty-five that one of her novels saw print. *Words by Heart* is the heart-warming story about twelve-year-old Lena, an African American girl who learns how hard it is to carry out her dying father's lessons on love and forgiveness. The book became an immediate popular and critical success.

After waiting so long to publish one of her novels, Sebestyen feared that she would not be able to write another. She was immensely relieved, therefore, when *Far from Home* was published. It is the

Submitting a Manuscript

When an author writes a book, the copy he or she writes, types, or prints from a computer is called a manuscript. Most authors work with an agent, a person who has professional relationships with editors and publishing companies and who knows what kind of books they like to publish. The agent will negotiate with an interested publisher and obtain a publishing contract for the author. The contract details the business arrangement and states how much money an author is to receive as an advance against future sales and from the sales of the book once the advance is paid out. If an author sends a manuscript directly to the publishing company, it may be returned unread or with a rejection slip.

story of Salty, a thirteen-year-old boy who is forced to fend for himself after the death of his mother. As in Sebestyen's first book, family love and loyalty sustain and complicate the character's life. Similar tensions also inform her next novel, *IOU's*, in which Stowe Garrett, also thirteen, struggles to break free from the mother he loves. In *On Fire*, a companion novel to *Words by Heart*, the tension flows out of Sammy's conflict between the love and rejection he feels for his older brother, Tater, whose lack of conscience and violent ways begin to alienate him.

Sebestyen's next novel shifted gears. *The Girl in the Box* is a taut psychological story of seventeen-year-old Jackie, who after being kidnapped and isolated examines and rearranges who and what count most in her life. Sebestyen then returned to a more familiar subject in *Out of Nowhere*, about a young adolescent in search of family. He eventually finds his family in a most unlikely set of quirky outcasts as a triumph of acceptance and love.

Once an insecure teenager herself, Ouida Sebestyen has written novels that affirm life, that encourage and inspire young adults to value the worth of self, strong family relationships, love, and forgiveness. She gives her multidimensional characters sensitivity and insight that move readers and make them long remember such traits as the moral courage of Lena or Harley's poignant search to fill his life's gaps. The quality of Sebestyen's writing has been recognized and honored through many awards, including the International Reading Association **Children's Book Award** and Library of Congress **Children's Book of the Year**, as well as American Library Association **Best Books for Young Adults** and **National Book Awards** for *Words by Heart*.

p.621

p.45

p.480

p.122

– Henry J. Baron

International Reading Association

The International Reading Association (IRA) is a professional organization whose members are dedicated to improving literacy around the world. The IRA works to improve the teaching of reading, to support research about reading, and to encourage reading as a lifelong activity. Members include teachers, reading specialists, administrators, university faculty, librarians, and parents. The organization is active in ninety-nine countries and reaches more than 300,000 people worldwide.

Neal Shusterman

Born: November 12, 1962; Brooklyn, New York

www.storyman.com

Neal Shusterman's popular young adult books are typically set in the world of the supernatural and do not flinch from exploring dark issues. Many of his teenage protagonists are gifted with special powers that carry with them a painful price.

Shusterman was born and reared in Brooklyn, New York. By the age of eight, he was reading widely and studying the techniques of his favorite authors. During his adolescence, his family moved to Mexico City, where he attended high school. He later earned a bachelor's degree in psychology and drama at the University of California at Irvine. After his graduation, he wrote a humor column that made him the youngest syndicated columnist in the United States. In 1987, he married Elaine Jones, a teacher and photographer, with whom he has had four children. The family settled in Los Angeles, California.

Shusterman's first novel, *The Shadow Club*, was praised for its treatment of teenage-related issues, such as violence, anger, and revenge. Its leading characters are seven junior high school students who form a secret club to seek revenge on classmates who are superior to them. In Shusterman's second novel, *Dissidents*, a fifteen-year-old boy is forced to deal with the problems of living in Moscow with his mother, the **American ambassador** to the Soviet Union. His ordeal turns to adventure and self-discovery when he helps a friend reunite with her father, a Soviet dissident.

What Daddy Did explores the power of love, with a couple forgiving the man who has murdered

p.2

p.62

their daughter; however, the man's son struggles with anger before finally forgiving his father, too. *Speeding Bullet* explores the nature of its teenage hero, who is unsuccessful with girls until he discovers that he has an extraordinary talent for rescuing people in trouble. However, he eventually learns that his special powers are a sham, and he must find a new source of strength. In *The Eyes of Kid Midas*, Kevin finds a pair of glasses that can create anything he wishes. The more he exercises this power, however, the more damage he causes. The moral is that one should be careful about one's wishes, for they might come true.

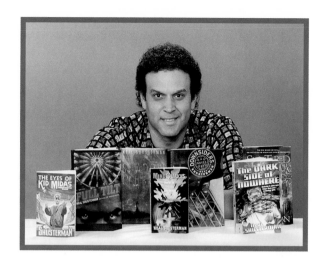

Shusterman continued to explore the dangers of supernatural powers in subsequent novels. In *The Dark Side of Nowhere*, a glove can shoot steel pellets with lethal force. The Star Shards Chronicles (*Scorpion Shards*, *Thief of Souls*, and *Shattered Sky*) follow the exploits of six teenagers, each of whom has a special power associated with an affliction. Tory, for example, suffers from acne and taints everything she touches. The group becomes divided, one side trying to eliminate the source of their power and the

American Ambassador

An American ambassador represents the U.S. in a foreign country, furthering the interests of the government and fellow citizens abroad. The official headquarters of the ambassador is the embassy. The ambassador meets with the government officials of the country as well as members of the business community to encourage good relations with the U. S. The U. S. government maintains diplomatic offices in more than 150 countries. Each post reports to the State Department and carries out instructions and policies of the president.

other exploiting it. By the final book, teenage angst has taken on universal dimensions as the forces of life and death battle for the fate of Earth. In the MindWorks series—which includes *MindQuakes*, *MindStorms*, and *MindTwisters*—Shusterman experimented with technique, using different voices, changing points of view, and shifting from satire to seriousness to fanciful flights.

Neal Shusterman's novels have regularly appeared on lists of top sellers and books most recommended for young adult readers. *The Shadow Club* received the **Children's Choice Award** from the p.621 **International Reading Association**. The **New** p.15 **York Public Library** gave both *Speeding Bullet* and *What Daddy Did* **Best Books for the Teen Age** awards. *Downsiders* received more than a dozen awards and became a television movie. Two short films that Shusterman directed won awards, and he p.62 has written for the *Goosebumps* television series.

– Bernard E. Morris

Goosebumps, the Television Series

The Fox Network produced a television series based on R. L. Stine's *Goosebumps* books, and it aired over three seasons from 1995 through 1998. The series was popular with readers familiar with the books, but many viewers found their own imaginations scarier than the images on television. Dreamworks, the movie production and technology company, has issued a *Goosebumps* computer game.

William Sleator

Born: February 13, 1945; Havre de Grace, Maryland

www.tycho.org/sleator.shtml

One of the most prolific writers of science fiction for young adults, **William Sleator** displays a knack for incorporating new and fascinating aspects of science into speculative fiction that is engaging, exciting, and thoughtful. Sleator's young protagonists not only encounter aliens, strange planets, and puzzling scientific phenomena but also encounter the limitations and possibilities of their own minds as they try to solve problems. Sleator celebrates the imagination, intelligence, and logic of his characters, who are often thrown into situations that no one has ever encountered before. Sleator's teenage characters must solve problems through their own ingenuity and without the help of adults.

Sleator was born in Maryland, and grew up in University City, Missouri, the son of two scientists. He studied English at Harvard University and then moved to London, England, where he studied music composition and worked as a rehearsal pianist for the Royal Ballet School. Although Sleator's interests were primarily artistic, he could not help but be influenced by living in a family of scientists. As a result, much of his writing explores the possibilities of science and how young people encounter and react to these ideas.

Sleator's best-known work is probably *Interstellar Pig*. Fourteen-year-old Barney becomes intrigued by the three mysterious and attractive neighbors who come to vacation next door to his family at the seashore. The strangers draw him into a board game known as Interstellar Pig, in which

aliens from other planets vie for the possession of the Piggy. Drawing together the history of the vacation home in which he is staying and the hints provided by the strangers, Barney realizes that the actions of the board game are real, and he is forced to fight a deadly battle with the aliens for the possession of the Piggy. In *Parasite Pig*, a sequel to *Interstellar Pig*, Barney is infected by an alien parasite and drawn to the planet where the Piggy now resides. There he must fight for his life to prevent himself and his friend from being served up as a gourmet meal for a race of alien crabs.

p.62

In other novels, Sleator pursues the concepts of strange attractors (*Strange Attractors*), the possibility of duplication of the self (*The Boy Who Reversed Himself*), time travel (*The Green Futures of Tycho*), and behavioral conditioning and the labyrinth of the mind (*House of Stairs*).

Royal Ballet School

The Royal Ballet School is the foremost training ground for classical ballet dancers in the United Kingdom. It maintains both a lower and upper school and trains pupils in both academic subjects and classical ballet. It was founded in 1926 and became associated with the Royal Ballet in 1956. In 2003, the upper school was relocated to studios next to the Royal Opera House in Covent Garden, London, and is now linked to the Royal Ballet. Dancers are trained to enter the Royal Ballet, Birmingham Royal Ballet, and international dance companies.

Parasite

A parasite is an organism that lives on or in another living organism and obtains food from it. Fungi are some of the most destructive parasites in the plant world. In the 1800's, outbreaks of late blight destroyed the potato crops of Europe. Millions of people who depended on potatoes as their primary source of food starved to death. Christmas mistletoe is a parasite that grows in trees, and if it is not removed, it can do damage to its host.

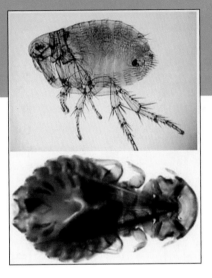

A collection of his stories, *Oddballs: Stories*, provides semi-autobiographical details about Sleator's life and family. Two other novels, *The Spirit House* and *Dangerous Wishes*, build upon Sleator's experiences living in Thailand. Each of Sleator's novels provides intricate twists and turns that take readers on exciting and suspenseful explorations of how his characters use their intellect and imagination to move through the sequence of solving life-threatening predicaments.

William Sleator's work has been widely recognized for its contribution to young adult fiction, including **Best Books for Young Adults** citations for *House of Stairs, Interstellar Pig, Singularity*, and *The Boy Who Reversed Himself*. He has also received **Best Book of the Year** awards from *School Library Journal* for *The Green Futures of Tycho, Fingers*, and *Interstellar Pig*.

– Ann M. Cameron

Betty Smith

Born: December 15, 1896; Brooklyn, New York
Died: January 17, 1972; Shelton, Connecticut

www.atreegrowsinbrooklyn.org

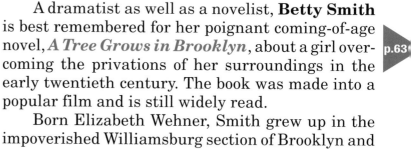

A dramatist as well as a novelist, **Betty Smith** is best remembered for her poignant coming-of-age novel, *A Tree Grows in Brooklyn*, about a girl overcoming the privations of her surroundings in the early twentieth century. The book was made into a popular film and is still widely read.

p.63

Born Elizabeth Wehner, Smith grew up in the impoverished Williamsburg section of Brooklyn and had to leave school at the age of fourteen in order to help earn money for her family. Although she never

went beyond the eighth grade, she was later admitted to the University of Michigan and Yale University drama school as a special student. Meanwhile, she worked in factories, retail sales, and clerical positions. She also did feature writing for a newspaper syndicate; was a columnist for the *Detroit Free Press*; and served as a reader, editor, and playwright for the Federal Theater during the Great Depression. Later she taught creative writing at the University of North Carolina, where a faculty member named Paul Green had a great influence on her. She eventually wrote 125 one-act plays and seven full-length plays and received a number of awards for her playwriting.

p.43

Smith wrote about what she

knew. In 1938 she began writing a novel, the semi-autobiographical *A Tree Grows in Brooklyn*. Even before the book was published, she tried to sell film rights to her story to Hollywood for five thousand dollars but was turned down. When the book was finally published in 1943, it became an immediate p.384 **best-seller**; it would eventually be translated into sixteen languages and sell more than three million copies. Meanwhile, Smith felt as if she had gone to bed one night as an obscure writer living quietly in a small town and awakened the next morning as a celebrity. Producers at **Twentieth Century Fox** of- p.629 fered her fifty thousand dollars for the film rights they had early declined for a tenth of that amount, but Smith turned them down. She relented only when the studio paid her an additional five thousand dollars to make up for its earlier rejection of her book.

A Tree Grows in Brooklyn is a highly autobiographical account of Smith's own childhood in Brooklyn. Smith modeled its heroine, Francie Nolan, closely on herself—even giving her the same birthday—and had Francie go through the same privations and learning experiences that she had gone through. The title of the book is a metaphor for its central theme: Francie's struggle to break through the concrete confines of her harsh surroundings, grow tall, and flourish. Smith's realistic depiction of inner-city squalor and Fran-

Twentieth Century Fox

Twentieth Century Fox produces, acquires, and distributes films. It was founded by William Fox in 1913, who produced the Movietone Newreels. In 1928, he acquired silent Western star Tom Mix's ranch in Los Angeles in what is now Century City and built studios and backlots. In 1935, Fox merged with Daryll Zanuck's Twentieth Century Pictures to become Twentieth Century Fox. The studio is now owned by Rupert Murdoch's News Corp., which also owns Fox Television Network.

cie's persistent optimism give the book a universal appeal.

Smith also used Brooklyn as the setting for her next book, *Tomorrow Will Be Better*. Her third novel, *Joy in the Morning*, was also semi-autobiographical. Smith set it in the Midwest, where she had attended the University of Michigan and lived with her husband when he was a law student. Although *Joy in the Morning* was adapted to the screen, neither it nor her second novel received the acclaim that *A Tree Grows in Brooklyn* had received. In later years Smith laughingly said that she wished she had written the three books in reverse order.

– Anita Price Davis

A Tree Grows in Brooklyn, the Movie

The screen rights to Betty Smith's novel were purchased by Twentieth Century Fox in 1944. The studio selected Elia Kazan, a director known for his work with the Group Theater in New York, as the film's director. As a New Yorker, he was drawn to the story about New York street life and the working class. The film was released in 1945 to good reviews. James Dunn won an Academy Award for Best Supporting Actor for his portrayal of Johnny Nolan, and Peggy Ann Garner received a special award for Outstanding Child Actress of 1945 for her portrayal of Francie Nolan.

Gary Soto

Born: April 12, 1952; Fresno, California

www.garysoto.com

Gary Soto's books take readers into the worlds of Mexican American teenagers growing up in California. His books have a sense of humor and stay focused on working-class families. Soto likes to include Spanish words in his stories, to reflect the speech of his young protagonists growing up in a bilingual world. As a consequence, many of his books have glossaries explaining the Spanish terms.

Soto has drawn on his own youth for much of his fiction. He was born and reared in central California, like the characters in *Living Up the Street* and *Baseball in April*. He attended the California State University in Fresno and graduated with a bachelor's degree in English. To the surprise of his family, he married a Japanese American woman, Carolyn Sadako Oda, just like his young protagonist in *Living Up the Street*. Soto also earned a master of fine arts degree from the University of California at Irvine. He then taught English at the University of California at Berkeley until the early 1990's, when he became a full-time writer. Since then, he has written children's and young adult fiction, poetry, drama, and novels for adults. His writing is connected to California's Mexican American community, and focuses on both the joys and hardships of its members.

Living Up the Street offers twenty-one interrelated short stories about a young Mexican American boy growing up in Fresno in the 1950's and 1960's. Although some of his stories deal with childhood adventures, the book is by no means a children's story.

.632

p.233

TITLES

Living Up the Street: Narrative Recollections, 1985

Baseball in April and Other Stories, 1990

Taking Sides, 1991

Pacific Crossing, 1992

Jesse, 1994

Buried Onions, 1997

Petty Crimes, 1999

The Afterlife, 2003

Mexican Americans in California

Mexican Americans have lived in California since it was settled by the Spanish Franciscan fathers who built missions along the coast. In more recent times, they have come across the border for jobs. The bracero program, created during World War II by the U. S. and Mexican governments to meet a demand for agricultural laborers, brought seasonal workers into the U. S., and farmers quickly became dependent on this low-cost source of labor. Between 1948 and 1964, some 4.5 million Mexicans were brought to the U. S. for temporary work. At the end of their contracts, many stayed on illegally. Since then, many have become legal residents and have become integrated into California life. The demand for workers continues to encourage Mexicans to enter the U. S. without papers. Mexican Americans now make up more than 30% of California's population.

The narration critically reflects the lives, hopes, aspirations and struggles of its protagonist, his family, friends, and adversaries, and speaks to sophisticated young readers. It won the **American Book Award of the** Before Columbus Foundation in 1985, and is widely read in American colleges. *Baseball in April* continues with similar stories set in Fresno during the late 1980's, and won the Reading Magic Award in 1991.

p.13

p.63

Taking Sides and *Pacific Crossing* follow Lincoln Mendoza, a fourteen-year-old Mexican American who moves into an Anglo suburb of San Francisco. Later he spends a summer as an exchange student in Japan, where he saves the life of his host's father. *Jesse* is set in 1968, when young American men were being drafted into the army to fight in the Vietnam War. At seventeen, Jesse leaves his alcoholic father, moves in with his older brother Abel, and starts college. Poverty and prejudice surround him and harden his life.

p.90

p.10

Buried Onions and *Petty Crimes* deal with poverty, violence, and a cycle of suffering encountered by their teenage protagonists. Nineteen-year-old Eddie imagines an onion buried under the earth causing all the tears of the humans he knows. His aunt challenges him to avenge the murder of his cousin, his jobs fail him, and the bleakness of his environment seems without redemption. The characters of the second book are slightly younger, but they appear headed to a similarly harsh future.

Gary Soto's fiction has a humorous side, but also portrays suffering among working-class Mexican American teenagers. His work has grown darker. Readers are rewarded with honest books that do not shirk away from confronting the sinister side of humanity.

– R. C. Lutz

Reading Magic Award

Parenting magazine publishes a list of books selected for the excellence of their writing or illustration. This list of the best books of the year is intended to help parents encourage a love of reading in their children by providing them with superior reading material from the more than 4,000 books published for young readers each year

Ivan Southall

Born: June 8, 1921; Canterbury, Victoria, Australia

http://ozlit.vicnet.net.au/writers.cfm?id=520

Ivan Southall was Australia's most prominent writer for children and young adults through the 1960's, 1970's and 1980's. After an **apprenticeship** writing conventional adventure stories about an air force pilot named Simon Black, Southall went on to develop a demanding **stream-of-consciousness** style for getting into the minds of his young **protagonists**, especially when they face sudden crises. He writes with great energy and expression. His subject matter is often controversial, following in the footsteps of the founder of Australian young adult fiction, **Ethel Turner**, whose *Seven Little Australians* (1894) portrayed children as rebellious but joyful.

Born in southeastern **Australia**, Southall worked as an engraver for a Melbourne newspaper both before and immediately following World War II. During the war, he served in the Royal Australian Air Force. In 1947 he decided to become a full-time writer, making his name with nine Simon Black adventures and a series of popular adult wartime novels. In the 1960's he began to tire of such writing and developed a more interior characterization and a more challenging style. His output, if anything, increased as he entered his maturity as a young adult author. In 1975 he gave a series of lectures on writing for children, published as *A Journey of Discovery*, the title giving the clue to his own career. He followed this in 1994 with an equally significantly titled essay, "An Inner Lifestyle."

Southall's first significant young adult novel was *Hills End*, in which a group of young people face

p.24

p.27

p.23

p.635

p.46

the dangers of a storm and flooding. Similar plots followed in *Ash Road*, in which three boys confront a bush fire, and *To the Wild Sky*, in which a group of people are stranded by an air crash. The latter novel proved controversial as Southall left it ending with no certainty of the people's being rescued. Many years later, however, Southall wrote a sequel, *A City Out of Sight*, in which the stranded people finally reach safety. It is a characteristic of his writing that his heroes show typical human failings; their heroism is muted by their weakness, usually the inability to work together.

The disaster in *Finn's Folly* is a truck overturning and spilling its load of cyanide canisters. The force of the story is its center around a mentally challenged boy. Southall's most successful novel, *Josh*, won him the **Carnegie Medal**. Set in rural Australia, it tells the story from the outsider's perspective. A sensitive city boy visits relatives: he is bullied by the local youth, and though he survives, he leaves town without reconciliation. Southall's other young adult novels deal with love affairs: *Walk a Mile and Get Nowhere* and *Matt and Jo*. Set in World War II, *The Long Night Watch* is about members of an Australian religious cult awaiting the fiery end of the world on a deserted South Seas island, on which Japanese troops land. *The Mysterious World of*

p.42

Ethel Turner

Ethel Turner was born in England in 1870 and immigrated to Australia with her mother and sisters when she was ten years old. She grew up loving books and writing, and in 1893 she sent her manuscript, *Seven Little Australians*, to a publisher in Melbourne. The book was published and has been in print for more than one hundred years. It has sold more than two million copies, been translated into more than eleven languages, and was also adapted as a movie and two television series. Turner went on to write more than forty books before her death in 1958.

IVAN SOUTHALL

Marcus Leadbetter concerns a teenager coming to terms with the death of his grandfather.

Ivan Southall has won numerous awards, including **the Carnegie Medal** for *Josh*, the **Australian Writers' Award** for *Matt and Jo*, and several **Australia Children's Book of the Year** awards. In 1981 he was awarded the **Australia Medal** for services to literature.

p.63

– David Barratt

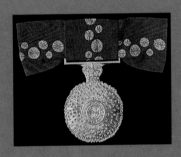

Australia Medal

The highest honor awarded in Australia is to be named a companion, officer, or member of the Order of Australia in either the general or the military division. Each award is accompanied by the Medal of the Order of Australia, often referred to as the Australia Medal. Individuals are selected for this honor because of outstanding service in a given field of endeavor.

Elizabeth George Speare

Born: November 21, 1908; Melrose, Massachusetts
Died: November 15, 1994; Tucson, Arizona

http://www.houghtonmifflinbooks.com/catalog/
authordetail.cfm?authorID=4099

Elizabeth George Speare wrote mostly about early America and created stories with believable and strong young characters who face the serious perils of their times and grow morally.

Born in Massachusetts and reared in New England, Speare nourished an interest in early American history, writing, and themes of interest to young people. She earned bachelor's and master's degrees from Boston University then began teaching high school English. As she raised her family, she wrote nonfiction articles for family-oriented periodicals and read widely in history.

Drawn to a book called *The Narrative of Captivity of Mrs. Johnson*, which was first published in 1807, she wrote her own first novel, a fictionalized account of Mrs. Johnson's younger sister. *Calico Captive* is set on the eve of the outbreak of the **French and Indian War** of the mid-eighteenth century. It presents Miriam, who with her sister's family, is captured by Native Americans, bartered to the French, and then ransomed to the English. During her captivity, Miriam experiences physical and mental hardship before being put out on the streets. These tests of endurance and ingenuity serve to develop her character as well as her appreciation for other cultures.

The spunky heroine of *The Witch of Blackbird Pond*, Kit Tyler, discovers at first hand the evil of fanaticism as she tries to fit into a new society. Forced to move from a free lifestyle with her grandfather to the restrictive life in **Puritan New England**, she

p.222

638

TITLES

Calico Captive, 1957

The Witch of Blackbird Pond, 1958

The Bronze Bow, 1961

The Sign of the Beaver, 1983

becomes an outsider subject to hostile suspicions. Kit learns to walk the narrow line between adapting to New England life and remaining true to herself.

Daniel Bar Jamin, the **protagonist** of *The Bronze Bow* also matures. This story, which is set in ancient Galilee, presents glimpses of Jesus and his message of love, an orientation to life that is the opposite of Daniel's. After the death of his parents at the hands of the Romans, Daniel becomes an intolerant zealot and outlaw. However, his experiences and his contact with Jesus inspire his moral growth.

p.23: p.639

In *The Sign of the Beaver*, thirteen-year-old Matt helps his father build a one-room cabin for their family in the woods of northern Maine. He assumes care for the place while his father goes back to Massachusetts to collect the rest of the family. His father's seven-week trip extends into deep winter. After being robbed by another white settler, Matt is befriended by the Native Americans whom he has previously feared. Like Speare's other protagonists, Matt develops survival skills and human understanding.

Elizabeth George Speare has been widely recognized as a significant contributor to historical fiction for children and young adults. She has won the prestigious Newbery

p.11

Puritan New England

The Puritans arose as part of the religious reform movement in England in the sixteenth century. They felt the Church of England needed to be purified. When they realized they had no power to reform the church, they left for the New World. The colony they founded in Massachusetts was an orderly society based on God's plan. The people valued hard work and scorned wasting time. From them, we inherited what is known as the Protestant work ethic. Hard work pleased God. Puritan life was structured around the congregation, and this place of discussion later led to the New England town hall meeting. Puritan society was one in which religion was part of political life.

Ancient Galilee

The ancient Middle Eastern region of Galilee is known as the place where Jesus Christ lived. It is a region approximately fifty miles long from north to south and twenty-five miles wide. It was a lush, fertile region in Biblical times and is again today. It is now the area of Israel north and east of the city of Haifa. The once fertile land became neglected and desolate until the return of Jews in the late nineteenth century. When the State of Israel was created in 1948, the citizens set about to again make it the "land of milk and honey." It is now home to most of Israel's collective farms and is filled with orange groves, vineyards, and fruit orchards.

p.102 Medal for *Calico Captive* and *The Bronze Bow*, and *The Sign of the Beaver* was a **Newbery Honor Book**. p.45 She has won **American Library Association** awards, the Scott O'Dell Award for Historical Fiction, and the **Laura Ingalls Wilder Award** for p.51 her lifetime contributions to children's literature.

– Bernadette Flynn Low

Jerry Spinelli

Born: February 1, 1941; Norristown, Pennsylvania

http://www.randomhouse.com/features/jerryspinelli

Jerry Spinelli's works typically involve conflicts between pressures to conform and be popular and desires to be an individual. Many of his central characters have little trouble following the dictates of their own consciences, but others feel powerful pressures to do otherwise.

Spinelli was born and reared in southeastern Pennsylvania. Many of his works are set in towns that resemble his hometown of Norristown and draw on his growing up there. Excelling in sports, especially baseball and track, he had little interest in reading and writing until he wrote a poem about a victory of his high school football team. After graduating from high school, he earned a bachelor's degree from Gettysburg College and then attended writing seminars at Baltimore's Johns Hopkins University, where he earned a master's degree. He took additional courses at Temple University in Philadelphia. In 1977, he married Eileen Masi, who had five children, and thereby gained a ready-made family.

Spinelli worked as a magazine **editor** and wrote four adult novels, but no one would publish them. He got the idea of writing a book for young people when one of his stepchildren ate some chicken he was saving for his own lunch. The resulting work, which Spinelli had little trouble getting published, was *Space Station Seventh Grade*. From then on, he concentrated on writing books for children and young adults. He later wrote a sequel to *Space Station Seventh Grade* titled *Jason and Marceline*. Both books explore the developing relationship be-

p.2

tween Jason and Marceline as Jason becomes less concerned with what others think and more concerned with pleasing himself.

Who Put That Hair in My Tooth-brush? concerns sibling rivalry, and *Night of the Whale* deals with high school seniors who come across a group of **beached whales** and try to save them. *There's a Girl in My Hammerlock* depicts Maisie Potter, a mature, self-sufficient young adult who does not accept the idea that only boys can be on her school's wrestling team. The book involves a sensitive treatment of gender issues.

Maniac Magee creates a figure based on American folklore. Like **Paul Bunyan**, Maniac Magee is larger than life. He turns the city of Two Rivers upside down as he flouts racial taboos, bridges generation gaps, and shows incredible athletic prowess. *Maniac Magee* won many awards, including the **Newbery Medal**. This p.102 book gained Spinelli recognition as a major figure in the field of children's and young adult literature.

Beached Whales

It is not common for whales to beach themselves. No one knows why they do this, but there are many unproven theories. Some speculate that sounds under water—explosions, earthquakes, or other loud booms—disrupt the whales' ability to navigate. Others attribute it to infections or stress. Still others theorize that they are chasing prey too aggressively and end up on shore. In some cases, humans are able to redirect the whales and return them to the ocean. In others, the whales die or are euthanized.

Stargirl is also about a person who refuses to conform. Equally important is the story's narrator, Leo Borlock, whom Stargirl loves. Leo, however, is concerned with conformity, so after a roller-coaster relationship, he does not invite Stargirl to the Ocotillo Ball. She attends alone and ultimately enchants the entire crowd of classmates, who follow her in a magical line dance. All the while, Leo—who does not attend the ball after all—watches from the shadows, feeling a mixture of shame and regret. Stargirl, who was first popular and then despised at school, is suddenly gone the next day. Leo learns that she has moved away; he never sees her again, but knows that she has changed his life forever. The book ends on a hopeful but enigmatic note as, years later and now a grown man, Leo receives an anonymous gift that makes him ponder about the mysterious Stargirl and if she might be still waiting for him somewhere.

Spinelli's books are popular with young adults. As the numerous awards he has won attest, his books are also well received by reviewers and literary critics. His works are full of conflict and humor of the sort that young people love.

– Richard Tuerk

Paul Bunyan

Paul Bunyan is one of the heros of American folklore. He is a giant of a man and is accompanied by his companion Babe, a blue ox. Bunyan is a lumberjack, and in his travels he is said to have created the Grand Canyon, the ten thousand lakes of Minnesota, and the barren landscape of North Dakota. All of Paul's adventures are exaggerated and comical. He is the hero of a collection of tall tales that were originally created as entertainment and later written down as literature.

Nancy Springer

Born: July 5, 1948; Montclair, New Jersey
www.stlf.org/ntc/11/nsinfo.htm

Nancy Springer first attracted a young adult audience with books about horses. Later she brought the same insights to realistic novels, mysteries, fantasies, and books set in the Middle Ages.

Springer was born Nancy Connor, the youngest child in her family and the only girl. Because she was small and shy during her childhood in New Jersey, she was often bullied. She escaped through reading and imagining fantasies about heroic characters. When she was thirteen, her parents moved to Gettysburg, Pennsylvania. There she attended high school and Gettysburg College. In 1969 she married Joel Springer, a fine-arts photographer. The following spring, she received her bachelor's degree. After teaching for a year, she stopped working in order to devote time to her family and two children. However, she soon began experiencing severe depression. As a last resort, she tried venting her feelings through writing. The experiment was successful. *The Book of Suns*, a **fantasy** written for an adult audience, appeared in 1977. More fantasies soon followed.

p.87

By 1981 Springer had published enough books that she was able to buy a horse. The fulfillment of this childhood dream inspired her to write a book directed at younger readers. *A Horse to Love* is the story of a shy teenage girl, much like Springer, who finds her own identity by taking care of a horse. Other books about horses followed as well as a vol-

TITLES

A Horse to Love, 1987

The Friendship Song, 1992

Toughing It, 1994

Looking for Jamie Bridger, 1995

I Am Mordred: A Tale from Camelot, 1998

Sky Rider, 1999

I Am Morgan le Fay: A Tale from Camelot, 2001

Rowan Hood: Outlaw Girl of Sherwood Forest, 2001

Separate Sisters, 2001

Lionclaw: A Tale of Rowan Hood, 2002

The Hex Witch of Seldom, 2002

Outlaw Princess of Sherwood: A Tale of Rowan Hood, 2003

Wild Boy: A Tale of Rowan Hood, 2004

Camelot

Camelot was the legendary castle of King Arthur. It was here that Arthur assembled his court of chivalrous warriors, the Knights of the Round Table. The knights' quest was for the Holy Grail, and Camelot is where their journey begins. In American politics, a legend was created around the presidency of John F. Kennedy. His White House was dubbed Camelot, and the legend of King Arthur was suggested by his group of confidantes.

ume of poetry entitled *Music of Their Hooves: Poems About Horses* (1993).

Springer has also written fantasies aimed at young adult readers. In *Sky Rider*, a ghost returns from the dead to heal an ailing horse. In *The Friendship Song*, two girls venture into the underworld of dead rock musicians in order to rescue their favorite lead singer. The **protagonists** of Springer's more realistic mysteries are also both brave and persistent. Although everyone else seems indifferent, the hero of *Toughing It* will not give up until he finds the murderers of his beloved older brother. The heroine of *Looking for Jamie Bridger* exhibits the same kind of courage when she sets off to find her father and to establish her own identity.

In 1998 Springer began publishing books for young adults based on medieval legends. In *I Am Mordred: A Tale from Camelot* and *I Am Morgan le Fay: A Tale from Camelot*, she took a new, more sympathetic look at familiar characters in the **Arthurian** stories who are traditionally presented as villains. For *Rowan Hood: Outlaw Girl of Sherwood Forest* and its sequel *Lionclaw: A Tale of Rowan Hood*, Springer created an entirely new set of characters who, like the legendary Robin Hood, flee to **Sherwood Forest** in order to escape tyranny.

p.23

p.644

p.4

p.64

In all of these genres, Nancy Springer creates strong characters, many of them women, and places them in situations that test their courage. Her books are popular with young adult readers and are also praised by critics. Both *Toughing It* and *Looking for Jamie Bridger* won **Edgar Allan Poe Awards** from the Mystery Writers of America, and *I Am Mordred* received an **American Library Association** Best **Books for Young Adults** citation.

p.72
p.45
p.480

– Rosemary M. Canfield Reisman

Sherwood Forest

Located near Nottingham, Sherwood Forest is the legendary home of Robin Hood and his band of Merry Men. Today, a Robin Hood festival is held in Sherwood Forest each year. The Major Oak attracts tourists to Sherwood Forest County Park. This tree that measures thirty-three feet around with a canopy of ninety-two feet is estimated to be some eight hundred years old. The forest once suffered from development but is now being returned to a natural state.

Suzanne Fisher Staples

Born: August 27, 1945; Philadelphia, Pennsylvania

www.suzannefisherstaples.com

Suzanne Staples's young adult books give readers a vivid sense of place. Whether she is describing a blinding dust storm or the onset of a deadly **cyclone**, she creates fascinating and detailed worlds that are populated by admirable characters. p.64

Born Suzanne Fisher, Staples explored her creative talents at an early age by writing poems and stories and creating a newspaper. Even though she loved creating stories, she did not think she could earn a living as an author, so she majored in journalism in college. After graduating, she began her career as a foreign correspondent in Asia for United Press International. She held that position for thirteen years.

From 1985 to 1988, she lived with a nomadic tribe in the **Cholistan Desert** in Pakistan, a mostly p.64 Muslim country that she later made the setting for two novels, *Shabanu: Daughter of the Wind* and its sequel, *Haveli*. In addition, she drew on stories she collected about rural women in **India** p.3 and Pakistan when she was a correspondent and when she worked with the U.S. Agency for International Development. As a result, her books have realistic female characters who are strong, resilient, and resourceful in dealing with complex social issues.

Shabanu relates the poignant coming of age of young Shabanu. Although her world is very different from the world that American youth experience, her longings, joys, and sorrows are universal. She is a complex and spirited young woman;

Cyclone

Cyclones are storms that form over tropical oceans. Hurricanes, known as the greatest storms on earth, begin as cyclones, caused when warm surface water, high humidity, and winds coverge. The circular motion of a cyclone is counterclockwise in the Northern Hemisphere and clockwise in the Southern Hemisphere. As a vortex of wind, water vapor, and clouds spin at an increasing rate, the eye of the hurricane forms. This is a calm area surrounded by the violent activity of the hurricane. In the Western Hemisphere these storms are called hurricanes; in the Western Pacific, typhoons; in the Indian Ocean, cyclones; in Australia, Willy Willys; and in the Philippines *baguious*.

however, she is bound to the traditions of a culture in which women are basically powerless to control their own destinies. With tremendous empathy, Staples explores Shabanu's internal conflicts when she is forced to sell her beloved camel and later loses her first betrothed when she is forced to marry a much older man to settle a blood feud.

Haveli is set five years after *Shabanu* and delves into more complex social dynamics. Shabanu's new world is replete with intrigue, conspiracies, betrayal, and violence. At the age of eighteen she is the youngest of her husband, Rahim's, four wives, and is his favorite. His older wives view her as an uncultured interloper. Afraid that she might destroy their security, they continually scheme to minimize her influence and eventually threaten the lives of both her and her daughter, Mumtaz. Shabanu's internal conflicts are intensified when she falls in love with another man, knowing that their relationship can never be actualized because of duty and family honor.

SUZANNE FISHER STAPLES

Cholistan Desert

The Cholistan Desert is located in the Punjab province of Pakistan. It is the country's largest desert. The dry Kakra riverbed runs through the desert, and there were many settlements along its banks during the period of the ancient Indus Valley civilization. Today, more than four hundred archaeological sites line the riverbed. The desert is sparsely populated by semi-nomadic people who, because of the scarce water supply, must frequently move from place to place.

Staples's third novel, *Dangerous Skies*, is set in a vastly different locale: the mud flats of Chesapeake Bay. Like Staples's female **protagonists**, this p.2 book's male protagonists confront such issues as prejudice and hypocrisy; they also face and overcome racism.

Pavarti, the protagonist in Staples's novel *Shiva's Fire*, is another spirited, independent young woman who was born with a gift, the gift of dance like the god Shiva himself. Because of her innate ability to charm birds, fish, and her magical abilities to dance, she is shunned. However, she is self-reliant and secure within herself.

Suzanne Fisher Staples's writing awards include a **Newbery Honor Book** award for *Shabanu:* p.1 *Daughter of the Wind* and an **American Library** p.45 **Association** **Best Books for Young Adults** award p.4 for *Dangerous Skies*.

– Sharon K. Wilson

John Steinbeck

Born: February 27, 1902; Salinas, California
Died: December 20, 1968; New York, New York

www.steinbeck.org/MainFrame.html

Although **John Steinbeck** did not write specifically for young adults, two of his books, *The Red Pony* and *The Pearl*, have all the hallmarks of young adult literature and are widely read in schools. Several of his adult novels, such as *Tortilla Flat* (1935), *Of Mice and Men* (1937), *The Grapes of Wrath* (1939), and *Cannery Row* (1945), also appear frequently on secondary school reading lists. However, many school districts view these books as too controversial to be suitable for required reading. *The Grapes of Wrath*, Steinbeck's most celebrated novel, is a family saga set in the grim social and economic context of the **Great Depression** of the 1930's. It won a **Pulitzer Prize** and still ranks high among the most significant twentieth century American novels.

Born in Northern California, Steinbeck developed an early interest in **Arthurian** legend. For his ninth birthday, his mother, a schoolteacher, gave him a copy of Thomas Malory's *Le Morte d'Arthur*, a fifteenth century collection of stories about England's legendary King Arthur and his Round Table. By the time Steinbeck was fifteen, he had vowed to become a writer. Attending Stanford University sporadically between 1919 and 1925, he failed to

TITLES

The Red Pony, 1937

The Pearl, 1947

The Short Reign of Pippin IV, 1957

.437

.137

.48

p.650 complete his undergraduate studies. He finally moved to the **Monterey Peninsula**, near where he had grown up, to pursue a writing career that would eventually produce eighteen novels, two collections of short fiction, eleven works of nonfiction, and six screenplays. In 1962 his vast and influential literary production was honored when he was awarded a p.231 **Nobel Prize in Literature**.

Steinbeck's *The Red Pony*, comprising three interrelated stories, is set in the Salinas Valley, a rich agricultural region in which much of the nation's produce is grown. The book's adolescent **protago-** p.2 **nist**, Jody Tiflin, receives a red pony from his father on the condition that he care for it properly. He depends on Billy Buck, a farm hand, to show him how to look after the pony. One day Billy tells Jody to leave his pony in the pasture, promising that if it rains, he will put it in the stable. It does rain, but Billy forgets his promise. The drenched pony sickens and dies, leaving Jody disillusioned, his innocence shattered.

The Pearl is also concerned with disillusionment and loss of innocence, themes that pervade Steinbeck's fiction. Kino, a Mexican pearl fisher, lives with his wife, Juana, and their young son in Baja California. Kino's existence is hand-to-mouth. When his son is stung by a scorpion, the village doctor refuses

Monterey Peninsula

Located on the California coast, the Monterey Peninsula is home to Cannery Row, the historic setting of John Steinbeck's novel of the same name. No longer a series of sardine canneries, Cannery Row is now a tourist attraction with restaurants, shops, and a world-class aquarium. Located a couple of miles south of the city of Monterey is the famous art colony of Carmel-by-the-Sea and the world-renowned golf course at Pebble Beach..

The Pearl, the Movie

John Steinbeck's story of a Mexican fisherman who finds a huge perfect pearl was filmed in Mexico and directed by a Mexican director, Emilio Fernandez, who is credited with creating the Mexican film industry. Fernandez's 1943 film, *Maria Candelaria*, won the Grand Prize at the Cannes Film Festival. *The Pearl* was honored with the International Prize at the San Sebastian Film Festival. The film was not a huge success with filmgoers at the time of its release.

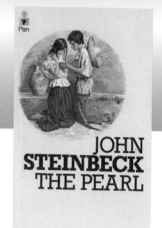

the sick child treatment because Kino is poor. Soon, however, Kino's fortunes improve: he finds an oyster that contains the largest pearl ever found in the region. Suddenly, everyone becomes Kino's friend. The doctor arrives offering his services. Then pearl merchants try to cheat Kino. Villagers try to steal the pearl. The disillusioned Kino ends up throwing his treasure back into the sea.

John Steinbeck's work is consistently marked by a sympathy for those living on the fringes of society. Although most of his characters are poor and uneducated, Steinbeck treats them with dignity and respect. He revels in their ability to survive in the face of what seem to be overwhelming odds. Most of Steinbeck's novels have been made into films. *The Pearl* was filmed in 1947, and *The Red Pony* in 1949.

– R. Baird Shuman

Robert Louis Stevenson

Born: November 13, 1850; Edinburgh, Scotland
Died: December 3, 1894; Vailima, near Apia, Samoa

www.kirjasto.sci.fi/rlsteven.htm

Robert Louis Stevenson's output of fiction was not great, but several of his novels rank among the most popular classics of all time. He is best known for his stories about pirates, and he created one of the seminal works of horror fiction.

Stevenson was a member of a family of lighthouse engineers—his father, two uncles, and grandfather were responsible for building fourteen lighthouses around the Scottish coastline in the nineteenth century. He himself, however, was born a sickly child, with weak lungs that plagued him all his life. He spent much of his youth bedridden, attending school only sporadically. Yet, even as a child he was writing stories with religious themes that were in keeping with his family's strict Scottish Presbyterianism. When he was sixteen, he enrolled in Edinburgh University intending to follow the family's lighthouse-engineering tradition but was soon living the life of a foppish undergraduate and, to his parents' dismay, declaring himself an **agnostic**. Nevertheless, by the time he graduated, he was already making a name for himself as a writer.

p.65

Stevenson's earliest writings were nonfiction travel works. Due to his bad lungs, he often traveled in search of warm climates. However, in addition to his medical needs, he also enjoyed the adventure of seeing new places. In 1876 he was at an artists' colony outside Paris when he met Fanny van de Grift Osborne, a married American woman more than ten years older than he who was temporarily separated from her husband. Stevenson fell in love with her. A few years after Fanny returned to America and her husband, she telegraphed Stevenson to join her in California. He left immediately. The trip almost killed Stevenson, but Fanny did divorce her husband and marry him in 1880. Along with Fanny's son, Lloyd, the newlyweds returned to Scotland the next year. Stevenson's perilous journey to win his wife became the material for two more travel books.

It was while playing with his young stepson that Stevenson drew an imaginary map that became the inspiration for his classic adventure story *Treasure Island*. After that novel became a **best-seller**, Stevenson turned his talents to writing children's adventures such as *The Black Arrow*, *Kidnapped*, and *Catriona*. His stories often drew upon Scottish history and locations, his family's long association with the sea, and a certain amount of extrapolation from his own travel adventures. His heroes undergo rites of passage when they are snatched from their safe childhood environments and must learn to fend for themselves among ruthless, violent, older men. However, rich treasures or inheritances are the rewards for navigating these waters successfully.

Agnostic

An agnostic believes that we do not have enough information to prove the existence of a God or a higher reality than our own. Likewise, agnostics believe that we cannot prove that God does not exist either. An agnostic relies on reason to know how to behave rather than relying on divine laws.

In 1886 Stevenson had a nightmare about a man taking some kind of powder that caused him to turn into a monster. Although his wife woke him before his dream ended, because he was screaming, he recognized that this was the stuff of a great tale. He turned that idea into *The Strange Case of Dr. Jekyll and Mr. Hyde*. The novel was even more of a success than any of his previous works, and has become one of the most significant works of modern horror fiction. It is a classic mad-doctor story, an allegory of the dangers of unchecked experimentation and scientific hubris that continues to strike a nerve in this modern age of cloning and ever more sophisticated pharmaceuticals.

p.654 The Stevensons spent 1888 and 1889 sailing the South Pacific, settling in Samoa in 1890. For the next four years, Stevenson was involved in the life and politics of Samoa, chiefly with the aim of preventing the islanders from being exploited by the Europeans. Robert Louis Stevenson died there from a stroke in 1894.

– Leslie Ellen Jones

Samoa

Samoa is a group of islands in the Pacific Ocean about halfway between Hawaii and New Zealand. Western Samoa, consisting of two medium-sized and seven small islands, was a territory of New Zealand until becoming an independent state in 1962. American Samoa, a group of six islands, became a territory of the U. S. in 1900. The native population of less than 250,000 in Western Samoa and less than 60,000 in American Samoa is Polynesian, and the people speak both Samoan and English. The majority of the population is Christian, having been converted by missionaries from numerous denominations. The islands are mountainous with rain forests and a coastal plain. Bananas and taro are the primary crops.

Todd Strasser

Born: May 5, 1950; New York, New York

www.toddstrasser.com

Characters in **Todd Strasser**'s realistic fiction face problems and conflicts familiar to those of most adolescents and young adults. He uses humor and romance to talk about serious teenage problems such as drugs, sex, alcohol and illness, and to explore adolescent fantasies such as what it would be like to be a rock-and-roll music star. His writing falls into three groups: realistic fiction for adolescents, humorous and historical fiction for younger readers, and novelizations of screenplays.

Strasser grew up on New York's **Long Island**. As a student, he liked science, but was not particularly good at English, and did not imagine he would ever become an author. After deciding to become a doctor, he enrolled in a premed program in college. However, he found that he was becoming more and more interested in writing and ended up taking time off from school to figure out what to do with his life. By the time he returned to college, he had decided to concentrate on writing. During his last semester in college he began work on his first novel, *Angel Dust Blue*.

Angel Dust Blue took six years of writing and rewriting before it was finished. It tells the story of a group of suburban teenagers who get in trouble with drugs. Its plot is based on events that Strasser himself had witnessed. Although Strasser's protagonists usually do not use drugs—although they may have friends who do—in this novel the main character, Alex Lazer, not only uses drugs, he also is a dealer, and must face the difficult and frightening consequences.

p.117

p.105

p.617

656

p.233

TITLES

Angel Dust Blue, 1979

Friends till the End, 1981

Rock 'n' Roll Nights, 1982

Workin' for Peanuts, 1983

The Complete Computer Popularity Program, 1984

Turn It Up, 1984

Very Touchy Subject, 1985

Wildlife, 1987

The Accident, 1988

The Family Man, 1988

How I Changed My Life, 1995

Girl Gives Birth to Own Prom Date, 1996

Playing for Love, 1996

The Boys in the Band, 1996

How I Spent My Last Night on Earth, 1998

Here Comes Heavenly, 1999

Give a Boy a Gun, 2000

Pastabilities, 2000

Con-fidence, 2002

Thief of Dreams, 2003

Can't Get There from Here, 2004

Impact Zone series:

Take Off, 2004

Cut Back, 2004

Close Out, 2004

Premed Program

Students interested a professional career in medicine are required to complete certain requirements before applying to medical school. These requirements can often be fulfilled in a premed program, either as an undergraduate or following completion of a bachelors degree. They include one year of biology, chemistry, organic chemistry, and physics, with the appropriate labs. There are also requirements for mathematics and English. A premed program also helps to prepare students for the Medical College Admission Test (MCAT), a standardized test required for admission to medical school.

Strasser kept writing after his graduation from college but also needed to work at other jobs to support himself. He worked in a public relations office, a newspaper office, and an **advertising agency**, and p.65 even owned a fortune cookie company before he could support himself by writing full time. His persistence paid off. The young boy who never did well in English became a popular and prolific author.

An example of how Strasser approaches adolescent issues is seen in *The Accident*. This book deals with the consequences one young boy must face when four of his friends are killed in a **drunk-driving** ac- p.5 cident. It is only by luck that the boy is not in the car at the time of the accident, and now he must uncover the real story behind what happened. In the process, he confronts his own values and answers difficult questions about truth and justice.

In *Friends till the End*, a group of typical teenagers deal with the realization of their own mortality when one of their friends is stricken with **leuke-** p.2 **mia**. In the rock-and-roll trilogy: *Rock 'n' Roll Nights*, *Turn It Up*, and *Wildlife*, the characters must learn that becoming rich and famous is not the answer to all of life's problems.

Todd Strasser has won many awards for his writing, including the **American Library Association's Best Books for Young Adults** citations.

p.45
p.480

– Deborah DePiero

Advertising Agency

A business that handles the advertising and promotional needs of other businesses is called an advertising agency. An agency consists of management and creative teams that develop campaigns to sell a company's products or services or to promote the company's image to the public. One of the jobs available in advertising agency is the creative director, who manages a project and team of coworkers. Working with the creative director are art directors and copy writers. The American Association of Advertising Agencies (AAAA), founded in 1917, is the national trade organization that provides guidance to agencies, with its members billing 75% of the advertising business in the U. S.

Noel Streatfeild

Born: December 24, 1895; Amberley, Sussex, England
Died: September 11, 1986; London, England
www.msu.edu/~thomp169/noel.htm

Mary Noel Streatfeild wrote more than eighty novels for both adults and children. Her best-known books are the "Shoes" novels. The books in this series do not follow a single set of characters but are instead united by their focus on children. The children in these books are often wrenched from safe, comfortable existences and must make their way in careers in the **performing arts**, such as dance, theater, films, ice skating, and the circus. In 1938 Streatfeild was awarded the prestigious **Carnegie Medal** for *Circus Shoes* (*The Circus Is Coming* in England). p.24 p.42

Streatfeild was born into a conventional English family. Her father, a **vicar** at the time of her birth, eventually became the bishop of Lewes. She herself, however, was an unconventional child who was expelled from school for challenging the headmistress's authority. She was then educated at home, where she excelled in parish pageants and other forms of amateur theatricals. After World War I, which she spent working in a munitions factory, she headed for London to study theater and worked as an actress and model for nearly a decade. After her father's death in 1929 she shifted her interests to writing, using her performing experiences as background for her novels. p.659

Streatfeild was the first children's novelist to depict glamorous and exciting professions such as dancing and acting as fields that require hard work, but work that is well worth the effort. Her **protagonists'** stories do not end with their first great suc- p.23

cesses but continue on to show young people grappling with the temptations of vanity and self-importance, with the flatness that follows triumphs, the necessity to discover one's own particular talent, and the need to find satisfying work as well as the value of being able to support oneself in an artistic career.

Ballet Shoes provided the model for the books to follow. Pauline, Petrova, and Posy Fossil are three unrelated girls who are adopted by an archaeologist named Matthew Brown. They adopt the name "Fossil" because fossils are what Matthew Brown generally brings back from his trips. He leaves the girls, one by one, to be raised by his great-niece Sylvia. When he disappears without a trace on one of his expeditions and the money he has left for the family's upkeep runs out, Sylvia starts taking in boarders. However, she cannot afford to send the girls to school. Fortunately, her boarders include two retired Oxford dons, who offer to teach the girls their lessons, and an instructor at Madame Fidolia's Children's Academy of Dancing and Stage Training, who arranges for the girls to become dancing students so that they can learn a trade. Pauline eventually discovers that she has a talent for acting, and Posy, the daughter of a ballerina, has no intention of being anything other than a dancer, but Petrova struggles dreadfully, since what she really

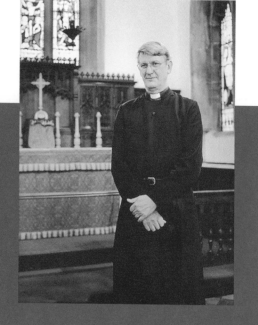

Vicar

A vicar is a Christian clergyman who has the authority to perform certain religious rites. In the Church of England, a vicar acts as the priest of a parish. The vicar is a common character in English literature, and generally plays a major part in village life.

NOEL STREATFEILD

Aviator

An aviator is someone who flies aircraft for business or pleasure. Some of America's most famous aviators include Charles Lindbergh, the first pilot to fly solo and non-stop across the Atlantic Ocean, in 1927; Amelia Earhart, who mysteriously disappeared with her plane over the Pacific Ocean in 1937; Howard Hughes, eccentric businessman and aviator who owned the "Spruce Goose"; and Chuck Yeager, who in 1947 was the first pilot to break the sound barrier in his experimental X-1 aircraft.

p.66

wants to be is an **aviator**. Eventually, all three girls are able to follow their chosen careers, but along the way they learn how much work each field requires.

An important theme of the novel is each girl's vow, repeated by her on her birthday, to make the name Fossil famous because it is a name they have chosen for themselves. Aside from the boarders Mr. and Mrs. Simpson, none of the residents of the Brown household are actually related to one another; however, together they form an extended family that supports and teaches each member. The boarders all pitch in to raise the Fossil girls to become self-sufficient adults and literally to make a name for themselves.

— Leslie Ellen Jones

Rosemary Sutcliff

Born: December 14, 1920; West Clandon, Surrey, England

Died: July 23, 1992; unknown

www.historicalnovelsociety.org/solander%20files/rosemary_sutcliff.htm

p.117

.662

p.314

p.530

p.233

663

Rosemary Sutcliff was one of the best-known writers of young adult historical fiction of the twentieth century. She was the daughter of a naval officer who sailed all over the world, but in her childhood she contracted a form of rheumatoid arthritis that progressively crippled her, so that she spent most of her life in a wheelchair. Although she trained as an artist and became an accomplished miniaturist, it was her love of reading—a way of transcending her physical disability—that led her to a literary career.

Sutcliff was particularly fascinated by the history, archaeology, and mythology of early Britain. Her novels utilize this interest in stories that focus primarily on Britain's Bronze Age and Roman and medieval eras. Her plots follow a basic adventure story pattern, in which the hero must overcome adversity not only to triumph over opponents but also to discover a sense of personal peace. Many of her protagonists are members of one ethnic group whose way of life and even family or tribe is destroyed by invading members of another ethnic group. For example, the Briton Aquila is enslaved in Denmark by raiding Anglo-Saxons in *The Lantern Bearers*. When Aquila finally escapes and returns home, he discovers that his sister has married a Saxon, an accommodation that he cannot accept. His Roman forebear, also named Aquila, in *The Eagle of the Ninth* travels north of Hadrian's Wall to recover his legion's lost standard. While these heroes may quest for specific objects, such as the lost

TITLES

Simon, 1953

The Eagle of the Ninth, 1954

The Silver Branch, 1957

Warrior Scarlet, 1958

The Lantern Bearers, 1959

Knight's Fee, 1960

Dawn Wind, 1961

The Mark of the Horse Lord, 1965

A Circlet of Oak Leaves, 1968

Blood Feud, 1976

Sun Horse, Moon Horse, 1977

Song for a Dark Queen, 1978

The Light Beyond the Forest, 1979

Frontier Wolf, 1980

The Road to Camlann, 1981

The Sword and the Circle, 1981

Bonnie Dundee, 1983

Flame-Colored Taffeta, 1985

Blood and Sand, 1987

standard, they also quest for metaphorical qualities, such as the honor and heroism that the standard represents.

Many of Sutcliff's novels are based on Celtic legends. *The Shining Company* (1990), while an original plot, is based on the doomed expedition against the Saxons mounted by Mynnyddog the Generous immortalized in the *Gododdin*, a Welsh poem by the seventh century poet Aneirin. Other Sutcliff novels are based on **Arthurian legends**, which Sutcliff often takes back to their Celtic roots. Thus, King Arthur becomes Artos the Bear, a Dark Age warlord, rather than the refined and chivalrous king of the High Middle Ages. Other novels revolve around p.48

Jacobite politics in Scotland and England in the seventeenth and eighteenth centuries (*Bonnie Dundee* and *Flame-Colored Taffeta*) and the English Civil War (*Simon*), while still others take place in Viking Russia (*Blood Feud*) and the Ottoman Empire (*Blood and Sand*).

What gives Sutcliff's novels their special place in so many readers' hearts is the depth of historical background that informs them. In contrast

Rheumatoid Arthritis

Severe joint inflammation is called rheumatoid arthritis. It usually begins in middle age and strikes women more than men. The inflammation occurs most frequently in the joints of the hands, hips, knees, or legs and is caused by infection or injury. Specialists suspect that the disease runs in families. Treatment involves rest, restricting use of the inflamed joints, and medications ranging from aspirin to stronger drugs to relieve the pain and reduce the inflammation. The disease continues to develop as those afflicted age, and most sufferers of rheumatoid arthritis will have some deformity or crippling caused by deterioration of the bone.

Hadrian's Wall

In 122 C.E. the Emperor Hadrian began building a rock wall along the northern boundary of Roman Britain. The wall took six years to complete and stretched seventy-three miles from what is now Wallsend-on-Tyne in the east to Bowness-on-Solway in the west. It stood some fifteen feet high and had guard posts every mile, with forts also built along the wall. To the north and south were defensive trenches. By the early 400's C.E., the Roman Empire was in decline, and the soldiers guarding the wall were no longer paid. As they left their posts, the wall ceased serving its original purpose of keeping people out. Instead, rocks were removed to build farm houses, walls, and even churches. Today, remnants of the wall still exist and attract tourists interested in Britain's Roman history. Hadrian's Wall has been designated a World Heritage Site.

to many Arthurian retellings, there is no fantasy in her Arthurian trilogy; Artos may become a legend, but he is a real person fighting simply to succeed in difficult times. Sutcliff wrote of past times as they were actually lived rather than as they are romanticized.

Rosemary Sutcliff's writing honors include Britain's prestigious **Carnegie Medal** for *The Lantern Bearers*, a Boston Globe-Horn Book Award for her children's book *Tristan and Iseult* (1971), **Boston Globe-Horn Honor Book Awards** for *Blood Feud* and *The Road to Camlann*, and a Phoenix Award for *The Mark of the Horse Lord*.

— Leslie Ellen Jones

p.42

p.747

p.147

Amy Tan

Born: February 19, 1952; Oakland, California

www.achievement.org/autodoc/page/tan0bio-1

Amy Tan is a superb storyteller, one who can capture in vivid detail a world that is unfamiliar to an American audience. All her novels draw on her upbringing as an Americanized daughter of a traditional Chinese mother with whom she was in constant conflict. Her principal themes probe the relationships among opposing traditions, cultures, and generations.

Tan was born in Oakland, California, across the bay from San Francisco, to a father who was a Baptist minister and electrical engineer and a mother who was a vocational nurse. Her parents, both Chinese immigrants, also had two sons, one of whom died of a brain tumor when Amy was fourteen years old. During the same year, Tan's father also died of a brain tumor. Her mother moved the family to Switzerland, where Tan finished high school in 1969. After the family returned to California, Tan entered Linfield College in Oregon, where she met Louis M. DeMattei, whom she married in 1974. She earned bachelor's and master's degrees at San Jose State University. She also attended the University of California at Berkeley, but left before earning a degree and spent five years working with **disabled** children. While doing **freelance writing** for

p.746

p.665

p.31

p.36

businesses, she also wrote fiction. One of her stories won her admission to a writer's workshop and was reprinted in *Seventeen* magazine. A literary agent encouraged Tan to write a volume of stories, and a trip to China with her mother in 1987 further inspired her to complete *The Joy Luck Club*.

   The Joy Luck Club tells the stories of four Americanized daughters who find it difficult to understand their Chinese mothers, who are trying to pass on to their daughters their traditional beliefs and wisdom. *The Kitchen God's Wife* focuses on generational conflicts as well as female victimization, covering a mother's life from 1925 through World War II in China to present-day San Francisco. In *The Hundred Secret Senses*, a young Chinese immigrant's supernatural powers enable her to envision past lives. Her Americanized half-sister develops the same power. When they go to the sister's native village in China, the American finally realizes that the past and present merge in her. In *The Bonesetter's Daughter*, a Chinese American woman finds a written narrative of her mother's life as a girl in China, a narrative that enables her to understand her mother's fears and superstitions as well as her own.

   Tan has also written two books specifically for children, *The Moon*

Chinese Immigration

Until the late nineteenth century, the U. S. allowed free immigration. Chinese immigrants, however, were not eligible to become naturalized citizens. In 1882, Congress excluded Chinese from immigrating to the U.S., an act of racial discrimination that was extended to most Asians in 1917. The Immigration Act of 1943 repealed the Chinese Exclusion Acts and established a small quota for Chinese immigration. It also made Chinese immigrants eligible for naturalization. In 1952, The McCarran-Walter Act removed all racial barriers to immigration.

Lady (1992), a picture book with text based on a story from *The Joy Luck Club*, and *The Chinese Siamese Cat* (1994).

In 1989, *The Joy Luck Club* won awards from the Commonwealth Club, the Bay Area Book Reviewers, and the American Library Association. p.4 It was adapted into a feature film in 1994. *The Kitchen God's Wife* was named an **Editor's Choice** of *Booklist* in 1991 and was nominated for the **Bay Area Book Reviewers Award**. p.143

Amy Tan's novels have been translated into twenty-three languages. In 1991, she received an honorary Doctor of Humane Letters degree from Dominican College. She lives in San Francisco and New York with her husband and performs in a celebrity-writer garage band called the Rock Bottom Remainders that raises money for charity. p.204 p.66

– Bernard E. Morris

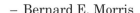

Rock Bottom Remainders

The Rock Bottom Remainders is a band made up of writers. It was founded by Kathi Kamen Goldmark, a book publicist, in 1992, and first performed at the American Booksellers Association convention in Anaheim, California. Among the members are well known authors Amy Tan, Scott Turow, Stephen King, Dave Barry, Ray Blount, Jr., and Matt Groening. They play around the country and at publishing conventions. Remainders is a term for books that do not sell at their original price and are discounted in order to sell the remaining inventory. The group's web site is www.rockbottomremainders.com.

Mildred D. Taylor

Born: September 13, 1943; Jackson, Mississippi

www.olemiss.edu/mwp/dir/taylor_mildred/

Mildred Taylor is best known for her award-winning novels about the Logan family. This five-volume saga traces the history of an African American family from the time of the Civil War to America's entry into World War II.

Taylor was born in Jackson, Mississippi. Shortly after her birth, her parents moved the family north to Ohio to escape the pervasive violence and racial hatred of the South. Taylor excelled in high school and served as the editor of her school newspaper. In 1965 she graduated from the University of Toledo and spent two years in Ethiopia in northeastern Africa as a member of the Peace Corps. She later completed a master's degree in journalism at the University of Colorado.

Roll of Thunder, Hear My Cry, perhaps the best-known work in Taylor's Logan family series, earned Taylor the American Library Association's Newbery Medal for its gripping depiction of eight-year-old Cassie Logan's growing awareness of racial oppression and violence in the Deep South during the 1930's. From her father, who struggles to keep the family safe against white gangs engaged in a campaign of terror against black families, Cassie learns the importance of her family's land to their survival and dignity.

Set in 1935, *Let the Circle Be Unbroken*, which won the American Library Association's **Coretta Scott King Award** and earned a **National Book Award** nomination, depicts several key issues that affected the lives of African Americans prior to the

.224

.102

.122

p.77

p.45

TITLES

Roll of Thunder, Hear My Cry, 1976

Let the Circle Be Unbroken, 1981

The Road to Memphis, 1990

The Land, 2001

Civil Rights movement

The Civil Rights movement refers to a period of time in U. S. history beginning in the 1950's during which prejudice and discrimination against the rights of minorities began to be reversed. In 1954, the Supreme Court outlawed racial discrimination in public schools in its *Brown v. Board of Education* decision. A few years later, an African American boycott of segregated buses in Montgomery, Alabama, launched a decade-long era of antidiscrimination campaigns that culminated in the first significant civil rights legislation in nearly a century, the Civil Rights Act of 1964. By the end of the 1960's, virtually all major forms of legally enforced or protected racial discrimination were outlawed.

Civil Rights movement. When T. J., a Logan family friend, goes on trial for murder, he must convince an all-white jury of his innocence. Suzella, Cassie Logan's cousin, attempts to "pass" for white with disastrous consequences. Mrs. Lee Annie and her family, neighbors of the Logan family, are finally driven from their home when they advocate extending **voting rights** to African Americans.

p.668

p.669

The third book in the Logan family series, *The Road to Memphis*, is set on the eve of the U.S. entry into World War II. Cassie Logan, now seventeen, puts her dreams of college and law school on hold to assist her friend Moe, whose life becomes threatened when he defends himself physically against white assailants. Knowing that he will face certain violence if he does not flee, Cassie, her brother, and a handful of friends decide to accompany Moe on the long journey to Memphis, where he will be safe. *The Road to Memphis* earned Taylor another **Coretta Scott King Award**.

p.66

The Land serves as a "prequel" to *Roll of Thunder, Hear My Cry*. Set in the years following the Civil War, the novel chronicles the life of Cassie Logan's grandfather, Paul-Edward Logan, the son of a wealthy white plantation owner and a slave woman. As a teenager, Paul-Edward flees his family home and arrives in Mississippi, where he hopes to purchase land. His setbacks and triumphs on the way to becoming a land owner, husband, and father, despite overwhelming odds, forms the substance of the book and fill in many details about the origins of friendships and rivalries in the earlier Logan family novels. *The Land* received numerous literary awards, including another **Coretta Scott King Award** and the **Scott O'Dell Award for Historical Fiction**.

p.51

Among Mildred Taylor's many other literary awards are the **Assembly on Literature for Adolescents' ALAN Award** for Significant Contributions to Young Adult Literature in 1997, one of the highest honors available to an author of young adult fiction.

p.162

– Philip Bader

Voting Rights Act of 1965

This legislation abolished a number of practices that had been used to disqualify African American voters, primarily in the South, including literacy, education, and character tests. It authorized the U. S. Attorney General to send federal examiners into areas where voter discrimination was suspected, allowing federal voting registrars to supersede state ones. Passage of the act resulted in a dramatic increase in African American voters and an increase in African American elected officials.

Theodore Taylor

Born: June 23, 1921; Statesville, North Carolina

www.theodoretaylor.com

Theodore Taylor is best known for his realistic and **historical fiction**. The main characters in his young adult books are usually adolescent boys and girls of various ethnicities who must cope with problems that threaten their survival. His action-packed adventures employ such literary techniques as flashbacks, alternating points of view, and epilogues. Many of his characters speak in dialects or use words from their native language. Taylor started writing at age thirteen as a sports writer for a local newspaper. His adult writing career included work as a radio network sports reporter, a press agent, a story editor, and an associate producer for films.

p.1

The Cay, Taylor's best-known book, won eleven literary awards including the **Lewis Carroll Shelf Award**, given to a book considered worthy enough to be on the same shelf as Carroll's *Alice in Wonderland*. In Taylor's book, Phillip Enright, a prejudiced white American youth is shipwrecked during World War II on a small island with Timothy, an elderly **West Indian** man. Their efforts to survive finally bring them to respect each other. *Timothy of the Cay*, which Taylor wrote twenty-four years later, both fills in the background to *The Cay* and continues its story.

p.67

Taylor explores a much different historical setting, the American frontier of the 1850's, in *Walking Up a Rainbow*. When fourteen-year-old Susan Carlisle's parents are killed, she inherits two thousand sheep and a large debt. To

West Indies

The West Indies is an archipelago of more than seven thousand mostly uninhabited islands, cays, coral reefs, and rocks that form the northern and eastern boundaries of the Caribbean Sea. There are coral islands such as the Bahamas; Greater Antilles islands such as Cuba, Puerto Rica, and Jamaica, which are worn-down peaks of sunken mountains; and the Lesser Antilles islands, an arc of smaller volcanically-formed islands. Sugar and bananas are the main crops, and tourism is a major source of revenue.

save her home, she decides to drive her sheep to California and sell them to the gold miners. Taylor wrote this book because his wife wanted him to write a story about an adventurous girl.

Taylor's writings reflect his interests in the environment, politics, and society. *Sniper* and its sequel, *Lord of the Kill*, feature Ben Jepson who must protect the animals in his family's nature preserve. In *The Bomb*, Taylor draws upon his personal experiences at **Bikini Atoll** in the South Pacific, where the United States tested two atomic bombs in 1946. Before the bombs were exploded, the Bikini islanders were forcefully removed from their ancestral homes. Taylor calls what happened to the islanders a modern-day "Trail of Tears"—the name by which the forced removal of the Cherokee people from North Carolina to Oklahoma during the 1830's is known. *The Bomb* won the 1996 **Scott O'Dell Award for Historical Fiction**.

Early in his life, Taylor served as both a merchant marine and a cargo officer in the U.S. Navy. While his love of the sea is evident in many of his books, *Rogue Wave and Other Red-Blooded Sea*

Bikini Atoll

Bikini Atoll is part of the Marshall Islands, a group of small islands located in the Pacific Ocean north of the equator in a region called Micronesia. Following World War II, the U.S. relocated the Bikini islanders to another atoll some 125 miles away and began a series of atomic bomb tests. The Bikinians were subjected to fallout from the bomb tests. Conditions on their new islands were unfavorable, and they suffered from malnutrition and subsequent relocations. Attempts were made to clean the island of radiation, and some

of the islanders returned to Bikini Atoll. There is still concern that residents eating a diet of local foods will suffer from high doses of radiation. Since 1996, the islanders have tried to make Bikini Atoll a diving, sport fishing, and tourist destination, assuring visitors that there is no longer any danger from radiation.

Stories, deals directly with this interest. Altogether, seventeen of Taylor's books are about ships and the ocean.

Theodore Taylor is a well-respected author who is always cited in major textbooks about adolescent literature. His book *The Cay* was made into a Universal film staring James Earl Jones. A long-time presenter at professional conferences, Taylor now mostly lets his personal Web site be his voice about his work. He lives in Laguna Beach, California, where he often goes fishing in the ocean.

– Kay Moore

Jean Thesman

Born: Date unknown; United States

www.jeanthesman.com

A popular writer with young adults, **Jean Thesman** creates realistic characters, usually adolescent girls, who live in the Pacific Northwest and feel self-conscious and out-of-step with their peers. Parents in her stories are often absent, dysfunctional, or uncaring, leaving the girls to rely on friends or romantic interests to help them through their problems. Although Thesman publishes most of her work under her own name, her Avon books have been published under the name T. J. Bradstreet.

Thesman keeps her personal life so private that even her place of birth is not publicly known. However, she now lives in Washington State. When she started publishing, she began in a flurry, completing an average of two novels a year and continuing this pace for over twenty years. In addition to her realistic coming-of-age novels, such as *The Last April Dancers* or *When the Road Ends*, Thesman also writes **fantasy**. Whether she is describing Julia Foster in *Cattail Moon* whose domineering mother tries to squash her daughter's musical interests or Keller Parrish in *Appointment with a Stranger* who suffers from severe asthma or Charlotte Thacker in *Between*, whose family is fragmented, Thesman grounds her stories in worlds that readers will recognize. The difference in these books, however, is that ghosts and supernatural beings step in to teach the **protagonists** what they need to know. In *The Other Ones*, Bridget Raynes even solves her problems with classmates, teachers, and family by accepting her own supernatural powers.

TITLES

The Last April Dancers, 1987

Running Scared, 1987

Appointment with a Stranger, 1989

Couldn't I Start Over?, 1989

Heather, 1990

Rachel Chance, 1990

The Rain Catchers, 1991

When Does the Fun Start?, 1991

Triple Trouble, 1992

When the Road Ends, 1992

Who Am I Anyway? Nancy's Story, 1992

Molly Donnelly, 1993

Cattail Moon, 1994

Nothing Grows Here, 1994

Summerspell, 1995

The Ornament Tree, 1996

The Storyteller's Daughter, 1997

Jamie, 1998

Meredith, 1998

Teresa, 1998

The Moonstones, 1998

The Other Ones, 1999

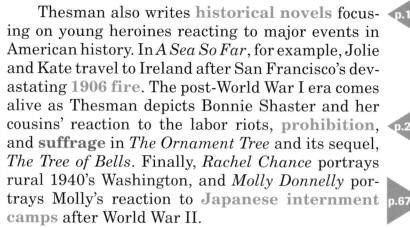

Thesman also writes historical novels focusing on young heroines reacting to major events in American history. In *A Sea So Far*, for example, Jolie and Kate travel to Ireland after San Francisco's devastating 1906 fire. The post-World War I era comes alive as Thesman depicts Bonnie Shaster and her cousins' reaction to the labor riots, prohibition, and suffrage in *The Ornament Tree* and its sequel, *The Tree of Bells*. Finally, *Rachel Chance* portrays rural 1940's Washington, and *Molly Donnelly* portrays Molly's reaction to Japanese internment camps after World War II.

Thesman has also written the Elliott cousin series. *Jamie*, *Meredith*, and *Teresa* focus on three fifteen-year-old cousins living in Seattle, these books are similar to *Heather* and *Triple Trouble* and are lighter reading than most of Thesman's other work.

Over the years Thesman has received awards from the American Library Association for *The*

p.1

p.674

p.14

p.2

p.67

p.4

San Francisco Fire of 1906

San Francisco was struck by a serious earthquake on April 18, 1906, at 5:12 A.M. but the most serious damage to the city was caused by the fires that immediately broke out. San Francisco had been gutted by fire six times prior to 1906 so many commercial buildings were now built of brick, stone, and steel. However, housing was still built primarily of wood. By noon, fifty-seven fires were

reported. The earthquake had broken the large water pipes serving the fire hydrants in the city, so little water was available to put out the blazes. The fires spread and continued to burn for four days. In the end, 4.7 miles of the city had burned. The death toll was estimated at 700, and more than 200,000 people were left homeless.

Japanese Internment Camps

In 1942, some 110,000 Japanese Americans living on the West Coast were relocated to ten internment camps away from the coast. Camps, such as Manzanar in the eastern Sierras, each housed approximately ten thousand people. The camps were surrounded by barbed wire and patrolled by armed guards. Residents lived in wooden barracks covered with tar paper. Each barrack contained a number of one-room apartments for families or groups of unrelated persons. The residents shared bathrooms, dining areas, and laundry rooms. In 1943, those who had obtained jobs away from the Pacific coast and could show acceptance by the local community were released. By the end of 1944, about thirty-five thousand evacuees had left the camps. After the presidential election of 1944, those remaining in the camps were allowed to leave. By the end of 1945, the camps were closed. In 1988, Congress formally apologized to Japanese Americans; there had been no military necessity to relocate them. A fund of $1.25 billion was set aside to be shared among camp residents who still survived.

Other Ones, The Ornament Tree, When the Road Ends, The Rain Catchers, Rachel Chance, and *The Last April Dancers.* In total, fourteen of Thesman's books have received awards for their merit, many of them garnering multiple awards. Five of her books have been noted as **Good Choices for Reluctant Readers**.

– Cassandra Kircher

Joyce Carol Thomas

Born: May 25, 1938; Ponca City, Oklahoma

www.joycecarolthomas.com

A successful poet and playwright during her early literary career, **Joyce Carol Thomas** achieved enduring fame with the publication of her first young adult novel, *Marked by Fire*, which has since become a classic.

Thomas was born in northern Oklahoma. Although she moved to the rural town of Tracy, California, at the age of ten, she would maintain an emotional connection to her roots in her birthplace of Ponca City, where many of her later novels were set. In California, Thomas often joined her parents and other **migrant workers** in the **cotton** fields and fruit orchards. In 1959 she married Gettis Withers and spent the following years raising four children, working as a telephone operator, and attending evening classes at San Jose State College, from which she graduated in 1966. A year later, she completed her master's degree in education at Stanford University and began a long career as an educator.

Between 1969 and 1980, Thomas published three volumes of poetry and four plays. She then published her first novel, *Marked by Fire*. Set in Ponca City, the novel depicts the early life of Abyssinia Jackson, a young African American girl who was born in a cotton field and scarred as an infant by a burning ember. At the time of her accident, a local healer predicted that her scar was an omen of a future life filled with great suffering and great joy. When

p.677

p.29

Abyssinia is raped at the age of ten, she begins a long period of emotional and physical turmoil. With the assistance of Mother Barker, a **faith healer**, Abyssinia eventually finds the strength to overcome her suffering. *Marked by Fire* won both **American** and **National Book Awards** for young adult fiction and the **Before Columbus American Book Award**.

p.678

p.122

Bright Shadow, a sequel to *Marked by Fire* depicts Abyssinia's life as a college student. Once again, her emotional life is shattered by a personal tragedy when she receives news of the brutal murder of her aunt. Set against her grief over her aunt's death is her burgeoning love affair with Carl Lee Jefferson. As in her first novel, Taylor emphasizes in *Bright Shadow* that suffering and happiness are pervasive and dynamic aspects of life.

The Golden Pasture explores the early life of Carl Lee Jefferson, the son of a Cherokee mother whom he never knows and an African American father, whose relationship to Jefferson is distant. Jefferson's greatest pleasure as a boy is the

Migrant Workers

Migrant workers travel from place to place working in the fields. The harvest seasons take them from one crop to another in order to make a living. They are not well paid, and living conditions are generally poor. During the Great Depression and following the terrible drought that turned the Great Plains states, like South Dakota and Oklahoma into the Dust Bowl, many people became migrant workers to survive. Often called "Okies," these poor families traveled to California in particular in search of work. Later, during World War II, with many men in the military, the governments of the U. S. and Mexico created a plan to bring Mexican workers temporarily into the U. S. to provide a work force for farmers. They then took the place of the American migrant workers.

JOYCE CAROL THOMAS

time he spends on his grandfather Gray Jefferson's ranch. An ex-rodeo star, Gray inspires young Carl with his stories of life in the rodeo. Carl's eventual triumph in the rodeo helps to mend the relationship with his father.

– Philip Bader

Faith Healer

A faith healer is a religious person who claims to be able to cure illnesses, mend broken or crippled limbs, and heal wounds by the strength of his or her faith in God. These individuals often draw crowds of believers at revival meetings or special religious gatherings.

J. R. R. Tolkien

Born: January 3, 1892; Bloemfontein, South Africa
Died: September 2, 1973; Bournemouth, England

www.tolkiensociety.org/tolkien/index.html

The scholarly **John Ronald Reuel Tolkien** was the unlikely father of modern fantasy literature. His epic *The Lord of the Rings* is generally recognized as one of the all-time great fantasy novels and continues to be read by both young and old.

Tolkien was born in South Africa to English parents. His father was a banker from Birmingham whose early death in South Africa left his family with little financial support. Tolkien's mother, Mabel, further alienated her family by converting to Roman Catholicism several years before she, too, died, of complications of **diabetes**. Tolkien and his younger brother Hilary were left to the guardianship of Father Francis Morgan, a well-meaning man who nonetheless had little sympathy for the teenage Tolkien's budding romance with a fellow boarder in the house where the Tolkien boys were living. The thwarted romance, which had an eventual happy outcome when Tolkien reached twenty-one and was free of Morgan's guardianship, became a strong theme in Tolkien's later writing.

Side by side with his romantic misadventures, Tolkien was a star student at King Edward's School and earned a **scholarship** to **Oxford University**, where he ended up majoring in English, concentrating on the history and linguistics of the lan-

p.87

p.104

p.236

p.380

p.173

The Inklings

J. R. R. Tolkien returned to Oxford University, from which he had earned a degree, as a professor in 1925. While there, he became part of a group of friends and colleagues named the Inklings. Included in the group were Neville Coghill, Hugo Dyson, Owen Barfield, Charles Williams, and C. S. Lewis, who became Tolkien's closest friend. The group gathered frequently for conversation and to read to each other from the books they were writing, asking for input from the other members. Tolkien remained at the university until his retirement in 1969.

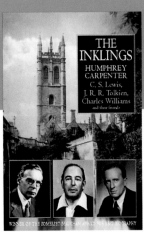

guage. Tolkien had been a creator of secret languages since childhood, and his studies in Old English, Middle English, Gothic, Welsh, Finnish, and many other medieval Northern European languages provided fodder for both his stories and the languages he invented for their denizens.

p.56

Tolkien served in World War I, wrote entries for the *W* section of the huge *Oxford English Dictionary* project, and taught for several years at the University of Leeds. In 1925 he was appointed to a professorship of Anglo-Saxon at Oxford and remained there the rest of his life. He became close friends with another medievalist, C. S. Lewis, and the two formed the core of a group of scholar-writers who called themselves the Inklings and met weekly to critique each other's work. Tolkien began bringing in sections of a bedtime story he had invented for his children, involving the adventures of one Bilbo Baggins, who belonged to a mythical race that Tolkien called hobbits. With the encouragement of the Inklings and the intervention of a friend of a former student who worked for the publishing company G. Allen & Unwin, *The Hobbit* was published in 1937 and became an almost instant classic.

p.68

It took Tolkien almost seventeen years to write and publish his "sequel" to *The Hobbit*, a novel called *The Lord of the Rings* so massive that it was published as three separate books: *The Fellowship of the Ring*, *The Two Towers*, and *The Return of the King*. Strictly speaking, however, it is a single novel,

p.551

not a trilogy. Its central story concerns the quest to destroy the One Ring of the evil **sorcerer** Sauron which, if recovered by him, would enable him to turn the entire world of Middle-earth into a wasteland. The world-preserving quest is carried out by a small and insignificant hobbit named Frodo Baggins, assisted by his gardener Samwise Gamgee, his cousins Merry Brandybuck and Pippin Took, as well as the humans Aragorn son of Arathorn and Boromir of Minas Tirith, the elf Legolas Greenleaf, the dwarf Gimli son of Glóin, and the wizard Gandalf the Grey.

681

The Lord of the Rings was well received upon publication in 1954 and 1955, but it was not until the mid-1960's that it became a worldwide **best-seller**. Tolkien's themes of the ability of the "little guy" to p.384 make a difference, his ecological concerns, and his heroic worldview made his work extremely attractive to the counterculture. His literary themes were enhanced by the enormous detail Tolkien invested in his Middle-earth, creating a world that seemed to exist outside the mere covers of a book. This was in part due to the fact that J. R. R. Tolkien had been inventing the mythology of Middle-earth since at least 1917, when he was recuperating from trench fever caught on the battlefields of World War I. His collected Middle-earth narratives were published after his death by his son Christopher Tolkien.

— Leslie Ellen Jones

Lord of the Rings, the Movies

There has long been a cult built up around Tolkien's *Lord of the Rings*, but with the completion of the movie trilogy, the movie cult now rivals that of the book. Directed by Peter Jackson and filmed in his native New Zealand, *The Fellowship of the Ring, The Two Towers,* and *The Return of the King* all captured the imagination of both moviegoers and film critics. The final film won eleven Academy Awards in 2004, including Best Picture and Best Director.

Terry Trueman

Born: December 15, 1947; Birmingham, Alabama

www.terrytrueman.smartwriters.com

Terry Trueman creates fiction from the material of his own life. When his son was born in 1979 with severe **cerebral palsy**, Trueman's world fell apart. Unable to cope with the situation, he left his family. His adult narrative poem, "Sheehan," tackles this subject from his point of view as a father while his young adult novel, *Stuck in Neutral*, imagines the same material from the son's point of view. Trueman uses the pain of this defining event of his life to create a thought-provoking, compassionate and heartfelt young adult novel.

p.68

Trueman was born in Birmingham, Alabama, and attended the University of Washington in Seattle. He received a master's degree in applied psychology and a master of fine arts degree in creative writing from Eastern Washington University. He has taught at colleges and universities in **Australia**, Honduras, and the United States. Although he knew that he wanted to be a writer when his high school creative writing teacher told him he had talent, it was not until he began *Stuck in Neutral* at the age of forty-eight that he thought of writing seriously as a profession. He has also written poetry and film and book reviews.

p.4

Cerebral Palsy

Cerebral palsy is a group of disorders that affect the brain at some time before a baby is one month old, resulting in a lack of normal control of movements. The problem is often not noticeable until the baby is nine or ten months of age. The motor problems can range from the inability to walk to symptoms so minor they are not noticeable. The disorder does not get worse over time. If detected early, it is possible for a child to improve to the point of not suffering from the disorder later in life. Cerebral palsy occurs more frequently in children born prematurely.

The first book that families should read.

CHILDREN with CEREBRAL PALSY

A Parents' Guide
Edited by Elaine Geralis
Foreword by Tom Ritter

Stuck in Neutral's first person narrator, fourteen-year-old Shawn McDaniel has severe cerebral palsy. He has no muscle control, and cannot walk, talk or communicate in any way. Readers, however, have access to Shawn's thoughts and realize what no one else can—that Shawn is a genius who remembers everything he ever hears. Although he appears to be a vegetable to the outside world, he is in fact happy to be alive and has a rich inner life. His father, a poet, is unable to handle his son's condition, and leaves the family. Fearing that Shawn suffers greatly, he considers killing him to end what he believes is a miserable existence. Shawn, who senses his father's thoughts, does not want to die, but has no way of communicating this feeling to him. An ambiguous ending leaves readers to draw their own conclusions and provides ample material for thought and discussion.

Terry Trueman received the prestigious **Michael L. Printz Honor Book Award** for *Stuck in Neutral*. The novel also received several other hon-

.488

Film Option

An individual or production company may approach an author of an article, book, play, or story with a cash offer for the right to adapt the work as a film. A time period will be set during which the producer must raise the money and sign agreements with the participants who will make the film. If the project cannot be organized, the rights return to the author, who can again option the film rights to another individual. Many books are optioned more than one time before they are adapted as a movie.

ors, including *Booklist*'s **Books for Youth Editor's Choice** and **Top Ten Youth First Novels**, American Library Association **Best Books for Young Adults** and **Quick Picks for Reluctant Young Readers** and the New York Public Library **Books for the Teen Age**. It has also been optioned as a feature film or television movie.

– Mary Virginia Davis

p.45

p.684

p.1

p.4

p.1

Mark Twain

Born: November 30, 1835; Florida, Missouri
Died: April 21, 1910; Redding, Connecticut

www.marktwainhouse.org

Regarded as a quintessential storyteller, humorist, and social commentator, **Mark Twain** is among American literature's most significant novelists and young adult authors. His characters, often drawn from people he knew, are depicted realistically and speak in plain language appropriate to their regions and social standing. Filled with adventure and comic incidents, Twain's deceptively simple novels explore deeper underlying themes, such as the questioning of authority, privilege, and the prevailing morals of society.

Mark Twain was born Samuel Langhorne Clemens in a tiny northeastern Missouri town. He spent his boyhood years in nearby Hannibal, on the Mississippi River. In 1863, while writing for a Nevada newspaper, he began signing the pen name "Mark Twain" to his work, taking the term from the steamboatman's term for two fathoms of water. His childhood memories furnish settings, stories, characters, and themes for many of his best-known books, including *The Adventures of Tom Sawyer* and *Adventures of Huckleberry Finn*. Although he had little formal education, his vast reading and diverse experiences as a printer, steamboat pilot, miner, reporter, lecturer, and world traveler provided a wealth of material for him to draw upon in his writings.

TITLES

The Adventures of Tom Sawyer, 1876

The Prince and the Pauper, 1881

Adventures of Huckleberry Finn, 1885

A Connecticut Yankee in King Arthur's Court, 1889

Pudd'nhead Wilson, 1894

.542

586

The Adventures of Tom Sawyer recounts the extraordinary adventures of an ordinary, but mischievous boy growing up in the 1840's in St. Petersburg, a Mississippi River town modeled on Twain's own Hannibal. Twain contrasts the idyllic nature of childhood with the more problematic adult world. Village life is filled not only with beauty, romance, and excitement, but also with hypocrisy, murder, and revenge.

Twain's first of several historical novels, *The Prince and the Pauper*, is set in England in 1547, at the end of the reign of Henry VIII. Young Tom Canty, a poor commoner, and Crown Prince Edward bear an uncanny resemblance to each other. Meeting by chance, the boys exchange places and are accidentally thrust into each other's worlds. Through their experiences, Twain explores issues of identity, wealth and poverty, social injustice, and the relationship between children and their parents.

p.11

A sequel to *The Adventures of Tom Sawyer*, *Adventures of Huckleberry Finn* is considered Mark Twain's best and most controversial novel because of its unique narrative perspective and its unflinching look at racial prejudice, slavery, and religious and social hypocrisy. Huck Finn struggles with his conscience and the racism of the antebellum South when he helps Jim, a runaway slave, to escape. Huck narrates his own story in unadorned language and is often unaware of the irony of the situations he reports. The racial epithets used by some of the characters make the novel a frequent target of censorship advocates who fail to appreciate the book's irony.

Mississippi Riverboat

Today, riverboats still cruise the Mississippi as they did In Mark Twain's day. Companies offer day trips, overnight trips, or extended cruises on the famous river. Traveling at about eight miles per hour, the leisurely trip attempts to recapture the pace, service, and entertainment of another era. Some boats are even floating casinos offering gambling onboard.

A Connecticut Yankee in King Arthur's Court combines elements of time-travel, comic adventure, burlesque, and social satire. The narrator, Hank Morgan, is a late nineteenth century American mechanic who is transported back to sixth century **Arthurian** England. Using Yankee ingenuity to gain power, he reorganizes the kingdom and tries to reform medieval Britain through modern technology and democratic principles. However, he finds the weight of custom and the power of the Church too strong to overcome.

p.48

Pudd'nhead Wilson (sometimes called *The Tragedy of Pudd'nhead Wilson*) gives the prince-and-pauper theme a different twist. A slave woman who to all appearances is white switches her own baby with that of her widowed master to save her son from the horrors of slavery. However, he grows up to become a callous tyrant and murderer. The novel is worth reading for its humor and unexpected turns, but it also raises fundamental questions about the meaning of racial identity.

Mark Twain's novels have provided material for numerous **film** and television productions. Unfortunately, most adaptations have focused on the humorous and adventurous parts of his stories and have almost uniformly failed to capture Twain's mastery of language, social criticism, satire, and the darker undercurrents found in his books. Readers will find his novels more complex than most film treatments and far more rewarding.

— Kevin J. Bochynski

Twain and the Movies

The movies love Mark Twain. Twain himself appeared in two silent films, *A Curious Dream* (1907) and *The Prince and the Pauper* (1909). Filmmakers have made movies of *The Adventures of Tom Sawyer* on numerous occasions throughout the history of film, with the first being a silent film in 1907 and the most recent, *Tom and Huck*, in 1995. There have even been television series using the character of Tom Sawyer, and in 1973 a musical movie was released. Tom has made his appearance in German, French, and Brazilian adaptations as well. The 1938 film version produced by David O. Selznick is noteworthy as an early Technicolor film.

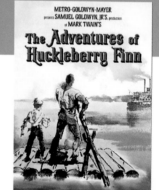

Jules Verne

Born: February 8, 1828; Nantes, France
Died: March 24, 1905; Amiens, France
www.phys.uu.nl/~gdevries/verne/verne.html

Jules Verne's name is almost synonymous with science fiction and particularly with stories about remarkable journeys. Many feel that Verne was the first true science-fiction writer. He certainly was the first exponent of "hard" science fiction, based on technology and explorations of alien environments such as outer space, the interior of the earth, and the depths of the sea. Although many of the scientific advances his books predicted have not become realities, his works are still read and enjoyed today.

Verne was the son of a middle-class lawyer in Nantes, France, and as a young man he went to Paris to study law in order to join his father's firm. However, while in Paris he also started writing short stories and plays. Even after passing his law

Stockbroker

A stockbroker is an individual who invests other people's money with the goal of increasing the value of the investment. Stockbrokers earn their own incomes from commissions paid from these transactions. In the U. S., he or she has passed an exam administered by the National Association of Securities Dealers (NASD). This allows him or her to buy and sell stocks, bonds, and mutual funds through the NASD and national stock exchanges. It is important for an investor to pick a stockbroker who has a track record of making good investments. Because the investor is trusting the stockbroker with his or her money, it is important to trust this individual and develop a good working relationship.

exams he remained in the capital, trying to support himself as a writer. In 1857 he married a widow with two children, and the need to earn a living through his writing became even more pressing than it had been in his bachelor days. He worked as a **stockbroker** for a while, until in 1862 he produced an adventure tale, *Five Weeks in a Balloon*, that caught a publisher's eye. That book's success led Verne to sign contracts to write one or two novels a year, many of which were first published in serial form.

p.688

p.197

Although Verne's early stories were comparatively realistic adventure tales, he quickly became interested in writing speculative stories based on ideas from the latest technological advances. These led him to predict inventions and advanced developments of such things as submarines, automobiles, space ships, and other wonders.

Even Verne's less fantastic adventure tales, such as *Around the World in Eighty Days*, involved imaginative advances on contemporary transportation technology, as well as encounters with exotic cultures. However, Verne's predictions were not the results of flashes of brilliant inspiration, but rather the result of a thorough and ongoing familiarity with current scientific thought and its goals. It was his awareness of the way that scientists and inventors were thinking that led him to predict the shapes that their experiments would eventually assume. At the same time, however, the popularity of his novels no doubt helped influence the scientists themselves to envision new inventions in certain ways.

For all of his scientific acumen illustrated in his novels and his ingenious, adventurous plots, Verne was not particularly good at, or interested in, creating unique and well-rounded characters. His heroes tend to exhibit typical nineteenth century imperialist virtues:

They are cool-headed in crises; they believe that science is the key to bettering human existence and, as the flip side of this belief, are apt to dismiss superstitious, religious, or "primitive" belief systems; and they are not particularly interested in women. Adventure is a man's business, and the women in their lives, if any, are left at home. The romantic interests that appear in film versions of Verne's novels have generally been added by the producers.

p.690

Two of Verne's characters have transcended this stereotypicality and captured his readers' imaginations. One is Phileas Fogg, the hero of *Around the World in Eighty Days*, who adds to the general character traits of a Verne hero an obsession with punctuality that may have been adopted from Verne's own father. The other is Captain Nemo, the nominal villain of *Twenty Thousand Leagues Under the Sea* and *The Mysterious Island*. Nemo, whose name means "nothing" in Latin, is said to exhibit many character traits of Verne himself. He is a classic example of a man whose obsession with his ends—halting the excesses of British imperialism—justifies his dubious means—destroying British ships and the lives of those who man them. In this character, Verne seems to warn of the dangers of too great a dependence on technology alone to solve the world's problems.

– Leslie Ellen Jones

Around the World in Eighty Days, the Movies

A film adaptation of *Around the World in Eighty Days* was first released in 1956. The film is an action-packed adventure, hilarious comedy, and around the world travelogue. The film had a large cast, long shooting schedule, and numerous locations in thirteen countries. It also is responsible for the term "cameo," a short apperance by a well-known personality. More than forty cameos appear in the film. The high production costs paid off. The film was a box-office hit and earned five Academy Awards, including one for Best Picture. The 2004 remake starring Jackie Chan had a less enthusiastic reception.

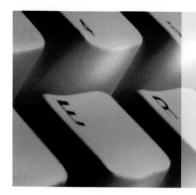

Elfrida Vipont

Born: July 3, 1902; Manchester, England
Died: March 15, 1992; Yealand Conyers, Lancashire, England

Elfrida Vipont writes from a committed Quaker position, which her novels reflect either explicitly or implicitly. Her books are typically coming-of-age stories that follow their heroines through childhood and adolescence, with particular reference to their schooling, until they attain settled values within their chosen particular careers.

Vipont was educated at England's Manchester High School for Girls and later at one of the country's most prestigious Quaker schools, Mount School, York. After studying history and music, she worked as a professional singer briefly and as a freelance writer and lecturer. In 1926 she married a researcher, R. P. Foulds, with whom she had four daughters. During World War II she became principal of the Quaker Evacuation School in northern Lancashire, in which she settled permanently. After the war she devoted her life to writing, not only young adult fiction, but also stories for young children, short stories and adult fiction. Sometimes she used her married name to publish literary biographies and Quaker histories and apologetics. She also compiled several anthologies of prayers and poetry.

Vipont's most successful young adult fiction centers around the Quaker Haverard family, which she modeled on her own family. Kit Haverard, the heroine of *The Lark in the Morn* and *The Lark on the Wing* parallels Vipont's own life, from her years at public school and the Quaker boarding school to her singing career. In the first novel, Kit's growing perception of the Quaker ethic of the inner voice

p.749

p.692

p.368

p.168

p.693

Mount School

Mount School in York, England, was founded by the Quakers in 1785. It was one of the first girls' schools to send its graduates to university. Today it has both boarding and day students. Its educational philosophy rests on the Quaker principle of taking care of each individual to bring out her best qualities. It is ranked as one of the top thirty schools in England.

mirrors her discovery of who she really is, her uniqueness. This is shown by Vipont to be a slow process of distinguishing the true from the false, characterized specifically by two music teachers. Even so, Kit learns that even the true musician, "Old Fish," has compromised her vocation, just as she learns her embittered great-aunt had also been forced to refuse a musical career through family pressure. In a touching scene, Kit manages to bring resolution to her aunt's lifelong frustration.

In *The Lark on the Wing*, Kit refuses such compromises and battles through a number of tests to become the singer her talents and her inner voice seem to promise. Both novels are set against an upper-middle class background of culture and genteel prosperity. In the third novel of the series, *The Spring of the Year*, Kit's niece, Laura, is educated at the local public school system as part of her father's egalitarian ideals. Laura goes through the two-tiered high school system that was typical in England at the time. Despising the exam she must take to enter the higher tier, she fails it. Laura's social prejudices over the lower tier system are overcome by the head teacher. Vipont's school principals are consistently wise figureheads, unlike her characters' fathers, who remain blind to their children's

p.32

needs. In the last two novels of the series, *Flowering Spring* and *The Pavilion*, Laura's family opposes her ambition to be an actress, trying to force her into teaching. Like her aunt, Laura prevails while learning artistic values.

Elfrida Vipont's novels succeed in combining fictions of career, self-discovery, and religious belief in lively and realistic ways. In 1950 *The Lark on the Wing* won Britain's prestigious **Carnegie Medal**. Vipont also won recognition for her collaboration with Raymond Briggs for *The Elephant and the Bad Baby* (1969), a picture book for young children.

p.42

– David Barratt

Inner Voice

The Religious Society of Friends, commonly known as the Quakers, was founded by George Fox in England in 1652. Unlike most religious groups, the Quakers believe that each individual is capable of grasping the word of God individually. By listening to the "inner voice," an individual will understand God's direction. Quakers do not believe in ritual, and their meetings are often silent and unstructured. Quakers believe that all individuals are equal. In the U. S., they supported the abolition of slavery and played a major role in the Underground Railway. They are also pacifists (opposed to bearing firearms), but they have served in the ambulance corps to help with the wounded in war. There are fewer than 150,000 Quakers living in the U. S. today.

Cynthia Voigt

Born: February 25, 1942; Boston, Massachusetts

www.randomhouse.com/highschool/authors/
voigt.html

Cynthia Voigt explores themes of courage, loyalty, friendship, self-determination, and maturation. She is best known for her resourceful, independent (usually) female protagonists who overcome adversity and grow p.23 up in the process. From the time she was a young adult, she knew that she wanted to write. She says her writing often begins with a question. She records ideas and lets them "stew" for many months before beginning to develop her characters. The books that have emerged from this process are as varied as the characters whom Voigt imagines and the themes her books explore.

Born in Boston, Voigt grew up enjoying reading and knowing that she wanted to become a writer. After earning a bachelor's degree at **Smith College**, p.39 she did graduate work at St. Michael's College and later got a teaching certificate. Through the 1970's she taught high school English in Maryland and became interested in writing young adult books. During the early 1980's she began writing full time and turned out at least one book every year.

Voigt's popular Tillerman series begins with *Homecoming*, in which the four young Tillerman children are abandoned by their mother. Led by the oldest, Dicey, the children search for a home and struggle to stay together, surviving through a heady

Boat Building

Boat building in modern society can be done by a large company or by an individual. It can involve building a canoe, a sailboat, or a power boat. In our modern world, we frequently turn to the Internet to find information, and that is the case with boat building. An excellent information source is www.boatbuilding.com, a site for builders and designers large and small. It is a place where people can exchange information, buy plans, read about construction details, or link to sites of suppliers. It is an excellent first stop for the beginning or experienced boat builder.

mixture of spirit, determination, and skill. The second book, *Dicey's Song*, begins with the children living with their grandmother on a Maryland farm. Dicey must now redefine herself as something other than the family's surrogate mother. Subsequent Tillerman books include *The Runner*, *Come a Stranger*, and *Sons from Afar*. The series ends with *Seventeen Against the Dealer*, in which the grown-up Dicey must draw upon her inner strength to save her **boat-building** p.695 business and her family.

Voigt's Kingdom series, set in an imaginary land inspired by medieval Europe, begins with *Jackaroo*. Gwyn, an innkeeper's daughter, is snowbound in a cabin with a young nobleman. Finding a costume like that worn by a legendary masked outlaw who helps the poor, Gwyn emulates the hero. Another innkeeper's daughter turns up in *On Fortune's Wheel*. She leaves the kingdom with a nobleman. In foreign lands, the pair faces capture, imprisonment, and slavery. In *The Wings of a Falcon*, a brave and resourceful slave boy flees his native land, only to become embroiled in a civil war in which he acts as a peacemaker. The Kingdom series ends with *Elske*, the story of a maiden who escapes almost certain

CYNTHIA VOIGT

The Homecoming, the Movie

The film version of *Homecoming* aired on television in 1996. It starred Anne Bancroft as the grandmother. Readers of the book were big fans of the movie. Out of necessity, some details of the book were left out of the movie, but viewers were pleased to find the book's characters portrayed as they had imagined them.

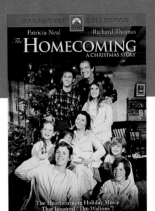

death in her native land and becomes a servant to an exiled princess. In helping her mistress regain her royal birthright, Elske learns the price of betrayal and the value of friendship.

Voigt often treats controversial subjects. *When She Hollers*, for example, follows seventeen-year-old Tish through the events of a single day—the day that Tish decides to end her stepfather's sexual abuse. In *Izzy, Willy-Nilly*, a pretty, popular fifteen-year-old girl goes to a party with a boyfriend who drinks and drives. The result is a horrific accident, and Izzy loses a leg. She learns to manage her disability and achieve both dignity and independence.

A master of all fictional elements—character, setting, and plot—Cynthia Voigt received the **Margaret A. Edwards Award** for Outstanding Literature for Young Adults from the Young Adult Library Services Association in 1995. Her many other awards include a **Newbery Medal** for *Dicey's Song*. *Solitary Blue* was both a **Newbery Honor Book** and a **Boston Globe-Horn Honor Book**. In 1996 *Homecoming* was made into a television movie that is available on video and DVD.

– Faith Hickman Brynie

p.339

p.696

p.10

p.747

Mildred Pitts Walter

Born: September 9, 1922; Sweetville, Louisiana

http://www.harperchildrens.com/catalog/
author_xml.asp?authorID=18931

Mildred Pitts Walter is best known for writing children's literature but has also written three novels for young adults, as well as one work of nonfiction, *Mississippi Challenge* (1993), which examines the civil rights struggle. In that book she explores the laws that fostered racism in Mississippi and the Civil Rights movement that forced the laws to change.

Born in Louisiana, Walter was the youngest of seven children in her family. She grew up in the Deep South and faced problems of poverty and racism on a daily basis. However, instead of allowing these problems to defeat her or make her submissive, she gained strength from them and became a teacher, a civil rights activist, and an award-winning author of young adult fiction.

The values instilled in Walter by her parents influenced the major themes in her novels: the value of self-respect and hard work, the necessity of courage when facing hardships, the importance of making choices and living by the consequences of those choices, and probably the most significant value, the importance of family as the sustaining, grounding force in one's life. These values provided Walter and the characters in her novels with the ability to overcome racism and prejudice.

In *Because We Are*, Walter conveys the importance of making good choices and accepting the consequences of making poor choices through the book's eighteen-year-old character Emma, a student who excels academically in her integrated school. How-

TITLES

Because We Are, 1983

The Girl on the Outside, 1992

Second Daughter: The Story of a Slave Girl, 1996

0.668

ever, Emma is forced to leave the school when she misinterprets and is too sensitive about a comment made by one of her teachers. When she accepts responsibility for her actions and stops blaming others, she matures.

The Girl on the Outside is based on the true story of a 1950's racial desegregation court case (*Brown v. the Board of Education of Topeka, Kansas*) that overturned many decades of "separate-but-equal" education. The protagonists are two teenage girls. Sophia, the white daughter of a wealthy family, fears the problems that racial integration will bring. Elizabeth, a fifteen-year-old black girl and a student at the Carver High School for Black Youth, is forced to leave her friends to attend the integrated school. Walter conveys the fear of change and the courage of both young women realistically.

Second Daughter is a fictionalized account of Elizabeth Freeman—called Mum Bett in the novel—a slave who took her owner to court in 1781 and won her freedom under the Massachusetts constitution.

p.698

p.401

p.233

Brown v. Board of Education

This landmark Supreme Court case struck down the "separate but equal" doctrine upheld by the Supreme Court in *Plessy v. Ferguson* (1896) and subsequent decisions, ending legal racial segregation in public schools. It was but one case dealing with segregation in public schools that came

before the Supreme Court in 1954. The cases all addressed excluding black children from all-white schools by state laws. Chief Justice Earl Warren stated that "separate but equal" schools did not exist and were "inherently unequal." The decision opened the way for laws endorsing segregation in other public places to be overturned.

Jane Addams Honor Book Award

The Jane Addams Book Award has been granted annually by the Women's International League for Peace and Freedom and the Jane Addams Peace Association. The selecting committee considers books for children up to age fourteen that promote the "cause of peace, social justice, and world community." In addition to the winning author and artist, the committee may also select Honor Books. The award has been given since 1953. The winning author and artist receive a certificate and a cash award.

While the historical aspects of the novel are entertaining, the real story is told through the eyes of Mum's sister, Aissa, who struggles to discover who she is and maintain her self-respect as a slave. The power of family to sustain life is another important theme in Walter's writing. When the sisters' father is beaten to death for protesting against the sale of his five sons, their mother dies of grief after Aissa is born. The girls are then sold and must rely on their tenacity and their extended family of slaves to survive.

While Mildred Pitts Walter provides readers with realistic characters, the themes and the plots individualize her works and bring them to life. Her novels have won several awards. *Because We Are* won the Parents' Choice Award and Honorable Mention from the Coretta Scott King Award from Social Responsibility Round Table of the American Library Association. In addition, her novel, *Second Daughter: The Story of a Slave Girl* received the Jane Addams Honor Book Award and the Virginia Library Association **Jefferson Cup Worthy of Special Note Award**.

p.153

p.66

p.45

699

– Sharon K. Wilson

H. G. Wells

Born: September 21, 1866; Bromley, Kent, England
Died: August 13, 1946; London, England

www.hgwellsusa.50megs.com/favorite_links.html

Herbert George Wells wrote more than one hundred books, including fifty novels, ten volumes of short stories, and the rest on history, science, world politics, and other subjects. He is best remembered, however, for his science-fiction novels, which helped to define the genre. Many of those books are still avidly read today, and they continue to inspire popular film adaptations.

Wells was the son of servants who rose from his family's **lower-class** status by winning a **scholarship** to the Normal School of Science, the first British school dedicated to providing scientific training for teachers. Although he attended the school for only three years and left without taking a degree, Wells was profoundly influenced by **T. H. Huxley's** teachings on **Charles Darwin** and his theory of evolution. Wells soon found work as a book reviewer for *The Saturday Review*, and between 1895 and 1897 he reviewed virtually every novel published in England. He gained a reputation as a thoughtful reviewer who considerably raised the standards of professional literary criticism, and he also learned a great deal about what made successful fiction work.

Wells was an ardent socialist, a political stance that he felt was a natural counterpart to the scientific

◄ p.32

p.38 ►

p.701 ►

p.42 ►

theory of evolution, in which he strongly believed. He intended a great number of his writings—both fiction and nonfiction—to promote and explore the ramifications of his political views. During his lifetime, he was, in fact, primarily known for his novels of social comedy and commentary, such as *Kipps* (1905), *The History of Mr. Polly* (1909), and *Ann Veronica* (1909). However, the novels that have best stood the test of time are his science-fiction adventure stories.

The Time Machine grew out of a story Wells wrote while still at school; it illustrates his theories of the end result of human evolution. His time traveler invents a machine that transports him to the year 802,701, where he discovers that the human race has split into two distinct species: the Eloi, childlike beings who live leisurely but pointless lives on the surface of the earth; and the Morlocks, evil beings who inhabit the underground. The Morlocks' advanced technology creates the paradisiacal lifestyle of the Eloi, but at the expense of the Eloi becoming the food of the Morlocks. Wells's moral seems to be that the only way to get a free lunch is to be the lunch yourself.

The Island of Dr. Moreau is another tale of the dangers of technology and science. Moreau believes that his experiments to create new species by a kind of Frankenstein surgery that grafts together animal and human parts will benefit the world. Instead he creates an island full of terrorized subhuman beings who worship him as a god in

T. H. Huxley

T. H. Huxley was a nineteenth century English biologist who called himself "Darwin's bulldog" for his defense of Darwin's theory of evolution. His ability to present his ideas in both lectures and essays had a positive impact on many educational and humanitarian causes. As a member of the London School Board, he strongly influenced British elementary education with his insistence that, in addition to the three R's, courses be taught in physical education, home economics, the arts, and natural sciences. He is considered one of the most influential figures in the history of modern science education. His grandsons, Julian and Aldous Huxley, each benefited from T. H.'s rich personality, the former as one of Britain's leading scientists and the latter as a novelist and metaphysical speculator.

p.702

a superstitious attempt to ward off his seemingly random attentions. After his death they revert to their animal state, losing all traces of their humanity. Similarly, the hero of *The Invisible Man* uses science to achieve the incredible—the ability to become invisible. However, his discovery drives him insane, partly because of the actual process of invisibility, but partly because his mind cannot cope with the sinister power that invisibility grants him.

The War of the Worlds is notorious not only as a novel but also as a radio broadcast made by actor Orson Welles (no relation to H. G. Wells) in 1938. When Welles broadcast a dramatic adaptation of the novel on the night of Halloween, many listeners missed the broadcast's disclaimers and thought they were hearing a real news broadcast of the invasion of Earth. Martian technology proves unstoppable by mere Earth technology; what kills the Martians and saves Earth from conquest is a simple bacterium. In some ways, Wells's story is an ironic reversal of the devastation that alien diseases such as **smallpox** p.33 created among Native Americans after Europeans began settling the Americas.

– Leslie Ellen Jones

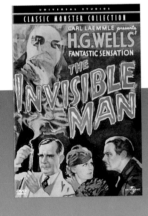

The Invisible Man, the Movie

The 1933 film version of *The Invisible Man* continues to fascinate film fans today. Director James Whale, who directed the hit film *Frankenstein* in 1931, was ready to try his hand at more elaborate special effects. He hired John Fulton to develop the "invisible" in Wells's story. Claude Rains, in his film debut, was hired to use his distinctive voice as Jack Griffin. Viewers hear his voice, but they see his face for less than a minute. Throughout the film he is either bandaged or, when the bandages are removed, invisible. His invisible presence is signaled by footprints forming in the snow, objects moving from one place to another without assistance, or empty pajamas walking about the room. It is only in death that Griffin becomes visible. These special effects owe much to the French film pioneer and stage magician Georges Melies, who built the first film studio in the 1890's. He developed many of the tricks and discovered ways to use the camera that later led to the sophisticated special effects achieved in film today.

Nancy Werlin

Born: October 29, 1961; Salem, Massachusetts

www.nancywerlin.com

Nancy Werlin's prose has been described as hard-edged and realistic. Her novels are highly regarded for their well-plotted suspense, psychological realism, and vividly drawn characters. Werlin has also been praised for her sensitive treatment of dysfunctional families, teenage suicide, guilt, fear, and budding adolescent emotions that include sexual attraction. The principal characters in her novels tend to be bright youngsters from well-to-do and well-educated families.

The daughter of a **computer engineer** and homemaking mother, Nancy Werlin was encouraged in her early years to read. She read science fiction, history books, classical works, and even encyclopedias. At the age of ten she decided to become a writer. Although she regarded school as a waste of time, she did well academically and finished her formal education at Yale University with a bachelor's degree. Afterward she did **technical writing** for computer software companies and later worked for eighteen months in Germany before returning to Boston, determined to become a writer. A year later she completed the draft of her first novel.

Werlin skillfully depicts young people trapped in harrowing situations. Her main characters are challenged psychologically and emotionally, eventually achieving self-discovery. **Autism,** which affected a member of Werlin's own family, afflicts the twin sister of the **protagonist** of *Are You Alone on*

p.705

p.3

p.704

.233

TITLES

Are You Alone on Purpose?, 1994

The Killer's Cousin, 1998

Locked Inside, 2000

Black Mirror, 2001

Double Helix, 2004

Autism

National Alliance for Autism Research

Autism is a lifelong mental disability which develops in children before the age of two. Its cause is unknown. Children diagnosed with autism show a wide range of symptoms, but all of them show difficulty with social relationships. They avoid eye contact or show little facial expression. They also have difficulty with language and communication, ranging from physically being unable to talk to having difficulty making conversation. A preoccupation with repetitive activity is also present, such as flapping the hands or being obsessive about hand washing or counting. Treatment depends on the degree of disability. One-on-one therapy to change behavior has proved the most successful form of treatment.

Purpose? Like Werlin herself, the novel's main characters are Jewish. Alison Shandling is the sister of an autistic twin, and her friend, Harry Roth, is confined to a wheelchair after a diving accident. Their emotions deepen into a mature affection as they discover that they both have been emotionally crippled by their dysfunctional parents. Together, they find a way to heal.

The teenage narrator of *The Killer's Cousin* is acquitted of murdering his girlfriend, but when he moves to Massachusetts to live with relatives, he is tormented by the sister of the girl he killed. Although he realizes that the sister is mentally deranged and may possibly be a killer herself, he nevertheless rescues her from a burning house and offers to help her fend off her own demons.

Locked Inside is set in a **boarding school**, p.1 where Marnie plays Internet games and tries to defeat her online enemy, Elf. One of her teachers, convinced that she is Marnie's half-sister, kidnaps and imprisons Marnie in a cellar. Marnie uses her computer-game skills to extricate herself, aided by Elf. *Black Mirror* returns to the boarding school setting and also involves the Internet, suicide, and drugs as the protagonist struggles to find self-worth as a half-Jewish, half-Japanese young woman.

Nancy Werlin's novels have won many awards. *Are You Alone on Purpose?* won the **Publishers Weekly** **Flying Start Award**; the American Library Association made the same book a **Best Books for Young Adults** selection and a **Teens' Top 10 Best Book Pick**. *The Killer's Cousin* won an **Edgar Allan Poe Award** for Young Adult Fiction and another for Best Young Adult Mystery. The novel was also selected as a **Best Books for the Teen Age** by the New York Public Library and was a *Booklist* **Editor's Choice** selection.

p.144
p.480
p.72
p.143
p.45
p.156

– Bernard E. Morris

Computer Engineer

Computer engineers design computer hardware and software, set up computer systems, and help keep computers running. A bachelors degree or a graduate degree is usually required to obtain employment, and job opportunities are good in our computer dependent society. People with training in computer science generalize or specialize in network administration, systems analysis, or database management.

Barbara Wersba

Born: August 19, 1932; Chicago, Illinois

Barbara Wersba grew up an only child, and feeling lonely and self-conscious. She began writing at an early age. However, her first career was not writing but acting. To escape her own life by playing the role of someone else, she began performing in community theater at the age of twelve. During her young adult life she performed in Off-Broadway productions, in summer stock, and on television and radio. Eventually she found that she disliked acting and began writing constantly, keeping journals and hiding them in her closet. When an illness forced her to leave acting, she began writing in earnest, realizing that it was the career she had wanted all along. Her first five published books were for children. Her sixth book, *The Dream Watcher* (1968), was her first young adult novel.

Wersba's stories are about relationships—either friendships or romances—but her characters never achieve harmony and understanding easily. For example, in *Whistle Me Home*, Noli, a high school junior who abuses alcohol and feels disaffected toward her mother, falls in love with T. J. When she discovers that he is gay, Noli must learn to express her love by leaving him. Wersba tells the tale in present tense, giving a sense of immediacy and urgency to this story about being honest and keeping secrets. *Whistle Me Home* was an **Honor Book** of the Society of School Librarians **International Book Award** in 1997.

Wersba has written more than twenty-five novels. In many, her young male protagonists are vul-

p.101

p.23

Psychotic

When we describe a person as psychotic, we are referring to someone suffering from a mental illness that damages that individual's sense of reality. The symptoms can be delusions, such as that he or she is being spied upon or plotted against; hallucinations, such as hearing voices; or thought disorder, such as using made-up words or jumping from one subject to another. Psychotic disorders can appear at any age. The most effective form of treatment is usually medication.

nerable and loving, and they must face how different they are from other boys. In *You'll Never Guess the End*, for example, fifteen-year-old Joel Greenberg sets out to locate the wealthy kidnapped girlfriend of his brother, JJ. Joel is a responsible, caring kid who gets good grades and helps the homeless, while his brother is the opposite. Lazy and a college dropout, JJ has suddenly became a best-selling author. Joel tries to solve his family problems while also solving the mystery.

Wersba's female protagonists are often eccentric misfits who must find their own way and battle against societal norms. A trilogy follows the life and loves of Heidi Rosenbloom between the ages of fifteen and eighteen. Heidi rebels against the security of her wealthy family. In *Just Be Gorgeous*, she falls **.732** in love with Jeffrey, a **homeless** and gay tap dancer who performs on the streets and has unrealistic expectations of stardom. In *Wonderful Me*, Heidi falls in love with her high school English teacher who turns out to be **psychotic**. In *The Farewell Kid*, she runs a dog-rescue service out of her apartment—an p.707 enterprise that Wersba herself undertook at one time. Heidi's failed romances lead her to reject men,

Sag Harbor, New York

Sag Harbor is a charming village located on a bay in the Hamptons, on New York's Long Island. The port was home to whaling ships in the seventeenth century, an industry that reached its peak in the mid-nineteenth century. The last whaling vessel left port in 1871. Today, Sag Harbor welcomes summer visitors and tourists. It's harbor is lined with shops and restaurants, and visitors wander through the historic winding streets. It is one of the most picturesque villages in the Hamptons, which is also the summer home to many New Yorkers.

but she changes her mind when she meets a photographer, Harvey Beaumont. The trilogy portrays Heidi and her misadventures with humor, while probing the more serious side of love, sex, and how teens come to find and accept themselves outside their parents' often unreasonable expectations.

Wersba explores the same themes in another trilogy about the life of Rita Formica. These humorous novels begin with *Fat: A Love Story*, in which Rita, an overweight teenager, falls in love with her employer, Arnold Bromberg, a cheesecake salesman twice her age. The romance continues in *Love Is the Crooked Thing*. Rita searches for Arnold, who has gone to Europe, and is reunited with him in Zurich. In *Beautiful Losers*, Rita sets up housekeeping with Arnold and pursues her dream of becoming a writer. Living in **Sag Harbor** on New York's **Long Island** p.61 (where Wersba lives and sets many of her books), Rita refuses to get married or go to college. Reality and romance butt heads, and Rita must make some difficult choices.

p.708

– Faith Hickman Brynie

Robert Westall

Born: October 7, 1929; Tynemouth, Northumberland, England

Died: April 15, 1993; Cheshire, England

www.norham.n-tyneside.sch.uk/westall

Robert Westall's many novels and short stories include World War II adventures, science-fiction stories of time travel, and tales of the uncanny. Despite their many themes, nearly all his stories feature adolescent characters compelled to make moral choices in settings in which support is not always forthcoming from parents, the community, or society in general. The worlds of Westall's stories are complicated by wartime violence, supernatural dangers, and the soullessness of modern technology. His young characters respond to the challenges of these worlds as adults would, making difficult life decisions and living with the consequences of their choices.

Robert Atkinson Westall was born in **Tynemouth**, a small town in northeastern England where he lived until his early twenties. After earning degrees from Durham University and the University of London, he taught art at several secondary schools and colleges between 1957 and 1985. He began writing full time in 1985 and continued until his death from complications of pneumonia in 1993.

During the early 1970's Westall set out to write a book that would let his son, Christopher, who was then turning twelve, know how he had felt when he was the same age. Drawing on his childhood experiences during World War II, he wrote *The Machine-Gunners*, about a group of teenage boys whose adventures include secretly removing a machine gun

710

from a downed German fighter plane. Although the boys plan to use the gun to shoot down enemy aircraft themselves, their action pits them against concerned adults and authorities, compelling them to form a silent fraternity held together by threats p.71 and intimidation as much as by loyalty. The novel earned praise for its realistic depiction of life during wartime but was criticized by some readers for its violence and frank language. Controversy over the book persuaded Westall to tone down the rawness of his later novels but also made him an outspoken critic of protective taboos that restricted the potential of young adult fiction.

A believer in younger readers' love of what he called "inevitable catastrophe," Westall revisited war themes in later books, including *Fathom Five* (1975), *Blitzcat* (1989), and *The Kingdom by the Sea* (1990). His second novel, *The Wind Eye* (1976), was his first to employ the supernatural, which Westall treats throughout his fiction as a type of chaos, similar to war, against which the conduct of his young protagonists can be measured. *The Devil on the* p.2 *Road* tells of a young man magically transported back to the seventeenth century who becomes the protector of a woman accused of witchcraft. The experience teaches p.3 him that the moral conflicts of the past differ little from those of the present. In *The Scarecrows*, Westall's most unusual

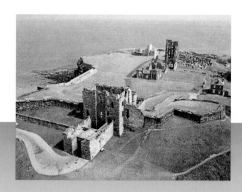

Tynemouth, England

Located on the Tyne River and the North Sea not far from Newcastle, Tynemouth is a popular British seaside resort. Its long sandy beach and a mineral spring contribute to its reputation as a health resort. Today, visitors flock to Tynemouth for its sandy beaches and historic buildings, such as the castle and priory. Robert Westall slightly disguised the village in his books, but the local libraries provide a guide to the Robert Westall Trail, allowing fans to visit the sites described so lovingly by this native son.

Fraternity

Originally from the Latin word *fraternus* (meaning "brother"), a fraternity is a group of people who gather because of a common interest, purpose, or pleasure. Most commonly, the term refers to male students at a university who join a social organization. A fraternity usually has an honor code, secret rites, and a name using Greek letters. The equivalent type of organization for women is called a sorority (from the Latin *soror*, "sister").

tale, a young boy's hatred of his stepfather channels the spirits of the long dead into the bodies of scarecrows who threaten to reenact a brutal drama from the past and force him to re-examine his feelings in order to stop them.

Westall's appeal to young readers lies in his credibly drawn teenage characters, his respect for their intelligence, and his faith that they will handle the unusual crises they face honorably. The honesty and realism of his writing has resulted in some of his work for young readers being reviewed as adult fiction.

p.42 Robert Westall's writing honors include Britain's **Carnegie Medal** and **Boston Globe-Horn Honor Book Awards** for both *The Machine-Gunners* and *The Scarecrows*. Several of his works have p.747 been adapted for television. Although his British settings have limited the popularity of some novels in America, his ghost stories have been widely anthologized.

— Stefan Dziemianowicz

Robb White

Born: June 20, 1909; Philippine Islands
Died: November 24, 1990; Santa Barbara, California

Robb White's stories deal with ordinary people who survive terrible hardships in wilderness and war settings. His usual heroes are teenage boys who are familiar with sailing or older boys serving in the navy. Often they seek sunken treasures that cruel enemies are determined to find first. White set his novels in a wide range of exotic backgrounds, particularly in the Caribbean and the South Pacific islands. He wrote twenty-one books, many of which were adapted into movies. He also scripted horror films and television shows such as *Perry Mason*. p.71

White lived a very adventurous life. He was born in the Philippines, where his father was an American missionary. Many years after, he was almost killed there when he was serving as a naval officer aboard a U.S. aircraft carrier during the **Battle of Leyte Gulf**. p.714 At the age of thirteen, White knew he would become a writer. After serving in World War II, in which he earned eight medals, he roamed from the snowy mountains of Kurdistan to the French Riviera to Eniwetok Island in the South Seas. Later, he and his wife, Rosalie or "Rodie," bought their own tropical island, Marina Cay, from the government of the British Virgin Islands for only sixty dollars. There they grew their own food.

White's best-known novel is *Deathwatch*, an often terrifying story about twenty-two-year-old Ben, who is hired by the creepy hunter Madec to show him where to shoot mountain goats. When Madec accidentally shoots an old prospector, he tries to kill Ben in order to keep his crime a secret. Forced to go on the run, Ben must survive a murderous south-western desert. He is determined to deliver the mad-man Madec to the authorities, but the broiling sun, lack of water and food, and his own Jeep and rifle are turned against him. *Deathwatch* won an **Edgar Allan Poe Award** and was named an **American Library Association** **Best of the Best Books for Young Adults** and a *New York Times* **Outstanding Book of the Year**. It is regularly taught in schools.

p.72
p.480
p.45

Another popular novel by White is *Fire Storm*, in which a park ranger accuses a teenage boy of starting a forest fire. The man is obsessed with im-prisoning the alleged arsonist, but as the flames close in around them, it turns out that the boy, Murdock, has the wits and skills to save both their lives. This dramatic story accurately describes the terrors and dangers of surviving a raging fire in the wilderness.

Perry Mason

The character of Perry Mason was created by mystery writer Earle Stanley Gardner and appeared as a lawyer in a series of books. Following a successful run as a radio serial, Perry Mason was brought to life on television in a weekly series. Beginning in 1957, actor Raymond Burr ap-peared as Perry Mason, assisted by his trusty secretary Della Street, played by Barbara Hale, and his detective sidekick Paul Drake, played by William Hopper. The show followed a set formula. In each weekly episode, a murder was committed, Perry Mason represented the suspected murderer, followed the clues, and solved the case, getting the guilty party to confess, usually while testifying in court. At the end of each episode, the characters would talk about the case and explain how it was solved. Reruns of Perry Mason still appear on cable networks today.

Robb White was proud that he wrote young adult novels that teenagers loved. His characters are brave and decent, as he knew young people usually are. His heroes and heroines must not only face human enemies but also the harsh realities of survival in the mountains, forest, desert, or wild seas.

– Fiona Kelleghan

Battle of Leyte Gulf

The Battle of Leyte Gulf in the Philippines took place in October, 1944 between Japanese and American naval forces. Invasion of the island was the first step in an Allied campaign to liberate the Philippine Islands from the Japanese. The Japanese planned to use air attacks against the American troops on land and strikes by the Imperial Navy to trap the invading army on the beaches of Leyte. The series of battles that followed resulted in an American victory even though the Japanese Central and Northern forces had escaped. They never regained the strength to challenge Allied control of the Pacific. However, the Japanese were encouraged by their first use of kamikaze squadrons, special suicide units whose pilots dove their planes and crashed into American ships. They continued to use this form of warfare in later World War II battles.

T. H. White

Born: May 29, 1906; Bombay, India
Died: January 17, 1964; Piraeus, Greece
www2.netdoor.com/~moulder/thwhite/index.html

Terence Hanbury White was born in India, the son of a British supervisor of police. When he was five, his parents separated, and he was taken to England by his mentally unstable mother. He had a precarious childhood because he grew up fearing his mother. When he was sent to school at Cheltenham College at the age of fourteen he was bullied by other students. He was admitted to Queen's College, Cambridge, and contracted tuberculosis during his second year, which required taking a year off to recover in Italy.

The continuing disasters of his life, as well as his ambivalence about his homosexuality, left White with an intense feeling of inferiority, for which he tried to compensate by excelling at whatever he tried. As a result, throughout his life he continued to learn skills and to master areas of information, not in any organized sense, as in an academic course, but whatever struck his fancy: archery, the Gaelic language, boating, or medieval bestiaries. After graduating from Cambridge, White taught English at a public school for several years. However, in 1936 he put together *England Have My Bones*, a book of his outdoors writing—hunting, fishing, and flying adventures—which became a **best-seller** and allowed him to leave teaching and spend the rest of his life as a writer.

p.5

p.522

p.57

p.716

p.384

TITLES

The Sword in the Stone, 1938

The Witch in the Wood, 1939 (also known as *The Queen of Air and Darkness*)

The Ill-Made Knight, 1940

Mistress Masham's Repose, 1946

The Candle in the Wind, 1958

The Book of Merlyn, 1977

Medieval Bestiaries

A bestiary is an illustrated book about animals, both real and imaginary. It first began in the second century, but it had grown in size and changed in message by the twelfth century. The illustrations presented elephants and lions, but also unicorns and dragons. Up to 150 animals could be included in a bestiary by the Middle Ages. In addition to the illustrations, the text relates tales in which each animal provides a moral or religious lesson for the reader.

White's best-known work is the **Arthurian** series based on Thomas Malory's fifteenth century *Morte d'Arthur*. *The Once and Future King* comprises *The Sword in the Stone*, *The Queen of Air and Darkness*, *The Ill-Made Knight*, and *The Candle in the Wind*. A fifth book, *The Book of Merlyn*, the culmination of this series that White wrote during World War II, was rejected by his publishers because they considered it too **pacifist**. The **manuscript** was later rediscovered and finally published in 1977.

p.4
p.5
p.620

The Once and Future King tells the story of King Arthur from his youth—before he discovers that he is the rightful king of England—until his death. *The Sword in the Stone* is the most lighthearted of the five books and the one most often read by itself. It introduces the absent-minded magician Merlin, who lives backward in time, aware of what has happened in the future but ignorant of the past. *The Queen of Air and Darkness* shows how Arthur sows the seeds of his eventual downfall when he sires his bastard son Mordred with his evil half-sister Morgause. *The Ill-Made Knight* tells the story of the quest for the

Holy Grail, focusing on the figure of Sir Lancelot. *The Candle in the Wind* tells of the final dissolution and destruction of Camelot, sapped from within by the affair between Lancelot and Guenever and attacked from without by Mordred. *The Book of Merlyn* is much less plot-driven than the other four novels, consisting mostly of a long discussion between Arthur, Merlin, and his menagerie of talking animals on the nature of war.

p.644

– Leslie Ellen Jones

Holy Grail

The Holy Grail is the cup from which Jesus Christ drank at the Last Supper. It was acquired by Joseph of Arimathea who later used it to catch the blood of Christ as he hung on the cross. The legend of the Grail has Joseph taking it with him to Britain, where it passes to his descendants upon his death. In the legends of King Arthur, it first appears around the twelfth century, and the quest for the Grail represents the highest spiritual pursuit for a Knight in King Arthur's court.

Thornton Wilder

Born: April 17, 1897; Madison, Wisconsin
Died: December 7, 1975; Hamden, Connecticut

www.thorntonwildersociety.org

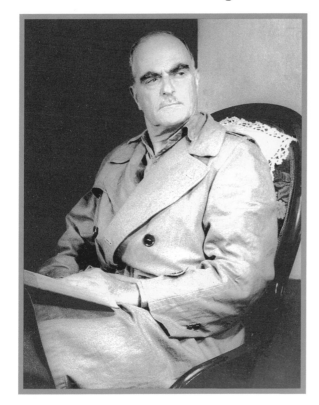

Thornton Wilder gained renown in 1927 when *The Bridge of San Luis Rey* was awarded the first of the three Pulitzer Prizes he would receive. His plays *Our Town* (1938) and *The Skin of Our Teeth* (1942), both of which are popular among young audiences, also won **Pulitzer Prizes**.

p.1

Wilder was born in Wisconsin to the daughter of a Presbyterian minister and a newspaper editor with values deeply rooted in his native New England. As he grew up, Wilder spent time living in Hong Kong, Shanghai, and Chefoo, China when his father's work took the family to Asia. He completed his secondary education in Berkeley, California, then entered Oberlin College in Ohio, before transferring to Yale University for his final two years of college. Solidly schooled in classical languages and literature, Wilder then spent a year at the American Academy in Rome and then earned a master's degree at Princeton University.

p.6

p.71

Wilder's first novel, *The Cabala* (1926), a fantasy set in Rome, reflects his classical background but is seldom read today. However, his next novel, *The Bridge of San Luis Rey*, enthralled the reading public. Set in colonial Peru in 1714, it poses the question of whether the collapse of a

p.8

American Academy in Rome

Following the World's Fair Columbian Exhibition of 1893 in Chicago, a group of architects and artists decided to create a center for the study of classical art and architecture in Rome. They received the support of Andrew Carnegie, J. P. Morgan, John D. Rockefeller, Jr., William K. Vanderbilt, and Henry Clay Frick, some of America's wealthiest men, and in 1894 the American School of Architecture was founded in Rome. The following year the American School of Classical Studies in Rome was founded by the Archaeological Institute of America. In 1913, the two merged to form the American Academy in Rome. This center for independent study in fine arts and the humanities grants the Rome Prize to thirty individuals each year based on their past achievements and a proposed research project. They become fellows at the American Academy in Rome. The director also invites residents—respected artists and scholars—to work at the Academy for periods of two to four months. There are no faculty members, and there is no course of study.

famous bridge over a deep ravine, resulting in the deaths of five people on the bridge, was an accident or a divine intention. Using Brother Juniper's report of the tragedy, the novel examines the lives of each person who was killed. The victims are the Marquesa Montemayor and her maid Pepita, Uncle Pio, and the two young brothers, Manuel and Esteban, both foundlings. The novel considers fate and explores love in its many manifestations. The universality of its themes assures the continued popularity of this work, which frequently appears on secondary school reading lists.

Wilder based *The Woman of Andros* on the Roman playwright Terence's *Andria*, which was written around 175 B.C.E. However, Wilder's own protagonist, Chrysis, reflects the religious tenets of classical Greek humanism. In his version of the legend, the Greek boy Pamphilus is forced to acknowledge that Glycerium, the sister of Chrysis is pregnant. Although she lives in Terence's comedy, Wilder's much more serious novel has her die.

Shakespeare's *Julius Caesar*

Julius Caesar is the first of Shakespeare's Roman plays and of his tragedies. It is more historical than his later tragedies and is drawn from Sir Thomas North's translation of Plutarch's *Lives of the Noble Greeks and Romans*. A comparison of Shakespeare's text with North's writing shows little more than a rephrasing of North's words. As the poet T. S. Eliot wrote: "Immature poets borrow; mature poets steal." Shakespeare's thievery is brilliant.

The Ides of March also reflects Wilder's fascination with ancient Rome. This novel examines Julius Caesar's final days. It considers how absolute power and popular resistance interact. Wilder documents this novel with imaginary letters, diary entries, and official reports and proclamations. These manufactured documents convincingly convey the political climate in Caesar's Rome and show a most determined Caesar, in sharp contrast to the indecisive Brutus who eventually betrays Caesar and is among the conspirators who stab him to death. Readers familiar with William Shakespeare's play *Julius Caesar* (pr. ca. 1599-1600) will find striking parallels and valuable illustrative material in Wilder's version of the story.

Thornton Wilder's novels consistently reflect his cosmopolitan outlook and his classical background. His characters, believable and frequently memorable, present the many faces of love and reflect Wilder's hope for humanity.

— R. Baird Shuman

Rita Williams-Garcia

Born: April 13, 1959; Jamaica, New York

www.ritawg.com

A strong voice for young black people today, **Rita Williams-Garcia** writes about both Caribbean and African American characters. Her narratives take on authentic cadences of urban language while her plots depict common conflicts and crises leading to self-discovery in her protagonists.

With a father who served in the army, Williams-Garcia moved several times during her childhood. Many of her formative years were spent in Seaside, California, where she experienced a pleasant childhood of daydreaming indoors and playing outdoors with her brother and sister. She began learning to read at the age of two and was already writing stories and poems before she entered school. When she was twelve, she moved back to her birthplace in Queens, New York. The change provided a culture shock that affected the themes of her later writing. Her new home had no backyard, and there was no safe haven at school. Williams-Garcia turned to her journal for solace. Soon she began submitting her writing for publication and sold her first story to *Highlights for Children* at the age of fourteen. During her senior year at Hofstra University she took a creative writing class in which she began the manuscript of what would become her first published novel, *Blue Tights*. It took her ten years to finish the novel and find a publisher, during which time she married Peter Garcia and had two children while

TITLES

Blue Tights, 1988

Fast Talk on a Slow Track, 1991

Like Sisters on the Homefront, 1995

Every Time a Rainbow Dies, 2001

No Laughter Here, 2004

p.233

working as a manager for a software marketer. She continued to work full time and do her writing before work and during her subway commute.

Blue Tights established Williams-Garcia's reputation as an honest and hard-hitting writer portraying the world of her characters in a genuine voice. p.722 Moody fifteen-year-old Joyce Collins loves to dance but is discouraged from **ballet** because of her curvaceous figure. Her talents are unleashed when she discovers African dance. In *Fast Talk on a Slow Track*, high school valedictorian Denzel Watson feels like a failure when he attends a summer session for minority students and discovers that he cannot shine by personality alone. He decides not to attend Princeton University in the fall as planned and spends the summer working, but through experiences on the street finds the courage to rise to the new challenge of attending college after all.

Williams-Garcia grappled with more controversial material in her next two books. Gayle, a fourteen-year-old mother, is pregnant for the second time in *Like Sisters on the Homefront*. The novel opens with her mother marching her to an abortion clinic, then sending her away from New York to religious relatives in Georgia. There Gayle learns another way to live. When

Ballet Dancers

Ballet dancers traditionally are long-legged and very thin. There are many biographies of dancers who develop eating disorders in order to maintain the dancer's ideal body type. However, there are also dance companies that break with tradition. The Bill T. Jones/Arnie Zane Dance Company includes dancers of all sizes, shapes, and colors. Tall, short, thin, and full-figured dancers create a remarkable impression as they perform the thoughtful, carefully choreographed dance pieces the company stages.

sixteen-year-old Thulani first appears in *Every Time a Rainbow Dies*, he is disconnected and introspective, mourning the death of his mother. The scream of a girl being raped awakens him to the world. He rescues the girl and they eventually fall in love. Their relationship heals old wounds for both.

Rita Williams-Garcia's books have earned numerous accolades, including several **Best Books for Young Adults** honors from the **American Library Association**. *Like Sisters on the Homefront* was a **Coretta Scott King Honor Book**, and Williams-Garcia has received the **PEN**/**Norma Klein Citation for Children's Literature**.

p.480

p.45

p.66

.723

– Lisa Rowe Fraustino

PEN

PEN (for poets, playwrights, essayists, editors, and novelists) was founded in 1921 by Mrs. C.A. Dawson Scott as an organization of writers working to advance literature, promote reading, and defend free expression. Today there are 130 PEN Centers worldwide and some 10,000 members. At least once a year, PEN hosts an international conference. PEN American Center is located in New York City and is the largest center with 2,700 members.

G. Clifton Wisler

Born: May 15, 1950; Oklahoma City, Oklahoma

www.harperchildrens.com/catalog/
author_xml.asp?authorID=19735

Gary Clifton Wisler writes exciting adventure novels set in a variety of historical periods and has also branched into science fiction. He is best known for his stories set during the American Civil War and in early Texas, where he grew up.

Born in Oklahoma, Wisler grew up in Dallas, Texas. In high school, he worked on the school newspaper. He always wanted to write novels because he had many interests, including the American Civil War, Texas history, and the Boy Scouts. Indeed, his novel *The Chicken Must Have Died Laughing* is about a summer when boy scouts encounter a camp leader called Mad Dog Malone.

Wisler enjoys writing about American Indians and their skills and pride. *Winter of the Wolf* tells of two teenagers, fourteen-year-old T. J. and the Comanche boy he saves during an Indian raid. T. J.'s farm is attacked by a gigantic wolf, the legendary Silver Devil, who cannot be killed except by two young warriors who are brave and true of heart. The wolf provides a test: If the boys are loyal to each other, they will kill the wolf. However, if one of them is weak, they will both die. In *The Wolf's Tooth*, teenager Elias moves to an **Indian reservation** and shares adventures with a Tonkawa boy. p.725

In *Buffalo Moon*, fourteen-year-old Willie Delamer runs away from his Texas ranch and stays with Comanche Indians to avoid being sent to school in New Orleans. His adventures with the Comanches are exciting, but equally dramatic is the sequel, *Thunder on the Tennessee*, in which Willie, now six-

.726

teen, goes to fight for the Confederacy during the Civil War. Wisler presents a grim portrayal of the devastating **Battle of Shiloh**. Wisler is one of the finest authors of Civil War novels for young readers. His most famous book on the war is *Red Cap*, the true story of Ransom J. Powell, a young Yankee drummer boy who shows enormous courage when he is captured by Confederate troops and sent to the horrifying Andersonville prison.

   The Raid resembles Mark Twain's *Adventures of Huckleberry Finn* (1884) in its depiction of fourteen-year-old Lige Andrews, who must discover whether he is brave or a coward as he journeys into Indian country with an African American to rescue his kidnapped brother. A similar book is *Caleb's Choice*, set in Texas in 1858. In that story, fourteen-year-old Caleb must choose whether or not to assist fugitive slaves in their run for freedom. Wisler also writes about other times and places. In *This New Land*, ten-year-old Richard Woodley describes his trip to the New World aboard the *Mayflower* in 1620

Indian Reservations

As the U. S. expanded and more white settlers moved westward, the displacement of American Indians to reservations was seen as the most efficient way to protect settlers while giving them access to more land. Most of the original Indian reservations were in the Plains or the deserts of the West, on land considered unsuitable for farming. As expansion pushed toward the west coast, Indians were relocated to the north and the south, leaving a safe path for travelers through the middle of the country.

and tells about the first year spent by the Pilgrims at Plymouth.

Wisler also writes science fiction. *The Antrian Messenger* features fourteen-year-old Scott, who loves astronomy and has precognitive dreams. An unusual friend tells Scott who he really is and explains to him how to use his special powers. However, Scott must risk his own life to protect the ones he loves. In *The Seer*, Scott continues to explore his new powers, and in *The Mind Trap*, his identity may be exposed when he is imprisoned in a research institute for psychic children run by a mysterious doctor.

G. Clifton Wisler received his first writing honors for his very first novel, *My Brother, the Wind*, which was nominated for the **American Book Award**. *Thunder on the Tennessee* won the Spur Award for Best Western Juvenile Fiction.

p.335

– Fiona Kelleghan

Battle of Shiloh

The Civil War Battle of Shiloh took place on April 6 and 7, 1862 in the northern Mississippi River military theater. Union forces under General Ulysses S. Grant and Confederate forces under Albert S. Johnston had engaged in a number of battles before clashing at Shiloh. The two-day slaughter ultimately resulted in a Southern retreat and Northern exhaustion. Both sides suffered heavy losses totaling approximately 23,000 soldiers. Johnston was killed and was replaced by Robert E. Lee.

Owen Wister

Born: July 14, 1860; Philadelphia, Pennsylvania
Died: July 21, 1938; North Kingstown, Rhode Island

www.kirjasto.sci.fi/owister.htm

Owen Wister's contribution to American literature and culture included helping to establish images of **cowboys** as rugged individualists and frontier heroes. Following in the steps of such writers as **James Fenimore Cooper** and Theodore Roosevelt, Wister helped establish the Western frontier, and the people who settled it, as uniquely American.

p.452

.728

Wister was born in Philadelphia to a physician father and a mother whose own mother was an actress. As a child, Wister attended schools in Switzerland and England before being enrolled at St. Paul's School in Concord, New Hampshire. After graduating from Harvard University, he spent two years studying music in Paris and then became a bank clerk. Because of his poor health, he went to the West to recuperate and then returned East to study law at Harvard University. He practiced law in Philadelphia before becoming a writer.

Lin McLean is made up of a series of connected stories about a wandering hero who both grows up and grows to know himself as he sheds his Boston past and embraces life on the frontier. While not as well plotted as Wister's later book, *The Virginian*, *Lin McLean* features excellent descriptions of the plains and deserts of

TITLES

Lin McLean, 1897

The Virginian, 1902

James Fenimore Cooper

James Fenimore Cooper was a historian of America. His novels span American history, dramatizing events from Columbus's discovery of the New World, through the French and Indian Wars and early settlement, to the American Revolution. His career was relatively short, from 1820 to 1851, but he left behind a large body of work. His purpose as both man and author was to work for the intellectual independence of his country. He felt Americans were influenced too much by foreign models. Most readers will be familiar with his Leatherstocking Tales and the characters of Natty Bumppo and his Indian friend Chingachgook. Cooper pictures an America which is moving away from the old European aristocratic order toward an order made natural through exposure to the American wilderness.

the western states, and is a good example of what is called **local-color** writing.

McLean also makes an appearance in Wister's most famous novel, *The Virginian*. Unlike the respected but slow-selling *Lin McLean*, *The Virginian* was an immediate success, establishing Wister's reputation as an author and giving him a level of financial security he had lacked earlier. The exploits of the character known only as "the Virginian" are told by an unnamed narrator, an easterner who is awed by the novel's hero. By using the Virginian as his example throughout the novel, the narrator becomes more manly, self-sufficient, and clear in his use of common sense as he sheds the baggage of his eastern upbringing.

As important to the novel as the narrator's personal growth is the continuing unfolding of the Virginian's character. The most manly of men, the Virginian is gallant, calm, trustworthy, and modest. He lives according to a frontier code that requires men to keep their word, protect women from harm, guard property against theft, and crawl for no one. Cool-headed, the Virginian even permits his implacable enemy, Trampas, to live until that man trifles with

p.12

his honor. Finally, after Trampas shoots him from behind, the Virginian kills him and returns to the waiting arms of his fiancé.

Owen Wister's **Virginian** became the basis for Hollywood notions of Americanness and masculinity. While the novel brought Wister financial success, it also complicated his literary career. Although he continued to write, he turned his attention to novels about college life and eastern manners. Many readers expected Wister to continue writing Westerns and were unwilling to read anything that did not meet this expectation. Thus, although Wister lived for thirty-six years after he published *The Virginian*, he never experienced that level of success again.

– Angela M. Salas

p.729

"You don't think I want to do this Molly? But you won't ask me to run away–"

THE Virginian

WITH GARY COOPER
WALTER HUSTON
RICHARD ARLEN
and MARY BRIAN
A VICTOR FLEMING PRODUCTION

a Paramount Picture

The Virginian on Screen

The Virginian was adapted as a movie five times. The most famous version was the 1929 black and white film starring Gary Cooper. It was one of the first talking movies to be filmed on location instead of on a set. A 1946 color film version, starring Joel McCrea, lost some of the "cowboy" language of the earlier film. In 1962, a television series based on Wister's novel, called *The Virginian, Men of Shiloh*, debuted in weekly ninety-minute episodes. The Viriginian was played by James Drury and Trampas by Doug McClure, both of whom continued in their roles for the full nine-year run until the final episode in 1971.

Ellen Wittlinger

Born: October 21, 1948; Belleville, Illinois

www.ellenwittlinger.com

Like most good writers of young adult fiction, **Ellen Wittlinger** appeals to adolescent readers who often feel awkward and out-of-place. She writes about the new kid, the gay teenager, and the middle-school nerd with understanding and humor. Her protagonists learn that being different is not necessarily bad and that the world is a very big place that dwarfs their problems and has room for all kinds of interesting people. p.23:

Wittlinger was born and reared in Illinois, the only child of parents who owned a grocery store. After graduating from Millikin University in Decatur, Illinois, she was eventually accepted into the Iowa Writer's Workshop at the University of Iowa. p.13

Avant-garde

Avant-garde is the French word for "vanguard," which means to be at the front of a movement or innovation, usually in the arts. It may be used to identify an artist or a group of artists who are breaking the boundaries of current artistic style. It is most commonly used in reference to music, art, film, and fashion.

There she earned her master of fine arts degree. She published a book of poetry in 1979 and also wrote plays but had difficulty getting them produced. After having children and working as a children's librarian she began reading young adult fiction and became inspired to write. She published her first book for young adults in 1993.

In Wittlinger's first young adult novel, *Lombardo's Law*, fifteen-year-old Justine Trainor has spent a friendless year after moving to a new town. When a beautiful new girl, Heather, moves in across the street, Justine's mother hopes the two can become friends. The two girls find they have little in common, but Justine does befriend Heather's thirteen-year-old brother, who shares her enthusiasm for avant-garde films. As their friendship begins to develop into something deeper, Justine must decide if she should let a two-year age difference—and a two-inch height difference—stand in the way of her true feelings.

In *Hard Love* another loner, high-school junior John Galardi, is the author of a homemade magazine, or "zine." When he meets fellow zine author Marisol, the two develop a close relationship. John, the lonely son of divorced and distant parents falls in love with Marisol, not realizing that she is a lesbian. The themes of unrequited love, difficulty with parents, and feelings of alienation common to many readers of young adult fiction are all addressed with sensitivity.

In *Gracie's Girl* Bess Cunningham, tired of being considered a dork, decides to start middle school with a stylish, trendy new image. Forced by her parents to volunteer at the homeless shelter with them, she meets Gracie, a homeless woman, and is

p.35

p.730

732

The Homeless

Homelessness has become a serious problem in America due to increased unemployment, high cost of housing, and cutbacks in government programs to aid the poor. The homeless are not only people who live on the streets and carry their possessions in a shopping cart, they also include single men, women, and families. All races and ages are represented among the homeless. Some have problems because of drug abuse, alcoholism, or mental illness. One thing they all share in common is poverty. Many homeless are visible, living on the streets, in parks, or in shelters. Others are not, living with friends or relatives or in their cars because they cannot afford to live on their own.

drawn into her life and problems. In the process, she learns that there are more pressing issues in the world than popularity in middle school.

Wittlinger has won American Library Association's Best Books for Young Adults awards for *Lombardo's Law* and *Hard Love*, and *What's in a Name*. She has also won the Michael L. Printz Honor Book and Lambda Book Award for *Hard Love*. Both *Gracie's Girl* and *Razzle* were **Junior Library Guild selections**.

 p.45 p.48 p.488 p.26

– Mary Virginia Davis

Virginia Euwer Wolff

Born: August 25, 1937; Portland, Oregon

stanleymusic.org/features/wolff_interview/
index.php

All of **Virginia Euwer Wolff**'s protagonists are outsiders. Whether they are poor or rich, mentally challenged or talented, they are all set apart in some way. Moreover, they all have to deal with challenges that most young adults will never face.

Born Virginia Euwer, Wolff was the daughter of a lawyer and a teacher who left Pennsylvania for a **fruit ranch in Oregon**. She was born in Oregon's largest city, Portland, and grew up in a log house that had no electricity but was filled with books and paintings. There was even a grand piano. Wolff was five when her father died, and her mother took over the ranch. On one of the family's occasional visits to New York, Wolff decided she would learn to play the violin. After attending a **boarding school**, she went to **Smith College** and earned a bachelor's degree in English. Afterward she married Art Wolff and accompanied him wherever his theatrical career led. When their two children grew older, she began teaching English and also took courses in creative writing.

After divorcing her husband in 1976, Wolff returned to Oregon, started teaching at a high school in Hood River, and wrote *Rated PG* (1980), her only adult novel. Seven years later, she began work on a story for young adults. The protagonist of *Probably Still Nick Swansen* is a sixteen-year-old **learning-disabled** boy, who is constantly ridiculed by other students. Nick is also haunted by the memory of his older sister's death, which he witnessed. However, Wolff emphasizes the fact

p.233
p.734
p.398
p.168
p.735

TITLES

Probably Still Nick Swansen, 1988

The Mozart Season, 1991

Make Lemonade, 1993

Bat 6, 1998

True Believer, 2001

that in many ways, Nick is no different from other high school students. He worries about such things as learning to drive and asking a girl to the prom; and after his date stands him up, he suffers agonies of rejection.

The heroine of Wolff's second novel, *The Mozart Season*, is set apart by her exceptional talent as a violinist. During a summer spent practicing for a rigorous competition, Allegra Shapiro learns much about being a musician and also about her own identity. Since she is Jewish, it is important for her to come to terms with her ethnic heritage. The same issue is dealt with in *Bat 6*, in which two softball players come into conflict because one of them is a Japanese American and the other lost her father in the Japanese attack on **Pearl Harbor**.

p.61

The problem faced by the characters in *Make Lemonade* and its sequel, *True Believer*, is not prejudice but desperate poverty. However, in both novels, strong young women prove that one does not have to remain a victim of unfortunate circumstances. Wolff wrote *Make Lemonade* in blank verse, which she felt would best reproduce the speech patterns of her characters. In another experiment in form, she used twenty-

Oregon's Fruit Industry

Oregon's settlers brought with them fruit trees in the mid-nineteenth century. One, Henderson Luelling, traveled to Oregon from Iowa with his family and more than 700 one-year old fruit trees. He set up a nursery near Milwaukie, Oregon, and also traveled throughout the territory, selling homesteaders fruit trees for their orchards. Oregon's river valleys have a climate well suited to growing fruit: the Rogue River Valley is home to many pear orchards; the Hood River Valley produces apples; and the Willamette Valley is ideal for sweet cherries. Oregon also produces plums, berries, and nuts.

one different narrators in *Bat 6*.

Although Virginia Euwer Wolff's novels deal with different challenges, all of them reflect her understanding of young adults and her optimistic spirit. Among the honors her books have won are the American Library Association's Best Books for Young Adults award for *Probably Still Nick Swansen*, *The Mozart Season*, and *Make Lemonade*; the Golden Kite Award for *Make Lemonade*; and a National Book Award for *True Believer*.

p.45
p.480
p.111
p.122

— Rosemary M. Canfield Reisman

Learning Disabilities

Learning disabilities are diagnosed in childhood or adolescence. These can include reading disorders, such as dyslexia; language processing disorders; Attention Deficit Disorder (ADD); physical disabilities such as blindness or deafness; and other conditions. The American Psychiatric Association estimates that 5 percent of public school students in the U.S. suffer from some form of learning disability.

Jacqueline Woodson

Born: February 12, 1964; Columbus, Ohio

www.jacquelinewoodson.com

Jacqueline Woodson writes mainly about young people who see themselves as outsiders, and tries to convey to readers a message of self-acceptance. Representing a variety of races, religions, and social classes, her characters fall in love across social boundaries, cultivate mixed-race friendships, and deal with abuse, parental abandonment, **homophobia**, racism, teenage pregnancy, and harsh family conflicts. p.26

Born in Ohio, Woodson spent her childhood first in South Carolina, and later in Brooklyn, New York, where her ethnically mixed neighborhood provided rich material for her future writing. Although an English major in college, Woodson did not take many writing classes, but learned to write by reading, something she suggests for aspiring writers. After college she worked as a **drama therapist** for runaway and **homeless** children, then turned to writing full time. p.737

Woodson's characters face complex moral choices. In *I Hadn't Meant to Tell You This*, a friendship forms between African American middle schooler Marie, the daughter of a college professor, and Lena, a poor white girl with a painful secret. As Marie watches Lena suffer, she cannot decide whether to reveal Lena's painful secret, and is shunned by her black friends for befriending a white girl. A sequel, *Lena*, provides resolution to the first book's uncertain ending. In *Miracle's Boys*, twelve-year-old Lafayette, devastated after his **diabetic** mother's death, is thrown into moral confusion p.23

p.732

when his brother, in prison for robbery, reacts to their mother Miracle's death by blaming Lafayette for not saving her. In *From the Notebooks of Melanin Sun*, the close relationship between fourteen-year-old budding writer Melanin and his law-student mother is shattered when his mother tells him she is in love with another woman. As Melanin grapples with his homophobic reaction, he also suffers through a crush on a girl he is too shy to telephone.

The poignant *If You Come Softly* also tells a story of young love, complicated by race, class, and religion. Jeremiah enrolls in an elite Manhattan prep school where, as a black teenager, he is an outsider. However, there he meets Ellie, a Jewish girl with whom he falls in love. The story ends in an act of police brutality, leaving readers pondering the grim realities of urban life for young black men. *Hush* again takes up police brutality, telling the story of Toswiah, a girl whose family enters the **witness protection**

.161

program when her father, the only black police offi-

Drama Therapy

Drama therapy combines the techniques of the theater with those of psychotherapy to help individuals with emotional or psychological problems. The therapist uses role playing, theater games, mime, puppets, improvisation and other techniques to act out situations with the goal of helping the patient. Therapy can be done one-on-one or in small groups. Drama therapists usually work in hospitals, schools, mental health clinics, prisons, and businesses.

cer in his precinct, receives death threats after witnessing the killing of a black teenager by fellow police officers. Toswiah's family moves away, and everyone changes: Her mother becomes a Jehovah's Witness, her father falls into suicidal despair, her sister plots her escape, and Toswiah (renamed Evie) grapples with her new identity as someone who must lie about both her past and her present.

Miracle's Boys won the 2000 Coretta Scott King Award, which honors African American authors of outstanding books for children and young adults. Several of Woodson's other books have been awarded honors from the **Coretta Scott King** and American Library Association Best Books for Young Adults award committees. Woodson also writes for children and adults, and her collaborative video *Among Good Christian People* won the American Film Institute Award.

p.6
p.48
p.45
p.73

– Jan Allister

American Film Institute

The American Film Institute (AFI) is a national organization dedicated to the advance and preservation of film, television, and other forms of the moving picture. At the Los Angeles Conservatory, students complete a five semester Masters of Fine Arts program in filmmaking, learning in a hands-on environment by making films. AFI also publishes the film catalog, reference books on films by decade. Preservation of classic films is also an ongoing activity. The AFI Washington National Theater at the Kennedy Center supports a film program introducing first run feature films and film festivals.

Patricia C. Wrede

Born: March 27, 1953; Chicago, Illinois

www.dendarii.force9.co.uk/Wrede

Patricia C. Wrede's young adult science-fiction novels fall into two groups: those chronicling adventures in the Enchanted Forest and those retelling well-known fairy tales and modern film stories. Wrede is important as one of the first science-fiction writers to depict the kind of strong female characters about whom young adults like to read. Noted for her frequent and effective use of humor, she also writes books for adult readers.

The eldest of five children, Wrede began writing when she was in the seventh grade. Although she majored in biology at **Carleton College** in Minnesota, she started her first novel after graduating in 1974. Five years later, after Wrede had completed her degree at the University of Minnesota, that book, *Shadow Magic* (1982), was accepted for publication. By then, Wrede was hooked on writing. In 1985, after having had more publishing successes, she left her business job and started writing for a living.

By then Wrede had begun the Enchanted Forest Chronicles, a four-volume series that became her most important work for young adults. The first volume in the series, *Dealing with Dragons*, describes the life of Cimorene, a sixteen-year-old princess who tires of her royal life and runs away to live with a dragon. Cimorene's antics continue in *Searching for Dragons* when she joins forces with Mendanbar, the king of the Enchanted Forest; she marries the king and helps battle wizards. In *Calling on Dragons*, while Cimorene is pregnant with Mendanbar's child,

.740

Carlton College

Carlton College is an independent liberal arts college located in Northfield, Minnesota, approximately forty miles south of St. Paul. It was founded in 1866 and today occupies a 900 acre campus. It is ranked as one of the top liberal arts colleges in the U. S. The student body of 1,800 study toward the Bachelor of Arts degree in thirty-four fields. The first graduating class consisted of two students: one man, one woman. Today, Carlton's diverse student body continues to be divided equally between male and female students.

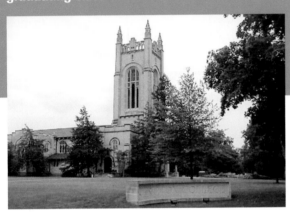

she helps subdue the wizards who have drained magic from the forest. Finally, in *Talking to Dragons*, Cimorene sends her sixteen-year-old son, Daystar, to rescue his father. All four books have evil wizards, fast-moving adventure, witty dialogue, suspense, humor, and entertaining characters.

In *Snow White and Rose Red* Wrede tells a new version of the classic Snow White fairy tale. Set in p.311 Elizabethan England, this story centers on the widow Arden who lives with her daughters, Blanche (Snow White) and Rosemond (Rose Red), on the edge of the forest between the mortal and fairy worlds.

Taking a completely different direction, Wrede has also "novelized" two of George p.1C Lucas's Star Wars movies: *The Phantom Menace* and *Attack of the Clones*. Besides giving young readers stories that are arguably better-paced than the film scripts on which they are based, Wrede's versions convey the thoughts of the characters. In these books, as in her more original stories, Wrede deals with an original, young heroine in Queen Amidala.

Book of Enchantments collects ten of Wrede's most entertaining stories, which straddle both types of her novels. Two of the book's stories are set in the Enchanted Forest of the dragon tales, and several more retell well-known fairy tales, ballads, and legends. In yet another departure, Wrede uses contemporary times as a setting in other stories.

Patricia C. Wrede's writing honors include Locus Poll Awards for *Snow White and Rose Red* and for *Dealing with Dragons* in 1991. In 1994 she was nominated for the **Mythopoeic Award** for *Calling on Dragons*.

– Cassandra Kircher

Locus Poll Award

The Locus Poll award is an annual award based on a poll conducted by *Locus* magazine. *Locus* is dedicated to the field of science fiction and fantasy. The award was established in the early 1970's and specifically honors publishers of winning works with certificates.

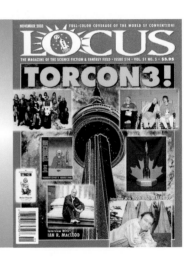

Tim Wynne-Jones

Born: August 12, 1948; Bromborough, Cheshire, England

www.collectionscanada.ca/pagebypage/t2-301-e.html

The young characters portrayed by popular Canadian author **Tim Wynne-Jones** deal with serious issues. They struggle to ensure their personal safety through perseverance and problem-solving skills. Faced with unique challenges, his protagonists resort to equally unique solutions. Often cared for by vulnerable and overwhelmed adults, the youths form unusual alliances to solve the mysteries that threaten them. Events such as murder, abuse, and mental illness thicken the suspense that Wynne-Jones generates in these stories.

p.2

Although he was born in Cheshire, England, Wynne-Jones grew up in Ottawa, Canada. While working as an instructor in **visual arts**, he participated in a research project focused on children's literature. He became interested in writing and soon published a picture book, *Madeline and Ermadello* (1977). He later finished his formal education with an advanced degree in fine arts. Although he continued to write for adults and children, his first young adult book did not appear until nearly twenty years after his initial publication.

p.74

Wynne-Jones's award-winning novel *The Maestro* opens with the unlikely vision of a grand piano being carried by helicopter across the skies of a Canadian forest. This striking example of Wynne-Jones's inventiveness is only the beginning. As the main character, Burl, watches the piano recede into the distance, he is attacked by his abusive father. Burl's only supporters are his drug-addicted mother and a teacher who can hardly imagine Burl's desperate situation. Burl escapes into the woods, where he forms an alliance with an eccentric maestro, a character patterned after a real-life Canadian musician.

Stephen Fair, Wynne-Jones's second young adult novel, features a protagonist haunted by nightmares. Fearing that he may be suffering a mental breakdown like his brother before him, Stephen records these experiences in a journal. Abandoned by his father and missing his brother, he goes on to form a friendship with a girl also suffering from an unstable home life. A later work by Wynne-Jones, *The Boy in the Burning House*, also involves a missing father and an improbable ally. Menaced by her stepfather, a troubled girl encourages the protagonist to solve an old mystery in hopes of blocking new violence.

Wynne-Jones has also published several collections of short stories, including *Some of the Kinder Planets*, *The Book of Changes*, and *Lord of the Fries and Other Stories*. Taking advantage of the freedom of the short-story form, these humorous works re-

Fraggle Rock

Fraggle Rock was a television series starring Jim Henson's Muppets that aired from 1983 through 1987. Doc, an inventor, and his dog Sprocket, discover the magical world of the Fraggles through a hole in the wall. The Fraggles are colorful, happy, furry creatures who play and tell jokes. There are two other types of creatures in their world, the Doozers and the Gorgs. To the Fraggles, human beings live in Outer Space and are called Silly Creatures. *Fraggle Rock* was very popular with young children and continues to have a loyal group of fans.

count zany adventures pulled off by resourceful characters.

Tim Wynne-Jones writes absorbing and well-crafted prose that combines Canadian settings and culture with universal realities. He is also recognized for his work as a lyricist for *Fraggle Rock*, a television program, and for his **radio plays**. His writing honors include a Canadian Library Association **Young Adult Book Award** and a Governor General's Literary Award for *The Maestro*, and the **Governor General's Award**, Canadian Library Association **Book of the Year for Children Award**, and Boston Globe-Horn Book Award for *Some of the Kinder Planets*.

– Margaret A. Dodson

 p.744

p.5

p.351

p.74

Laurence Yep

Born: June 14, 1948; San Francisco, California

www.harperchildrens.com/authorintro/
index.asp?authorid=12929

In **Laurence Yep** books, readers may fight alongside a dragon princess, face growing up Chinese American, or struggle to survive in the mining camps of the Wild West. His young **protagonists** use intelligence, spunk, and imagination to solve mysteries and win fantastic battles. Drawing on his knowledge of Chinese history and folklore as well as on his Chinese American heritage, Yep's fiction is quite extraordinary.

Yep was born in an African American neighborhood of **San Francisco**. His Chinese American father was a postal clerk. His mother had moved there from the Midwest and the South. *Star Fisher* and *Dream Soul* fictionalize his mother's experience. When she was fifteen, she and her family were the only Chinese Americans in a small town in **West Virginia**. Yep himself did not speak Chinese. He

p.233
p.746
p.602

TITLES

Sweetwater, 1973

Dragonwings, 1975

Child of the Owl, 1977

The Mark Twain Murders, 1982

Dragon of the Lost Sea, 1982

Liar, Liar, 1983

The Serpent's Children, 1984

Dragon Steel, 1985

Mountain Light, 1985

Dragon Cauldron, 1991

The Star Fisher, 1991

Dragon War, 1992

Dragon's Gate, 1993

Hiroshima, 1995

Thief of Hearts, 1995

Ribbons, 1996

The Khan's Daughter: A Mongolian Folktale, 1997

Dragon Prince: A Chinese Beauty and Beast Tale, 1997

The Cook's Family, 1998

The Amah, 1999

p.87

studied English in college and earned a doctorate from the State University of New York at Buffalo.

Yep's first book, *Sweetwater*, is a science-fiction novel with a strong ecological edge. *Dragonwings* is based on the true story of the Chinese American **aviator** Fung Joe Guey, who flew across Oakland in a homemade biplane in 1909. When *Dragonwings* won a **Newbery Honor Book** award, Yep launched his successful career writing young adult fiction often rooted in Chinese and Chinese American themes. He later married his former editor, Joanne Ryder. p.6 p.1

Yep likes to write his books in series. His four **fantasy** volumes begun with *Dragon of the Lost Sea* and ending with *Dragon War* feature the dragon princess Shimmer and the thirteen-year-old human boy Thorn fighting powerful adversaries. Yep also revisits his teenage protagonists in later books. *Child of the Owl*, which won the 1977 **Boston Globe-Horn Book Award** for fiction, tells how twelve-year-old Casey has to live with her Chinese grandmother Paw-Paw after her gambling father is hospitalized because of a brutal beating. After Casey realizes that her grandmother is not cruel, she learns the truth about her dead mother and her own Chinese heritage. Set thirty years later, *Thief of Hearts* portrays Casey's daughter, Stacey. In Chinatown, Stacey must find the p.747

San Francisco's Chinese American Community

The Chinese came to California, as did many others, in search of gold. However, most of them ended up providing services to the miners such as cooking, laundry, and other labor. In 1849 there were fifty four Chinese men in California; by 1876, there were 116,000 Chinese living in California. The largest Chinese community was in San Francisco. That Chinatown burned down in the 1906 earthquake. It was rebuilt on the same site in central San Francisco and continues to be home to many Chinese Americans who preserve their traditions by living in this community of some dozen city blocks. Chinatown also has become a tourist attraction that draws visitors to San Francisco.

Boston Globe-Horn Book Award

The Boston Globe-Horn Book Award has been presented annually since 1967 to three books which represent excellence in literature for children and young adults. A committee of three children's literature specialists evaluate books published in the United States the previous year. They select winners in the categories of Picture Book, Fiction and Poetry, and Nonfiction. They also can select up to two Honor Books in each category. The prize is sponsored by the *Boston Globe* newspaper and *The Horn Book Magazine*, the first magazine dedicated to children's books and reading.

The Horn Book, Inc.
Publications About Books for Children and Young Adults

thief who has framed her new friend Hong Ch'un, who originally made fun of Stacey as a mixed-race girl in their middle school.

Yep's award-winning series *The Serpent's Children*, *Mountain Light*, and *Dragon's Gate* begins in southern China and moves to **California's gold rush** of the mid-nineteenth century, with its action set among Chinese and American miners.

Ribbons introduces twelve-year-old ballerina Robin. After her grandmother arrives from Hong Kong, her parents can no longer afford to pay for her dancing lessons, so she must rethink her plans for her life. In *The Cook's Wife*, Robin and her grandmother act as the long-lost family of a homesick cook in Chinatown. *Angelfish* sees Robin working for a pet-fish shop after her backpack has smashed the shop's window. She learns that the grumpy shop owner, Mr. Tsow, has a sorrowful secret, and is not unkind.

Laurence Yep's books have believable characters and a wide range of exciting plots and settings. His teenage protagonists encounter fascinating adventures, whether in old China, outer space, or America.

— R. C. Lutz

Jane Yolen

Born: February 11, 1939; New York, New York

www.janeyolen.com

Jane Yolen is the star of the revival in children's and young adult folktale literature that began in the 1980's. She began publishing in 1963 and has written books for preschoolers through adults, more than three hundred volumes in all. She was a voracious reader of folk and fairy tales as a child and also became an enthusiastic folk singer, immersed in the ballads of English, Scottish, and Appalachian tradition. These folk narratives still deeply influence her storytelling.

Yolen grew up in a Jewish family but was also exposed to Roman Catholicism by a close friend in high school and to **Quakerism** at summer camp. The **pacifism** of the Quakers influenced her moral outlook on life, while Catholicism appealed to her through its rituals and the illumination that it cast on medieval legends, especially those of **King Arthur**. After graduating from high school, Yolen attended **Smith College**, a woman's college in Massachusetts, where she majored in English and Russian and minored in religion. She also gained a reputation as a talented writer, which led to her first encounters with the publishing world when she was recommended to a book editor at **Alfred A. Knopf**. When asked if she had any **manuscripts**, Yolen lied and said yes; when she was then asked to send them in for the editor to see, she panicked and produced several off-the-cuff children's book manuscripts.

p.749

p.56

p.4

p.398

p.750

p.620

The editor was not interested, but having written them, Yolen began to consider children's literature as an outlet for her fiction-writing talents.

Yolen's novels are too numerous to describe individually, but they often begin from folktales, fairy tales, and legends and the creatures and heroes that inhabit them—dragons, magicians, princes and princesses. She turns them into real, if adventurous, stories about believable people. Her Young Merlin trilogy (*Passager*, *Hobby*, and *Merlin*) tells the story of the magician's youth, before he became the **sorcerer** who stage-managed the youth of King Arthur, and *The Dragon's Boy* tells of Arthur's first encounter with Merlin. Likewise, *Odysseus in the Serpent's Maze*, *Hippolyta and the Curse of the Amazons*, and *Atalanta and the Arcadian Beast* tell stories of heroes and heroines from Greek mythology in their adolescent years which prefigure the myths that made them famous.

Books in Yolen's Tartan Magic series (*The Wizard's Map*, *The Pictish Child*, and *The Bagpiper's Ghost*) belong to the genre of normal contemporary children stumbling upon magic in a new environment—in this case, American twins Peter and Jennifer Dyer and their little sister Molly, who encounter sorcerers, witches, and ghosts on trips to Scotland. The Pit Dragon trilogy (*Dragon's Blood*, *Heart's Blood*, and *A Sending of Dragons*) belongs more on

p.551

Quakers

Founded by John Fox in 1652 in England, the Religious Society of Friends, also known as Quakers, was part of a greater religious awakening. Fox appealed to a group called the Seekers who were dissatisfied with the Church of England. He unified them in a denomination founded on simple worship services, honesty, and equality. Today, the Quakers continue to work for peace, human rights, and social reform.

the science fiction end of fantasy, taking place on a p.87 planet where dragons are trained to fight as companions of humans.

Although Jane Yolen's stories convey strong messages of self-reliance, loyalty, and friendship for both male and female protagonists, she never lets p.23 her message get in the way of good storytelling. Her writing honors include a Golden Kite Award for p.11 Fiction, several **Golden Kite Honor Book** awards, and a **Christopher Award**, which affirms values of the human spirit.

– Leslie Ellen Jones

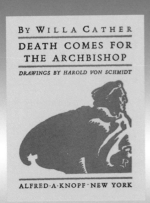

Alfred A. Knopf

Alfred A. Knopf is a distinguished publisher of both fiction, poetry, and nonfiction books. Founded in 1915 by Alfred A. and Blanche W. Knopf, the New York publishing house has published books by twenty-one Nobel Prize winning authors. Knopf is also the publisher of the Everyman's Classics, a series of affordable hardcover editions of classic works of world literature. In 1960, Alfred A. Knopf became part of Random House, which is now a division of the German media company Bertelsmann AG.

Paul Zindel

Born: May 15, 1936; Staten Island, New York
Died: March 27, 2003; New York, New York

www.edupaperback.org/showauth.cfm?authid=86

When **Paul Zindel** published *The Pigman* in 1968, the only comparable young adult novel was S. E. Hinton's ***The Outsiders***, which came out a year earlier. This new genre was to prove fruitful to both Hinton and Zindel. By 2001 Zindel had published twenty-nine young adult novels. *The Pigman*, which has sold more than one million copies, remains a young adult classic.

Born in New York City, Zindel was the product of a broken home presided over by a strict and bitter mother. At the age of fifteen, Zindel contracted **tuberculosis** and spent eighteen months in a **sanatorium**. He returned home and completed secondary school, having attended four high schools. He then entered Wagner College, where he prepared to teach high school chemistry, but where he also took a playwriting elective taught by **Edward Albee**. Zindel taught chemistry at Tottenville High School for ten years, but with the success of *The Pigman*, he resigned to become a full-time writer.

The Pigman shocked many adults. It is about the growing relationship and burgeoning trust between two teenagers, John and Lorraine, both from dysfunctional families, and Mr. Pignoti, whom they originally intended to exploit but who soon wins their friendship. The book's two main characters narrate alternating chapters, creating dual voices. When Pignoti is hospitalized, John and Lorraine, without authorization, throw a party in his house. Considerable destruction ensues. After Pignoti returns home unexpectedly early, disenchantment

p.338

p.522

.752

.753

sets in. However, the two friends take Pignoti to the zoo to visit Bobo, his favorite baboon. The baboon, however, has died. The shock of this loss is too much for Pignoti, who collapses and dies. This story is typical of Zindel in that it has a realistic rather than a happy ending and that it suspends moral judgment.

Zindel's next novel, *My Darling, My Hamburger*, deals with teenage pregnancy and abortion but is actually more about the impasses that often exists between young adults and their parents. Problems of communication pervade much of Zindel's writing. *Harry and Hortense at Hormone High* focuses on two misfits and their slightly off-center classmates. Zindel firmly asserts that teenagers need to rebel. In his novels, he demonstrates to them that there is nothing unique in rebellion; it is part of growing up.

Zindel's later novels are increasingly optimistic in their presentations of young people, although they do not question their need to rebel against adults. In *A Begonia for Miss Applebaum*,

Sanatorium

A sanatorium is a resort or hospital where people go to recuperate from an illness or to undergo a program that will make them healthier. In the 1920's, many sanatoriums were built for the care of people suffering from tuberculosis, a lung disease. It was believed that rest, dry climate, and quiet would help cure the disease. Discovery of medicines to treat tuberculosis replaced a stay in a sanatorium as a treatement for tuberculosis, and over time most of these facilities closed. Thomas Mann, a Nobel-prize-winning German writer, set his novel *The Magic Mountain* in a Swiss sanatorium.

Henry and Zelda lose their favorite teacher when cancer forces her early retirement. As her health declines, the two friends learn valuable lessons from her about life and about dying with dignity. In *Loch*, quite uncharacteristically, it is the children who help their father regain his self-respect.

Paul Zindel's greatest contribution as a writer is his realistic treatment of adolescent concerns. He reproduced typical teenage vocabulary convincingly. He understood how tedious school can be for teenagers and how parents and other authority figures can seem unkind and unfeeling. Despite the controversy his book *The Pigman* aroused, it received a Boston Globe-Horn Honor Book award.

– R. Baird Shuman

Edward Albee

Edward Albee, a famous American playwright, was born in 1928 and adopted by a wealthy family when he was two weeks old. His father was part owner of a theater chain, and Edward grew up attending matinees and Broadway plays. Three of his plays, *A Delicate Balance, Seascape,* and *Three Tall Women* have won the Pulitzer Prize. His 1962 play *Who's Afraid of Virginia Woolf* has been performed around the world, was made popular through a film version, and is considered a classic of the twentieth century theater.

Awards List

There are many awards and honors given to authors each year. There are also many lists highlighting the "best" books as selected by an association or a publication. The Awards List, drawn from the awards mentioned by our contributors in this book, identifies many of these honors. Check the Subject Index to find the awards **highlighted in color** below for more information.

Alex Award

American Book Award

American Library Association Best Books for Young Adults

American Library Association Distinguished Book

American Library Association Gay, Lesbian, Bisexual, and Transgendered Book Award

American Library Association Notable Book

American Library Association Quick Pick for Young Adults

ALAN (Assembly on Literature for Adolescents) Award

Atlantic Monthly Creative Writing Award

Before Columbus Foundation American Book Award

Booker McConnell Prize

Booklist Best Book

Booklist Editor's Choice

Booklist Reviewer's Choice

Boston Globe-Horn Book Award

Brachmann Prize

California Young Reader Medal

Canadian Library Association Young Adult Book Award

Capitol Choice Award

Carnegie Medal

Child Study Association Children's Books of the Year

Children's Book Award

Christopher Award

Compton Crook Award

Coretta Scott King Award

Daedalus Award

Delacorte Press Prize for a First Young Adult Novel

Dorothy Canfield Fisher Children's Book Award

Edgar Allan Poe Award for Best Young Adult Novel

Golden Kite Award

Governor General's Literary Award
(Canada)

Guardian Award

Hans Christian Andersen Award

Horn Book Award

Hugo Award

International Reading Association
Children's Book Award

James Tait Black Memorial Prizes

Jane Addams Honor Book Award

Janet Heidinger Kafka Prize

John and Patricia Beatty Award

Knickerbocker Award

Lambda Literary Awards

Laura Ingalls Wilder Award

Lewis Carroll Shelf Award

Margaret A. Edwards Award

Mark Twain Award

M-G-M Literary Award

Michael L. Printz Award and Honor
Book

Mildred L. Batchelder Award

Nancy Block Memorial Award

National Book Award

National Book Award of South Africa

National Council for the Social Studies
Award

National Intellectual Freedom Award

National Medal of Arts

Nebula Award

Nene Award

**New York Public Library Best Books for
the Teen Age**

Newbery Medal and Honor Books

Nobel Prize in Literature

Obie Award

Oklahoma Book Award

Parents' Choice Award

P.E.N. Center West Award

Phoenix Award

Premio Quinto Sol

Publishers Weekly Best Book

Pulitzer Prize

Pura Belpré Medal

Regina Medal

Robert B. Downs Intellectual Freedom
Award

School Library Journal Best Book

Scott O'Dell Award for Historical
Fiction

Shrout Short Story Prize

Smarties Prize

**South Carolina Association of School
Librarians Young Adult Book
Award**

Tir na Og Award

Top Ten Young Adult Books

**University of Southern Mississippi
Silver Medallion**

Whitbread Children's Book of the Year

William Allen White Award

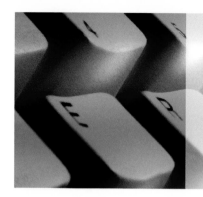

Photo Credits

African Studies Assocation: 492

American Library Association: 74, 102, 108, 465, 468, 488

American Pictures: 48

American Red Cross: 387

Americorps: 422

AP/Wide World Photos: 2, 8, 9, 17, 18, 21, 23, 30, 35, 44, 45, 53, 56, 59, 63, 65, 66, 68, 69, 71, 74, 81, 83, 89, 90, 92, 101, 120, 122, 130, 131, 133, 135, 137, 146, 150, 155, 156, 158, 159, 164, 170, 173, 179, 180, 184, 185, 186, 192, 200, 201, 203, 204, 206, 209, 218, 221, 224, 225, 226, 228, 230, 231, 236, 237, 240, 242, 244, 246, 248, 249, 250, 253, 255, 263, 272, 273, 275, 278, 283, 290, 291, 292, 296, 299, 300, 302, 309, 314, 317, 320, 323, 324, 326, 328, 330, 332, 334, 336, 341, 344, 347, 348, 356, 359, 366, 369, 371, 374, 380, 381, 389, 398, 400, 402, 405, 407, 413, 416, 419, 425, 429, 432, 435, 452, 453, 458, 459, 464, 466, 470, 471, 474, 476, 477, 489, 497, 501, 502, 515, 516, 518, 528, 534, 539, 540, 545, 548, 563, 565, 566, 567, 571, 579, 581, 584, 591, 594, 595, 596, 598, 600, 602, 603, 604, 614, 623, 628, 632, 639, 641, 666, 668, 669, 672, 677, 678, 695, 698, 722, 725, 727, 732, 734, 737, 738, 746, 752, 753

Arkent Archives: 542, 686

Baltimore Science Fiction Society: 288

Bibliothèque Nationale de Canada: 484

British Broadcasting Corporation (BBC): 6

California Library Association: 62

Canadian Children's Book Centre: 390

Carlsen Press: 142

Children's Literature Association: 147

Chris Ogle: 5

Corbis: 270, 456, 461, 491

Courtesy of Aidan Chambers: 118

Courtesy of Alan Garner: 268

Courtesy of Chris Crutcher: 175

Courtesy of Diana Wynne Jones: 363

Courtesy of Donna Jo Napoli: 494

Courtesy of Ellen Wittlinger: 731

Courtesy of Eve Bunting: 109

Courtesy of Gillian Cross: 172

Courtesy of James Haskins: 313

Courtesy of Jean Ferris: 236

Courtesy of Jerry Spinnelli: 641

Courtesy of Joyce Carol Thomas: 676

Courtesy of Joyce Hansen: 308

Courtesy of Karen Cushman: 178

Courtesy of Katherine Paterson: 526

Courtesy of Linda Sue Park: 523

Courtesy of Lois Duncan: 214

Courtesy of Lois Lowry: 430

Courtesy of Marion Dane Bauer: 55

Courtesy of Mary Downing Hahn: 302

Courtesy of M. E. Kerr: 368

Courtesy of Mel Glenn: 279

Courtesy of Monica Hughes: 350

Courtesy of Natalie Babbitt: 38

Courtesy of Neil Gaiman: 257

Courtesy of Robert Newton Peck: 542

Courtesy of Rodman Philbrick: 547

Courtesy of T. A. Barron: 47

Courtesy of Terry Brooks: 104

Courtesy of Terry Trueman: 682

Courtesy of Theodore Taylor: 670

Courtesy of William Sleator: 626

David Alford: 193

Subject Index